MANAGING FINANCE AND RESOURCES IN EDUCATION

This book, **Managing Finance and Resources in Education**, is the reader for the core module *Managing Finance and External Relations*, one of the core modules of the MBA in Educational Management offered by the Centre for Educational Leadership (formerly EMDU), University of Leicester.

The other modules in this course are:

Leadership and Strategic Management in Education
Human Resource Management in Schools and Colleges
Managing the Curriculum
Research Methods in Educational Management

For further information about the MBA in Educational Management, please contact the Centre for Educational Leadership and Management at celm@le.ac.uk. For further information about the books associated with the course, contact Paul Chapman Publishing at http://www.sagepub.co.uk.

University *of* **Leicester**

MANAGING FINANCE AND RESOURCES IN EDUCATION

Edited by
Marianne Coleman and Lesley Anderson

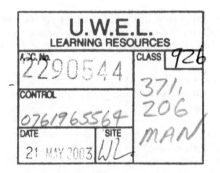

P·C·P

Paul Chapman
Publishing Ltd

Chapter 1 Rosalind Levačić
Chapter 2 Brian J. Caldwell
Chapter 3 Lesley Anderson
Chapter 4 Anne West, Hazel Pennell, Robert West and Tony Travers
Chapter 5 Jacky Lumby
Chapter 6 Tony Bush
Chapter 7 Derek Glover
Chapter 8 Kevin McAleese
Chapter 9 Fergus O'Sullivan, Angela Thody and Elizabeth Wood
Chapter 10 Tim Simkins
Chapter 11 Les Bell
Chapter 12 Ed Baines
Chapter 13 Marianne Coleman and Ann R. J. Briggs

First published 2000
Reprinted 2002

Paul Chapman Publishing Ltd
A SAGE Publications Company
6 Bonhill Street
London EC2A 4PU

SAGE Publications Inc
2455 Teller Road
Thousand Oaks, California 91320

SAGE Publications India Pvt Ltd
32, M-Block Market
Greater Kailash - I
New Delhi 110 048

British Library Cataloguing in Publication data

A catalogue record for this book is available from the British Library

ISBN 0-7619-6556-4
ISBN 0-7619-6557-2 (pbk)

Library of Congress catalog card number available

Typeset by Dorwyn Ltd, Rowlands Castle, Hants
Printed and bound by Athenaeum Press, Gateshead

CONTENTS

Series Editor's Foreword   vii
Preface   ix
Notes on Contributors   xiv

Part I: A National and International Perspective

1   Linking Resources to Learning Outcomes   3
  Rosalind Levačić
2   Local Management and Learning Outcomes: Mapping the Links
  in Three Generations of International Research   24
  Brian J. Caldwell
3   The Move Towards Entrepreneurialism   41
  Lesley Anderson
4   Financing School-Based Education in England: Principles and
  Problems   59
  Anne West, Hazel Pennell, Robert West and Tony Travers
5   Funding Learning in Further Education   81
  Jacky Lumby

Part II: Within the School and College

6   Management Styles: Impact on Finance and Resources   99
  Tony Bush
7   Financial Management and Strategic Planning   117
  Derek Glover
8   Budgeting in Schools   132
  Kevin McAleese

 9   The Role of the Bursar   148
     Fergus O'Sullivan, Angela Thody and Elizabeth Wood
10   Cost Analysis in Education   168
     Tim Simkins
11   The Management of Staff: Some Issues of Efficiency and
     Cost-Effectiveness   186
     Les Bell
12   Managing Information as a Resource   200
     Ed Baines
13   Management of Buildings and Space   215
     Marianne Coleman and Ann R. J. Briggs

Index   229

SERIES EDITOR'S FOREWORD

The emergence of self-governing schools and colleges in many countries at the end of the twentieth century has served to emphasize the importance of leadership and management. This is certainly true of financial and material resources which are now largely under the direct control of managers and governors. Traditional patterns of organization place the main responsibility for finance with national, regional or local government. Self-management requires a different approach where the role of government is limited to the allocation of budgets to schools and subsequent audit to ensure that public money has been properly spent. The internal deployment and management of these funds are the responsibility of governing bodies, and their international equivalents, and senior managers. They have the right and the responsibility to determine the appropriate resource mix and are uniquely placed to ensure that the budgeting process is linked to the specific needs and objectives of the school or college. While government can allocate resources only on the basis of perceived national or local needs, school managers and governors can target spending much more precisely to the benefit of pupils and students. They are also much more likely to ensure that spending is both efficient and effective by, for example, being prudent in the use of energy and by viring expenditure across budget heads to maximise value for money.

There is now a significant body of research on the impact of self-governance on funding and financial management and much of this work is reflected in this volume. Less attention has been given to the management of those human and material resources which are employed once the budgetary decisions have been made. However, this volume examines these key aspects of implementation as well as the broader aspects of strategic financial management.

The development of effective managers in education requires the support of literature which presents the major issues in clear, intelligible language while drawing on the best of theory and research. The purpose of this series is to examine the management of schools and colleges, drawing on empirical evidence. The approach is analytical rather than descriptive and generates conclusions about the most appropriate ways of managing schools and colleges on the basis of research evidence.

The aim of this series, and of this volume, is to develop a body of literature that:

- is directly relevant to school and college management;
- is prepared by authors with national and international reputations;
- adopts an analytical approach based on empirical evidence but couched in intelligible language;
- integrates the best of theory, research and practice.

Managing Finance and Resources in Education is the fifth volume in the series and its underlying rationale is that the core business of education is teaching and learning. Judgements about the effectiveness of financial and real resource management have to be made primarily on the basis of their impact on learning and teaching. This necessarily implies that funding decisions are not separated from curricular and pedagogic issues but are integrated with them in a way that best meets the requirements of the school or college, and its pupils or students. 'Joined up' management, linking finance, real resources, teaching and learning, is an important aspect of the intended purpose of self-governance and an essential part of building and sustaining successful schools for the new millennium. This book provides valuable insights for all those interested in the vital relationship between resource management and school improvement.

Tony Bush
University of Leicester
October 1999

PREFACE

In order to achieve their objectives, all educational organizations must both receive and manage finance and resources. This book is primarily concerned with the ways in which institutions manage their resources, although the area of national funding in England and Wales is explored by Anne West *et al.* in respect of schools and Jacky Lumby in respect of colleges in Chapters 4 and 5.

Whilst considering national funding within the UK, it is salutary to note the international context. In the Organization for Economic Co-operation and Development (OECD) countries in 1990:

> recurrent expenditure per student was ... forty times that of countries in sub-Saharan Africa, thirty times that of countries in eastern Asia, twenty times that of countries in south Asia, ten times greater than that of the Arab states of the Middle East and seven times greater than that of Latin America and the Caribbean.
>
> (UNESCO, 1994, p. 19 quoted in Harber and Davies, 1997, p. 12)

Such international inequities mean that for many schools in developing countries, the overwhelming problem is one of inadequate resources and over-full classrooms. However, even in the most difficult circumstances, the ways in which the resources are managed, as well as the amount of the resources, are likely to impact on the students and their achievements. A study of schools in South Africa (Christie *et al.*, 1997) identified schools that were 'resilient' and were able to manage the problems of poverty and unemployment more successfully than other, similar schools. It would therefore appear that even in countries where education is relatively starved of funds, the way in which a school or college is managed impacts on the quality of education that the student receives.

In many of the better funded parts of the world, notably the UK, New Zealand, Victoria in Australia, Hong Kong, Canada and parts of the USA, there has been evidence of what Caldwell and Spinks (1992) refer to as a 'megatrend'. This is a move towards decentralization of funding and increased autonomy for schools and other educational institutions which has placed a greater emphasis on the management of the individual institution. Caldwell and Spinks (1992, p. 14) go on to say that: 'it is simply more efficient and effective in the later twentieth century to restructure systems of education so that central bureaucracies are relatively small and schools are empowered to manage their own affairs within a centrally determined framework of direction and support.'

In the UK and elsewhere, this argument has been linked to the belief that increased autonomy, or school-based management, would lead to a better quality of education and improved standards (Levačić, 1995). A major reason for this belief was that there would be a more efficient use of resources where decisions are taken at a local school or college level. The increasing autonomy experienced by schools and colleges in the UK and elsewhere is inevitably an important theme in this book. However, the current concern for raising standards in education and improving educational processes and outcomes leads us to focus on two interconnected issues:

1) The potential relationship between the input of resources, both financial and real, and the learning outcomes that result.
2) The impact of management on the optimal deployment of these resources, particularly within a context of institutional autonomy.

Whilst both of these issues have importance for educational institutions in all countries, the contributions to this book have been written largely within the context of education in the developed, industrialized world.

The book is divided into two parts, the first of which includes five chapters that are concerned with national and international trends and with the national system of funding schools and colleges within England and Wales. The second part of the book is concerned with aspects of management of finance and other resources as practised within the individual institution.

In Chapter 1 Rosalind Levačić sets the scene by outlining a framework for resource management and offering definitions that provide important tools for analysis in the field of financial and resource management. The chapter is entitled 'Linking Resources to Learning Outcomes', and Levačić makes the useful distinction between 'learning outputs' being: 'direct effects . . . on . . . students in terms of their acquiring knowledge, skills, beliefs and attitudes' (p. 4), and 'learning outcomes' which are defined as: 'longer-term impacts on individuals and on society of the educational provision received at some earlier date' (p. 4).

The area of learning outcomes and links with resources is developed by Brian Caldwell in Chapter 2, who, through 'third generation' studies, is able to map those inputs which have a direct impact on student learning: professional development of teachers, implementation of a curriculum framework and monitoring. In this chapter, Caldwell breaks fresh ground, and for the first time 'Links between local management and learning outcomes are modelled and mapped' (p. 25).

The cultural change that accompanied the devolution of funds to schools and colleges encouraged new ways of thinking. Increasing independence on expenditure decisions, including the opportunity to vire funds, was matched by greater freedom to exploit alternative means of funding. The existence of a quasi-market encouraged competitiveness between educational institutions and a more innovative climate within which schools and colleges operate. In Chapter 3, Lesley Anderson explores some of the implications of these changes by examining the climate of entrepreneurialism in education.

In Chapter 1, Levačić defines the four 'e' words, 'effectiveness, efficiency, economy and equity', and in Chapter 4, Ann West *et al.* consider the principles, including equity, that underlie the national funding context. Basing the chapter on empirical research, West *et al.* are able to trace the process of the distribution of funds from central to local government, the determination of the budget at local level and the distribution of funding by the local authority to the schools. Within the schools, they further focus on the ways in which schools use money for special and additional educational needs. Finally, they present three alternatives to the present national system of schools funding.

In Chapter 5, Jacky Lumby gives particular consideration to the impact of the national funding system on colleges of further education. In doing so, she starts to bridge the gap between the national overview and the working of the individual organization. Her research in 11 general colleges of further education reveals the 'shift in culture' that has taken place as a result of changes in the method of funding since 1993. Whilst the overall impact of the changes cannot be underestimated, the conclusion from the research is largely optimistic, with both financial and curriculum objectives being considered together by managers of finance.

Part II of the book starts with a classic overview by Tony Bush, in Chapter 6, of how models of management styles may impact on the management of finance and resources. The analysis is in the context of the impact of autonomy resulting in a changed setting for resource allocation. Much of the chapter is given over to rational models of management and this sets the scene for Chapter 7 by Derek Glover. In this chapter, Glover focuses on the implications for the middle manager of autonomy in financial management and considers how the middle manager may work within an overall strategic plan that links with financial management.

Kevin McAleese is the headteacher of a school and, in Chapter 8, he presents what is, in effect, a case study of the setting of a budget in a large secondary school. In doing so, he is able to draw on comparative data from a large number of other secondary schools who subscribe to the National Information Exchange which he co-ordinates. McAleese is able to explain the nature of the annual process of budget-setting with reference to the need for practical considerations relating to staffing and other issues to be taken into account.

In the following chapter, Fergus O'Sullivan and his co-writers present empirical work relating to the role of the bursar or finance manager, an emerging role that mirrors the growth of school-based management. As schools (and colleges) become more autonomous, the authors hypothesize that the role of the bursar (resource manager) will grow to encompass greater elements of leadership as well as management and administration.

The analysis of costs in education is vital for informed decision-making and in Chapter 10, Tim Simkins considers such important concepts as opportunity cost, the alternative resource that has been forgone, and cost-benefit analysis. The latter, which requires that outcomes as well as inputs into education be measured in monetary terms, remains difficult to apply in the field of education. However, consideration of such aspects of costing may be illuminating for educational managers.

As the title of the book implies, the management of resources goes beyond the management of finance alone and, in the final chapters of the book, the nature and management of resources other than finance is considered. Caldwell and Spinks (1992, pp. 4–5) include amongst resources: knowledge (to underpin decisions); power (decentralization of decision-making); materiel (use of facilities and equipment); people (deployment of human resources) as well as finance. In Chapter 11, Les Bell gives particular consideration to the implications of the deployment of human resources. His analysis relates to both teaching and support or associate staff and he highlights issues of cost-effectiveness and efficiency in relation to the management of this most expensive resource. Some of the issues developed in this chapter link clearly with the practicalities of staffing outlined by McAleese in Chapter 8.

Chapter 12 picks up on a theme that runs through much of the book. Decision-making requires access to information and the management of information as a resource in education is developed by Ed Baines. The importance of having national data against which to compare the performance of the individual school is stressed by Levačić in Chapter 1, whilst in Chapter 5 Lumby reports on the importance of having accurate internal information in order to measure whether the college is on course or not. The work of McAleese in managing the budget process reported in Chapter 8 is dependent on accurate information within the institution and the collection of data from a range of secondary schools serves to provide a base against which such processes can be measured. The importance of information for decision-making in regard to staffing issues is stressed by Bell in Chapter 11. In considering the impact of information and communications technology (ICT) on school management, Baines draws a parallel with the impact of ICT on the classroom and raises the question of how the information technology revolution may affect management structures in education.

In the final chapter, Marianne Coleman and Ann Briggs consider the implications of the category 'materiel' mentioned by Caldwell and Spinks. The costs associated with buildings are second only to staffing and this chapter gives some attention to the possibility of innovative thinking to exploit the potential of buildings. There are links with Chapter 3, as innovation is likely to imply an entrepreneurial approach. Empirical research carried out for this chapter indicates that a plan to develop buildings may be an important strand in planned school improvement.

Throughout the chapters, there is an understanding that the core business of education is that of teaching and learning. The management of finance and other resources aims to provide a context in which the conditions that maximize learning and teaching prevail.

The editors are grateful to all the contributors to the book for their willingness to co-operate in its production. We also wish to thank Tony Bush as series editor, Marianne Lagrange of Paul Chapman Publishing for her support and advice, our colleague Ann Briggs for her valuable help and Christopher Bowring-Carr for his proofreading, index and advice. Finally, we would like to thank the members of the support team at the Educational Management Development Unit (EMDU), particularly Clem Little, Joyce Palmer and Tracy Harazdiuk.

Marianne Coleman and Lesley Anderson
October 1999

REFERENCES

Caldwell, B. and Spinks, J. M. (1992) *Leading the Self-Managing School*, London, Falmer.

Christie, P. and Potterton, M., with French, A., Cress, K., Lanzerotti, L. and Butler, D. (1997) *School Development in South Africa: A Research Project to Investigate Strategic Interventions for Quality Improvement in South African Schools*, Johannesburg, University of the Witwatersrand.

Harber, C. and Davies, L. (1997) *School Management and Effectiveness in Developing Countries: The Post-Bureaucratic School*, London, Cassell.

Levačić, R. (1995) *Local Management of Schools: Analysis and Practice*, Buckingham, Open University Press.

NOTES ON CONTRIBUTORS

Dr Lesley Anderson is a Lecturer in Educational Management at the Educational Management Development Unit (EMDU), University of Leicester. She is an Office for Standards in Education (OFSTED) inspector of both secondary and primary schools and an assessor for the National Professional Qualification for Headteachers. She is co-author of *Opting for Self Management: The Early Experiences of Grant-Maintained Schools* (1992, Routledge).

Ed Baines was head teacher for over ten years of Montagu School, a large grant maintained secondary comprehensive school in the East Midlands. Montagu's piloting of General National Vocational Qualifications, with their emphasis on new ways of working, for both teachers and students, and its ground-breaking investment in the development of ICT-based learning, including Internet and integrated learning systems, provoked interest from colleagues world-wide. He currently organizes and delivers modules of the University of Leicester's Educational Management MBA programme and lectures and tutors for De Montfort University in their MA in Educational Management.

Professor Les Bell holds a second chair of Educational Management within the EMDU/School of Education. He has teaching experience in both primary and secondary schools and academic experience at both Warwick University and Liverpool John Moores University, where he was Professor of Educational Management, Director of the School of Education and Dean of the Division of Health, Education and Community Studies. He has published extensively on many aspects of educational management.

Ann R. J. Briggs is a Lecturer in Educational Management at EMDU. Her special responsibility is as course leader for the campus-based MBA in Educational

Management. She has considerable teaching experience in secondary and further education. Her management responsibilities have included departmental leadership, curriculum development and learning resource management. Her research interests include the accessibility of learning and learning resources, and middle management in further education.

Professor Tony Bush is Professor of Educational Management and Director of the EMDU at the University of Leicester. He was formerly a teacher in secondary schools and colleges and a professional officer with a local education authority (LEA). He was Senior Lecturer in Educational Policy and Management at the Open University before joining Leicester in January 1992. He has published extensively on several aspects of educational management. His main recent books are *Managing Autonomous Schools: The Grant Maintained Experience* (with M. Coleman and D. Glover, 1993, Paul Chapman), *The Principles of Educational Management* (with J. West-Burnham, 1994, Longman) and *Theories of Educational Management* (1995, Paul Chapman).

Professor Brian J. Caldwell is Dean of Education at the University of Melbourne where he holds a Personal Chair in Education. He is co-author of several books that have guided educational reform in a number of countries, most notably the Falmer Press trilogy on self-managing schools, with Jim Spinks: *The Self-Managing School* (1988), *Leading the Self-Managing School* (1992) and *Beyond the Self-Managing School* (1998).

Dr Marianne Coleman is Senior Lecturer at the EMDU and has extensive experience in education, mainly teaching in secondary schools, and also working in the advisory service of a large LEA. She is co-author of *Managing Autonomous Schools: The Grant Maintained Experience* (with T. Bush and D. Glover, 1993, Paul Chapman). She has also published a range of materials as part of EMDU's distance-learning MBA, including 'Marketing in education' and 'Women in educational management'. She has published articles on gender issues in management and contributed chapters to the widely read *The Principles of Educational Management* (T. Bush and J. West-Burnham, 1994, Longman). She has also written on the subject of mentoring.

Dr Derek Glover was for 18 years headteacher of Burford School and Community College in Oxfordshire. He took early retirement in 1990 to complete his PhD in school and community relationships but soon became caught up in teaching and research work with Keele and the Open universities. He is tutor for the University of Leicester's MBA in Educational Management. He has particular interests in resource management, external relations and the preparation of distance learning materials.

Dr Rosalind Levačić is Reader in Educational Policy and Management at the Open University. She has written widely on financial and resource management in schools and quasi-markets in education, including *Local Management of Schools: Analysis and Practice* (1995, Open University Press). She is currently working on the Impact of Competition on Secondary Schools (ICOSS) Study funded by the Economic and Social Research Council (ESRC), a study of 'Needs Based Resourcing in Education' funded by the International Institute for Educational Planning and a European Union (EU) Programme for Harmonization and Reform in Europe (PHARE) project on decentralization of school finance in Poland.

Jacky Lumby is a lecturer in educational management at the EDMU at the University of Leicester. She has previously taught in a range of educational settings, including schools, community and further education. Prior to joining the University of Leicester, she worked in a training and enterprise council with responsibility for the development of managers in both business and education. She has published within EMDU's distance-learning MBA and has published widely on management in further education.

Kevin McAleese, CBE has been headteacher of Harrogate Grammar School since January 1992. This is his second headship. In 1996 the Harrogate Grammar School was listed by Her Majesty's Chief Inspector as being *outstandingly successful*, following an OFSTED inspection. He is a regular contributor to educational conferences and seminars, as well as writing in *Managing Schools Today*. Kevin's other publications include *Balancing the Books* (1998, The Questions Publishing Company), 'Creating a More Positive Learning Environment' in *Maintaining Excellence in Schools* (1997, Cornforth and Evans) and *Managing the Margins* (January 1996, SHA). In April 1995, he founded the National Information Exchange between secondary schools.

Fergus O'Sullivan is Director of Bursarship Development in the International Educational Leadership Centre at the University of Lincolnshire and Humberside, England, where he has developed and leads the first MBA in the UK for school bursars. He is joint director of the International Educational Leadership Centre's research project on school educational resource management and its future. His previous experience includes deputy-headship of a large comprehensive school, succeeded by senior LEA officer and inspector posts and course leadership in higher education.

Hazel Pennell is a Research Fellow at the Centre for Educational Research at the London School of Economics and Political Science. Her research interests include education policy and its impact on equity, market reforms and the relationship between local and central government. She has also held senior positions in local government.

Tim Simkins is Head of the Centre for Education Management and Administration in the School of Education at Sheffield Hallam University. He has more than 20 years' experience teaching, consulting, researching and writing on education planning and management both in the UK and in a number of overseas countries, and is currently Chair of the British Educational Management and Administration Society. His particular interests are in strategic and resource management in education and the management of educational change in developing countries.

Professor Angela Thody is Professor of Educational Leadership at the International Educational Leadership Centre and Faculty of Business and Management Research Director, University of Lincolnshire and Humberside, England. She leads the taught and research doctoral programmes in education leadership and is joint director of the centre's research project on school educational resource management and its future. She is the first female President of the Commonwealth Council for Educational Administration and Management, a member of the International Committee of the British Educational Management and Administration Society, and was a council member of the latter for three years and editor of one of its journals, *Management in Education*, for five years.

Tony Travers is Director of the Greater London Group at the London School of Economics. He has been expenditure adviser to the House of Commons Select Committee on Education and Employment (and its predecessor committees) since 1980. He has also been adviser to a number of other parliamentary committees. He was a member of the Audit Commission from 1992 to 1997 and was an associate commissioner for the National Commission on Education. He has written and co-authored a number of books and writes regularly for the national press.

Dr Anne West is the Director of the Centre for Educational Research at the London School of Economics and Political Science. Her research interests include: education policy and practice and their effects on equity; education reforms; education policy in a European context; and the financing of education, including new modes of funding education and training. She previously worked as a research officer in the former Inner London Education Authority.

Robert West is Professor of Psychology at St George's Hospital Medical School. He has undertaken research into smoking, traffic accidents, music perception and education, and has published more than 150 scientific papers, books and book chapters. He has taught statistics, acted as statistical adviser on a range of projects and written a textbook on statistics and computing for psychologists.

Elizabeth Wood is a research assistant in the International Educational Leadership Centre at the University of Lincolnshire and Humberside. She has an MBA in Education Management for Bursars and is an accomplished administrator in higher education. Her previous experience includes 15 years as a manager of a small business. She is currently a researcher on the centre's project on school educational resource management and its future. She has presented conference papers and written journal articles on this topic. She also has several years' experience as a school governor and member of Parent Teacher Associations.

Part I: A National and International Perspective

1

LINKING RESOURCES TO LEARNING OUTCOMES

Rosalind Levačić

DO RESOURCES MATTER?

There is a paradox concerning the relationship between expenditure on education and outcomes. While parents, students, teachers and managers are convinced that with more resources they could produce better educational outcomes, the findings of academic research on the link between educational expenditure per student and educational outputs at the school, college or system level are still subject to much controversy. Eric Hanushek, a leading US researcher in this field, concluded from literature surveys that: 'The close to 400 studies of student achievement demonstrate that there is not a close or consistent relationship between student performance and school resources' (Hanushek, 1997, p. 141). However, in an analysis restricted to good quality US studies, Laine, Greenwald and Hedges concluded:

> resource variables such as per pupil expenditure show positive, strong and consistent relations with [student] achievement. Smaller classes and smaller schools are also positively related to student achievement. In addition, resource variables that attempt to describe the quality of the teachers (teacher ability, teacher education and teacher experience) show very strong relations with student achievement. Indeed the most consistently positive relation is that of teacher ability.
>
> (Laine, Greenwald and Hedges, 1996, pp. 57–8)

In the UK, we do not have the range of research on resources and learning outcomes that is funded in the USA to draw upon in order to inform practice and policy. However, the Labour government, demonstrating a belief that both the quantity of spending and what it is spent on matter, increased educational spending by £19 billion over the years 1999–2002. It also introduced a number of specific expenditure programmes, such as reducing all classes of 5- to 7-year-olds to 30 or below.

What we do have in the UK is considerable discretion at school and college level to determine the allocation of a delegated budget. This power places great responsibility in the hands of school and college managers and governing bodies to allocate resources to the best possible effect. Schools and colleges are held accountable for the quality of their resource management, through external financial audit and inspection. Thus great reliance is placed on the quality of the professional judgements of decision-makers in educational organizations.

Given the state of knowledge, this chapter cannot provide a blueprint for efficient patterns of resource allocation in education. Rather the chapter aims to clarify thinking about the relationship between resources and learning outcomes in order to promote better understanding and improved decision-making.

LEARNING OUTCOMES

In this chapter 'learning outcomes' is used as a catch-all term to refer to desired impacts on students' learning as a consequence of experiencing a formal programme of education. This learning includes both cognitive attainment, as can be measured by tests and examinations, as well as the development of desirable skills, attitudes and behaviour. The latter in particular are difficult, if not impossible, to measure. Consequently, those learning outcomes that can be measured predominate in quantitative research on the relationships between resource inputs and learning outcomes. However, when determining resource allocations, education managers and policy-makers need to take into account both measurable and intangible learning outcomes.

Learning outcomes also differ according to the time-scale over which they occur. Education economists usually distinguish between educational outputs and outcomes. The outputs of an educational organization are the direct effects it has on its students in terms of their acquiring knowledge, skills, beliefs and attitudes. Educational outcomes are the longer-term impacts on individuals and on society of the educational provision received at some earlier date. The additional income individuals earn as a result of their education is a direct private monetary benefit. Other learning outcomes are less easily measurable, such as the enjoyment of cultural activities, and include those outcomes that benefit society as a whole as well as the individual, such as adherence to moral codes of behaviour and participation in democratic institutions.

Thus the term 'learning outcomes' is used in this chapter to include both outputs and outcomes and has a particular focus on the learning outcomes of the school, college or university for its students. Because of the greater ease of measurement, examination results, test scores and student destinations (to employment or to the next stage of education) are the most frequently used measures of outputs of educational organizations. Given the importance of students' prior attainment and social background factors in determining their later educational attainment, educational organizations' outputs can only be fairly measured using value-added statistical techniques which take account of these factors. As these measures are statistical estimates they cannot be treated as precise measures of educational outputs, but only as reasonably good indicators within a stated range of probability.

The danger of focusing on measurable outputs is that the less easily measured and intangible outputs, which are nevertheless important, get neglected. Another problem for educational organizations is what relative weight to give to different educational outputs (e.g. knowledge in depth of mathematics and language compared to breadth of knowledge over a wide range of subjects; knowledge of academic subjects versus personal and social skills). Sometimes different outcomes can be produced together (e.g. co-operative learning can promote both social and cognitive objectives) but at other times one learning outcome can be produced only at the expense of less time spent on another. Also what is viewed as desirable educational outputs and outcomes is contested, affected as it is by customs, values and interests.

Despite all these difficulties, policy-makers and educational managers have to make choices and decide how best to use the resources over which they have discretion in order to achieve learning outcomes for students. This book aims to assist in clarifying thinking about these important issues and in providing guidance for such decision-making.

The rest of the chapter is split into the following sections:

- Organizational perspectives: this examines how resource management is conceived from different organizational perspectives.
- An organizational framework for understanding resource management: this includes a review of key terms, such as efficiency, effectiveness and equity.
- Linking resources to learning outcomes at organizational level.
- System-level incentives.

ORGANIZATIONAL PERSPECTIVES

The organization and its operational core

Organizational theory informs our understanding of the nature of links between resources and learning in schools, colleges and universities. We need to consider both the links that are internal to the organization and those which connect the organization to its external environment. Every organization concerned with the production of goods or services has what Mintzberg (1979) refers to as its operational core, where the primary activity, which is the purpose of the organization, takes place. For educational organizations the operational core is teaching and learning. Teachers and students are members of the operational core and the 'core technology' is teaching and learning.

The organization's resources that are directly utilized in teaching and learning are clearly teachers, classroom support staff (e.g. teaching assistants, laboratory and information technology (IT) technicians) and curriculum support resources[1] (i.e. books, stationery, materials and equipment).

In order to support its operational core, an organization has to provide other functions (Mintzberg, 1979). One is leadership and management, including the strategy of positioning the organization in relation to its external environment. The operational core also needs support staff who provide services such as routine administration, cleaning and maintenance of the premises and an environment conducive to the work of the core. The key point is that some resource management is not concerned directly with learning but with providing the environment within which learning can take place. It is unlikely that direct links between the amount of expenditure on the learning environment and the learning outcomes of students can be established, though this expenditure is still necessary to support learning.

The distinction between the operational core and the support services part of the educational organization is an important one. There is a tension between the proportion of the budget that should be spent on each. Judgements have to be exercised on the appropriate division and to what extent expenditures on support functions are justified by the needs of the operational core.

Also crucial for resource management is the impact of the external environment on the educational organization. Hoy and Miskel (1989, p. 34) define the external environment to 'consist of those relevant physical and social factors outside the boundaries of the organization that are taken into consideration in the decision-making behaviour of individuals in that system'. The relationship of the organization with its external environment is crucial in relation to resources. The more open an organization is to its external environment and the more dependent it is on securing support from its stakeholders, the more its survival and success depend on sustaining a flow of resources into the organization and providing stakeholders with the services they demand.

The three key layers of organizational structure are depicted in Figure 1.1. These layers interact. The nature of the external environment is in part dependent on the way in which the educational system as a whole is organized for allocating resources to its constituent organizations – schools and colleges. Thus the introduction of quasi-market arrangements, whereby school and college budgets depend largely on the numbers and

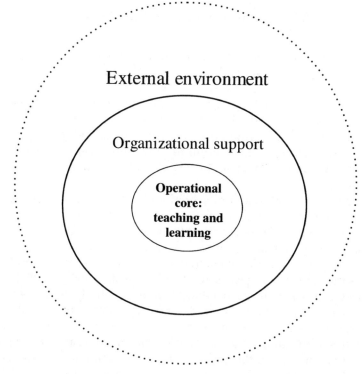

External environment

Organizational support

Operational core: teaching and learning

Figure 1.1 Organizational structure: core, support services and external environment

types of students recruited and where students have choice of institution, has greatly increased organizational dependence on the external environment. In turn, the advocacy of quasi-market arrangements for schools and colleges has been largely predicated on a view that financial incentives will induce educational organizations to improve their performance, just as they do for commercial organizations.

ORGANIZATION PERSPECTIVES AND EFFECTIVENESS

How one conceives of the linkage of resources to learning outcomes depends on the organizational perspective adopted. Three broad perspectives are frequently identified, as, for example, by Scott (1987) and Scheerens (1999), who relate organizational theory to school effectiveness research. These perspectives are:

- rational systems;
- natural systems or human relations approach;
- open systems.

The organization as a rational system

In this view the organization is defined as a collectivity with a distinct purpose. It has clear aims and goals, which are pursued through formal structures and rational decision-making. This requires the evaluation of alternative courses of action using relevant information and the selection of the alternative judged likely to be most successful in achieving the organization's goals. From the rational perspective organizational effectiveness is assessed in relation to how well organizational aims and objectives are achieved. The rational model is discussed further in Chapter 8.

A technical-rational model of school and college management has been promoted and strengthened by the educational policies pursued by governments around the world since the late 1980s. In the UK, for example, schools, colleges and universities are now held accountable through inspection for their educational standards. It is manifest, for example, in the OFSTED inspection framework (OFSTED, 1995a; 1995b; 1995c). Schools are expected to have clear aims and objectives, which should include the pursuit of high academic standards and the moral, social and personal development of students as reflected in the ethos of the school. The 1992 Education Act introduced the requirement that schools and colleges should be evaluated not only for the quality of their educational provision, but also for the efficiency of their resource management. Similar developments have occurred in Australia, New Zealand, Hong Kong, Singapore and in an increasing number of US states and Canadian school districts.

Organizations as natural systems

Whereas the rational perspective conceives of the organization as a goal-pursuing entity, the natural systems perspective focuses on the organization as a social unit and on the processes of social interaction between members. The organization is seen to exist in order to serve the human needs of its members. Thus its effectiveness is judged in relation to its ability to satisfy these needs and to promote social harmony between members. Staff morale and support are key measures of effectiveness. Management is therefore primarily concerned with human relations and with the creation and maintenance of social harmony. In Chapter 8, Tony Bush examines three models of management which are within the natural systems perspective. These models are:

- collegial;
- political;
- ambiguity.

Open systems models

In the open systems perspective the organization is dependent for its functioning on its external environment. The organization exists to satisfy external stakeholders, as well as its own members; its goals are influenced by or even set by external agents; its technical process involves taking inputs from the external environment and releasing outputs back to it. The approach emphasizes organizational complexity, both of the internal functioning of the organization and in its relationships with the external environment, with which its boundaries are permeable and ill-defined.

The open systems perspective is consistent with both rational and natural systems approaches. It adds an extra dimension: the organization lives, survives and adapts via its interlinkages with the external environment. From an open systems perspective an effective organization is one which adapts well to changes in its external environment and continues to serve the latter's needs.

The open systems approach is particularly appropriate for the analysis of educational organizations that have faced a continuing onslaught of changes designed to strengthen both consumer and government control. The creation of quasi-markets has increased the need for compliance with external stakeholders' preferences. In order to attract resources and to survive or even prosper, educational organizations must secure support from parents and students by producing educational outputs which these constituencies deem more attractive than those available from alternative providers. At the same time, the type and quality of these educational outputs are increasingly regulated by governmental agencies.

Implications of organizational analysis for resource management

How resource management is conceived – what its purpose is and how it is or should be undertaken – depends on the organizational perspective from which it is viewed. It is particularly important that this is appreciated by those involved in resource management as professionals and governors in educational organizations, because almost all of the official pronouncements on the subject are made from a rational perspective and are very often normative in nature.[2]

The idea that learning outcomes are related to the quantity and mix of resources deployed is an educational example of relating inputs to outputs or means to ends. These are all taken from the rational perspective. From a rational perspective there should be a tight coupling of resource and financial management to the operational core of teaching and learning. However, educational organizations often find this difficult to achieve. The main reasons for this are:

- ambiguity in defining and measuring educational outputs;
- ambiguity in relation to causal links between inputs of educational resources and educational outputs and outcomes;

- complexity because of the diverse kinds of outputs produced by educational organizations;
- the existence of a range of stakeholders in the educational organization who have different priorities concerning the outputs they desire (students, parents, employers, government agencies, staff members);
- the operation in practice of non-rational models, in particular political and ambiguity models.

Each perspective or model is likely to be in operation to some degree in an organization at the same time, and each provides a distinctive way of perceiving and understanding the organization (Bush, 1995; and Chapter 6 of this book).

When resource management is the focus of attention, then the normative issue of which perspective to favour can be resolved by seeing the rational perspective as predominant (Scheerens, 1999). For example, from the natural systems perspective it is important to develop and maintain an 'integrated organizational culture', i.e. where all staff members share organizational values, aims and objectives. Resource management includes personnel management which, to be effective, creates social harmony, job satisfaction and an awareness of being valued. The open systems perspective contributes the organizational processes for collecting information from the external environment, processing it and acting upon it so that the organization adapts as necessary for long-term survival. Hence strategic management is a vital part of resource management.

AN ORGANIZATIONAL FRAMEWORK FOR UNDERSTANDING RESOURCE MANAGEMENT

This section presents an organizational framework for understanding financial and resource management. The framework is predominantly rational, but draws on open systems and natural systems perspectives as well. Key terms needed for understanding resource management are also explained in the context of this framework.

An open systems model of the educational organization is depicted in Figure 1.2. It shows the educational organization as a system, which transforms inputs taken from the external environment into learning outcomes, which are delivered back to the environment. We start on the left-hand side of the model with the inflow of resources into the organization. The external environment can be subdivided into a general external environment made up of economic, political, social and technological influences and its 'task environment' (Butler, 1991) which relates to the specific purposes which its stakeholders wish the organization to serve. The interrelationship of the organization with its task environment is particularly crucial in influencing the inflow of resources to the organization and what it does with these resources.

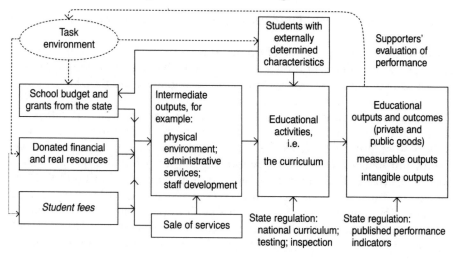

Figure 1.2   An educational organization as an open system

Financial and resource management is made up of four key processes:

1) Obtaining resources (marketing in the widest sense).
2) Allocating resources (planning and budget-setting).
3) Using resources (the implementation phase).
4) Evaluating the past use of resources and feedback of this information for future decision-making.

Although these processes are sequential they are also closely interrelated. The allocation of resources, for instance, depends on plans for their utilization and should be decided upon using information from evaluations of the outcomes of past resource use decisions. In this way the organization responds to feedback mechanisms and adjusts over time to changes in its task environment.

Obtaining resources

One of the major functions of resource management is to attract resources into the organization. Figure 1.2 shows the major types of resource inflow. When an organization operates within a market, resources initially enter in the form of money, which is then transferred into real resources – that is, staff, services and physical goods. Public sector and voluntary organizations also acquire real resources directly, for example in the form of donations of time from volunteers or of books and equipment. Financial resources come in the form of grants (mainly via the government), voluntary donations, from fund-raising and charging fees for educational services or, in a more minor way, from the sale of non-educational services, such as renting premises. Fund-raising and bidding are discussed further in Chapter 3.

Grants are the main source of financial income for public sector schools, and less so for colleges and universities which charge tuition fees. Different rules regarding the allocation of grants are designed to elicit different forms of behaviour from the recipients. The vast proportion of school and college grant income is determined by formulae in which the numbers and types of student are the main determinants of the amount of grant income received. This type of grant is 'unhypothecated'. This means it can be spent for any lawful purpose. Categorical or hypothecated grants have to be spent for a specific purpose. Department for Education and Employment (DfEE) Standards Funding in recent years has been made up of various categorical grants which have to be spent on items such as professional development, school improvement projects or newly qualified teacher induction. Funding principles for schools and colleges are examined in Chapters 4 and 5 respectively.

Allocating resources

Resource allocation concerns how both financial and real resources are deployed. In Figure 1.2 we move from the acquisition of financial resources to their transformation into real resources – staff, services and goods. Budget-setting is only part of the resource allocation process. The budget is concerned with transferring financial resources into real resources – teachers, support staff, services and physical resources. This budget-setting process in schools is examined by Kevin McAleese in Chapter 8.

Usually, the important decisions of how to deploy staff and physical educational resources to achieve specific learning outcomes do not appear in financial statements and are sometimes not even explicitly considered in the course of budget-setting. Typically in educational organizations, financial allocation decisions and real resource allocation decisions are not tightly coupled (Weick, 1976). This is not necessarily a criticism, as information and time for decision-making are limited. What is required from a rational perspective is that the teaching and learning in the operational core is organized and conducted effectively and supported to the greatest degree possible through the deployment of available resources. To do this requires that the processes of educational planning (school and college strategic and development plans) are explicitly tied into financial planning. The absence of precise knowledge on how particular quantities and mixes of resources affect learning outcomes, and the importance of the local context in mediating the link between inputs and educational outputs, mean that the quality of decision-making at school and college level is crucial for effectively deploying resources to achieve the best possible learning outcomes. Derek Glover examines these issues in more detail in Chapter 7.

Using resources

As indicated in Figure 1.2, resources fall into two main categories: those used to provide support services and those for the operational core of teaching and learning. Support services, such as the running costs of the building, administration and management, are intermediate outputs. These, in turn, are inputs into the operational core, where learning takes place. The educational activities of teaching and learning produce learning outcomes. The costs of financing the operational core are known as direct costs, whereas those of the support services are indirect costs. Tim Simkins examines costing further in Chapter 10.

Evaluating the use of resources to produce learning outcomes

The four 'e' words, effectiveness, efficiency, economy and equity, are concepts much used in the evaluation of resource usage. The next section considers what these concepts mean and how they relate to the issue of linking resources to learning outcomes.

Effectiveness

We have already noted that effectiveness depends on the organizational perspective being used. The usual definition of effectiveness (Audit Commission, 1984) – the extent to which intended outcomes are achieved – derives from the rational perspective. What is effective clearly depends on what objectives were set or, alternatively, on what objectives the evaluator desires.

Efficiency

Efficiency and economy are sometimes confused. Economy refers to minimizing the costs of a particular activity, whereas efficiency refers to the relationship between output and the costs of the inputs used to produce that output. An efficient use of resources is one which produces a given quantity or value of output at least cost. Equivalently, efficiency is attained when the maximum amount of output is produced for a given cost (Wyndham and Chapman, 1990, ch. 7). Economy is not a particularly useful concept. Reducing the cost of an activity is not an appropriate goal in itself, unless it at the same time improves efficiency. Cost-cutting for its own sake can make an organization less effective and less efficient.

Educational outputs, like any other goods and services, depend on the quantity of inputs used, their quality and the proportions in which they are used. The proportions in which different resources are used are referred to as the resource mix. For example, classes of children could be taught to read by spending the same sum of money on three different resource mixes. Method 1 is a smaller class and one fully qualified teacher, method 2 is a larger class with a fully qualified teacher and a teaching support assistant, method 3 is a larger class with a teacher and an integrated learning computer system. In principle, one could experiment with all three methods, with three groups of similar children, and see which produced the greatest progress in reading. The method which produced the most reading progress for the given sum of money would be most efficient, say it is method 2. However, if the relative prices of teachers, support assistants and integrated learning (IL) systems changed, say the IL system became much cheaper, then method 3 could become the most efficient.

The most efficient use of resources therefore depends on:

- the 'technical' relationship between the combinations of inputs and learning outcomes (e.g. how much reading progress is achieved for different learning methods);
- the prices of the various inputs.

Value for money

It is important to appreciate that efficiency is a normative concept. What way of allocating resources is deemed efficient depends on what kind of output is being produced. To assess schools' efficiency in terms of students' progress in specific forms of learning is to make a value judgement. It is quite possible to produce output of little value to society but to produce it efficiently. It is also possible to be effective in producing output which is desired, but to produce it inefficiently.[3]

Value for money is achieved when the production process is both effective and efficient (Audit Commission, 1984).

Equity

Though not part of the standard public accountant's three 'e's, equity is a crucial concept for guiding the allocation of resources. Equity is analogous to fairness and justice. A standard definition of equity in relation to education (Swanson and King, 1997, p. 323) is that 'expenditure is distributed in such a way that each child can access an education appropriate to his/her individual learning potential and needs'. The importance of judgement, and hence subjectivity, in the definition is evident from the use of the words 'appropriate', 'potential' and 'needs'.

There are two main equity principles:

- *Horizontal equity* is the principle that people with similar needs should be treated similarly. It therefore requires that children with similar learning needs should have the same quality and quantity of educational provision. This usually implies that roughly equal amounts should be spent on each child's education.
- *Vertical equity* is the principle that students should be provided with an education which matches their different learning needs. Those with learning difficulties require additional spending in order to have access to the standard of education provided for the majority of children.

Educational managers need to make equity judgements when allocating resources between different age groups, different curriculum areas, different courses and students' with different learning needs. An example of such an equity judgement is that of Ousedale School which received an allocation of £51,962 for non-statemented and statemented special needs students but spent £131,381, of which £122,709 was for staff. This provided 222 hours per week of support time for 218 students throughout Years 8 to 11. This additional spending contributed to the learning outcomes of students with statements, who achieved on average 6.7 GCSE passes each (Ousedale Governors, 1997).

LINKING RESOURCES TO LEARNING OUTCOMES AT ORGANIZATIONAL LEVEL

Education managers are exhorted to manage effectively and efficiently, and even equitably. They are faced with the problem of achieving effectiveness across a range of learning outcomes using limited resources which are difficult to augment. The education production process is characterized by considerable ambiguity and controversy over the best 'technology' of teaching and learning to use. However, both educational research on school and teacher effectiveness, and increasing prescription by government of literacy and numeracy strategies, are providing more specific guidance on how resources should be deployed than used to be the case.

The absence in education of the equivalent of technical blueprints for how to combine resources most efficiently for producing learning outcomes is reflected in OFSTED's inspection framework for the efficiency of the school. Though OFSTED defines efficiency in standard input-output terms, it does not attempt to measure efficiency in this way. Instead the framework requires evidence that schools are following rational decision-making processes which are consistent with the search for the most effective and efficient deployment of resources (Levačić and Glover, 1997; 1998). These include, in particular, the creation and implementation of development plans, systematic evaluation of resource deployment and the operation of sound financial systems.

Resource management and effectiveness in secondary schools

A study of the association between resource input and management process variables on the one hand, and educational effectiveness measures on the other hand, was undertaken by Levačić and Glover (1998). From a sample of 117 OFSTED inspection reports produced in 1994, we assembled a dataset of indicators of (1) resource inputs into schools, (2) management processes for rational decision-making on resource allocation, and (3) educational effectiveness.

Input variables were the pupil–teacher ratio, teachers' class contact ratio, teaching time, unit costs, educational resource costs, percentage of pupils entitled to free meals, percentage of pupils with special educational needs and whether the school had grant maintained status.

The variables concerned with processes for rational decision-making with respect to resource allocation are referred to as the rational decision-making (RDM) variables. These relate to:

- rational planning processes at school level;
- departmental planning;
- staff deployment;
- resource deployment;
- financial management.

The RDM variables were rated by us on a scale of 1 to 3 according to the inspectors' comments. Category 3 indicated commendations of good practice by inspectors; category 2 referred to satisfactory comments with suggestions for refinements; category 1 indicated critical comments.

Educational effectiveness was measured in terms of variables available in the inspection reports. These included:

- the proportion of students gaining five or more GCSEs grade C or better;
- percentage of lessons in which learning is rated as good by inspectors (variable LG);[4]
- percentage of lessons in which teaching is rated as good by inspectors (TG).

We examined the relationships between the input and management process variables on the one hand and the outcome variables on the other hand in a number of different ways. These included:

- placing schools into one of three groups according to values of each of their RDM variables and comparing group means (using an analysis of

variance test) for percentage of lessons in which learning was rated good (LG) and percentage for which teaching was rated good (TG);
- multiple regressions with LG and TG as independent variables and the RDM and input variables as dependent variables.

All the tests showed evidence of positive association between scores for educational effectiveness variables and the RDM variables. None of the input variables, except free school meals, was significantly related to educational effectiveness. Examples of the findings are reproduced in Table 1.1 (see also Levačić and Glover, 1998).

Table 1.1 Comparison of group scores for resource decision-making and percentage of learning rated as good and percentage of teaching rated as good

Resource decision-making variable groups	Means of Group 3		Means of Group 2		Means of Group 1	
	Learning good	Teaching good	Learning good	Teaching good	Learning good	Teaching good
Rational planning	47.9	46.6	41.9	41.4	32.2	30.9
Departmental planning	57.4	52	41.6	41.7	37.9	36.9
Staff deployment	47.1	46.8	41.2	40.4	26.3	26.9
Resource deployment	51.1	47.9	41.2	41.6	27	27.1
Financial management	44.6	42.6	39.7	41.3	26.2	23

Note: Analysis of variance (ANOVA) tests showed that the differences in means for the three groups were significantly different at $p < = 0.05$.

We concluded from the findings of this study that there was evidence of an association between rational decision-making processes and indicators of educational effectiveness: schools which are managed in ways consistent with rational decision-making also appear to be more educationally effective.[5]

Benchmarking

While we do not yet have research-based knowledge on the most effective resource mixes for specific learning outcomes, there is increasing availability of comparative or benchmarking data on learning outcomes and, separately, on resource mixes and spending patterns of schools of comparative phase and size.

An essential step in effective and efficient resource management is assessing the learning progress of individual students in relation to their prior attainment benchmarked against large national samples of pupils. Such value-added analyses of pupil performance data are being increasingly used, particularly now that schools are required to set targets at Key Stages 2 and 4. Value-added analysis gives schools and colleges information on relative strengths and weaknesses, where good internal practice exists which can be disseminated, and where weaknesses can be addressed by importing improvements tried out in other schools and colleges. However, to address efficiency as well requires schools to make conscious assessments of the costs of alternative approaches to improving learning outcomes relative to their likely effectiveness and to examine ways in which the budget can be used more flexibly to finance new developments. These issues are addressed further in Chapter 7.

Schools can also check their resource mix patterns of expenditure against those of other schools using the Performance and Assessment Report (PANDA) data provided by OFSTED, some of which are reproduced in Table 1.2. These data give guidance as to whether expenditure patterns are near the median or within the interquartile ranges or whether they are

Table 1.2 Expenditure patterns at LEA maintained schools (for financial year 1997/98) as percentage of total expenditure

	Primary schools (> 50 pupils)			Secondary schools		
	Lower quartile	Median	Upper quartile	Lower quartile	Median	Upper quartile
Staff						
Teachers	66.9	70.8	74.5	68.1	71.0	73.8
Supply teachers	1.1	1.9	3.1	0.7	1.2	1.8
Education support	3.7	5.9	8.8	1.9	2.9	4.0
Admin./clerical	2.7	3.4	4.4	2.6	3.3	4.3
Other staff costs	2.2	3	3.9	0.7	1.0	1.5
Supplies and services						
Learning resources	3.2	4.1	5.4	4.4	5.4	6.5
Staff development	1.1	1.5	2.0	0.6	0.8	1.1
Catering and other	1.1	1.9	3.1	1.2	1.9	3.0
Premises and facilities						
Buildings and grounds maintenance and repair	1.2	1.9	3.0	1.4	2.0	3.1
Cleaning and caretaking	3.4	4.3	5.3	3.0	3.6	4.3
Other occupancy costs	2.9	4.2	5.6	3.7	5.1	6.2

Sources: OFSTED (1999a, p. 29, table 7.1.2; 1999b, p. 34, table 7.1.3).

unusually high or low, in which case expenditure items in question need careful examination to ensure that there are good reasons for them.

Future improvements

In order to improve the links between resources and learning outcomes – in other words, to improve effectiveness and efficiency – schools and colleges need to move towards a more systematized professional knowledge base through:

- better systems within schools for evidencing their own practice;
- better support from external agents (LEAs, universities, research institutes and consultants) undertaking data collection, analysis and promoting the use of management information by schools;
- further research on school and teacher effectiveness, with more explicit focus on resource use and cost;
- better dissemination of benchmarking data and research findings.

SYSTEM-LEVEL INCENTIVES

The efficiency and effectiveness of resource use is also affected by the incentives and sanctions signalled to schools and colleges by the methods for allocating resources which operate at the national or system level. There is considerable controversy over the most appropriate way to structure resource allocation at the system level. These issues are outlined here briefly, in order to complete the framework for the analysis of resource management and its links with learning outcomes.

Two 'ideal models' can be distinguished – bureaucratic resource allocation and market allocation. In practice, in any educational system, some combination of both methods is used.

Bureaucratic allocation

In this system educational organizations are allocated resources in kind by central or local government bodies using administrative rules. The outputs of schools and colleges are prescribed by government, as are rules concerning their use of inputs (e.g. pay and conditions of teachers, class size). In a highly centralized system, teachers are selected and allocated to schools by central or local government departments. Since the 1970s there has been a reaction against bureaucratic organization of services on the grounds that it provides insufficient incentives for providers to satisfy the preferences of service users (either direct customers or political leaders who act 'on behalf' of service users) or to operate efficiently.

Market allocation

Under a pure market system, schools and colleges determine their own curriculum, set their admissions policies including fees, raise capital for investment and decide whether to enter or exit the market. If the state wishes to intervene to ensure that all parents can afford to send their children to school, then it will provide vouchers that may be means tested or taxed. Market allocation is advocated on the grounds that it promotes choice and diversity and ensures that educational organizations are efficient and effective, or else they cannot survive. Resources will be linked to the learning outcomes of schools and colleges via market signalling. The main criticisms are that market allocation of education is inequitable; it increases social stratification and does not ensure all children receive the kind of education valued by society.

Quasi-market

The quasi-market is a hybrid which has features of bureaucratic and pure market allocation. A distinguishing feature is that the provider of educational services (the school or college) is separated from the purchaser. This is done in the UK system by funding schools and colleges largely according to the number and objective characteristics of their students. It is notable that a number of education systems have been restructured along quasi-market lines (for example, Sweden, Australia, New Zealand, Chile and school districts in the USA and Canada). Schools and colleges have resource management delegated to them, face a degree of competition from other providers and are held accountable for the quality of education they provide as assessed against government defined standards. Performance related pay is a further example of attempts to link resources to learning outcomes via the use of financial incentives. Quasi-markets in education are also characterized by a considerable degree of state bureaucratic regulation; e.g. of the curriculum, tests, inspection procedures and the provision of information to service users.

The advocacy or condemnation of particular types of allocation mechanism is generally related to ideologically informed views of what constitute preferred social systems. This is not the place to discuss these complex issues. The main point being made is that different combinations of bureaucratic and market allocation result in particular configurations of incentives and sanctions for colleges and schools which influence how they allocate resources internally and what kinds of learning outcomes result. System-level allocation mechanisms are often designed to steer or control educational organizations in an attempt to make them deliver what policy-makers want. The system-level allocation mechanism is a key feature of the external environment of educational organizations and is highly influential in determining how resources are managed internally and to what effect.

CONCLUSION

This chapter aims to provide a reasonably comprehensive framework for the analysis of resource management in educational organizations. It draws on major theoretical traditions to demonstrate that the main purpose of resource management and how it is or should be conducted depend on the organizational perspective adopted. The main perspective adopted here is an open systems version of the rational model. This takes account of the importance for the educational organization of the system-level allocative mechanism within which it operates.

The usual approach to resource management, which also predominates in this chapter, is the rational perspective. The link between resource inputs and learning outcomes is conceived of as a production process, characterized by a distinct production technology, located in the operational core of the organization. The key sequential processes of resource management – obtaining, allocating, using and evaluating resources – feed into this production process.

The key concepts in resource management, particularly those of effectiveness and efficiency, are derived from the rational perspective and its conception of an education production process. Owing to the difficulties of valuing a highly diverse and intangible range of learning outcomes, and the lack of precise knowledge about the education process itself, the concepts of effectiveness and efficiency are not easy to operationalize for educational organizations.

However, from a rational perspective these concepts need to be made operational. This requires the establishment of appropriate management processes and the application of professional judgements. Knowledge from research on school and teacher effectiveness needs to be combined with considerations of resource use and costs. Schools and colleges need further support and encouragement to develop evidence-informed decisions on resource allocation in order to make it more effective and efficient. At the same time, the insights of other perspectives on resource management should not be neglected.

NOTES

1 OFSTED refers to books, stationery, equipment and materials as educational resources. I prefer to use the term 'curriculum support resources' as in this chapter educational resources really refers to all types of resource used in education.

2 By normative is meant that they are pronouncements of what 'should be' and therefore embody value judgements.

3 In economic theory efficiency is defined in such a way that includes effectiveness, because it is assumed that the output being produced is what society values. For example, Wyndham and Chapman (1990, p. 60)

state that 'efficiency exists where the desired mix of outputs (effectiveness) is maximised for a given level of inputs (cost)'. However, on page 225 they recognize that the concept of efficiency has to be operationalized in some specific value-laden manner. For operational purposes, then, analytical clarity is served by distinguishing efficiency from effectiveness, as practised in public sector accounting (see Audit Commission, 1984).

4 These ratings follow the guidance given to inspectors so that assessment is based upon a common set of criteria. The inspection reports give the percentage of lessons and teaching rated as good.

5 A discussion of assumptions and caveats is to be found in Levačić and Glover (1998).

REFERENCES

Audit Commission (1984) *Code of Local Government Audit Practice for England and Wales*, London, HMSO.

Bush, T. (1995) *Theories of Educational Management* (2nd edn), London, Paul Chapman.

Butler, R. J. (1991) *Designing Organisations: A Decision-Making Perspective*, London, Routledge.

Hanushek, E. K. (1997) Assessing the effects of school resources on student performance: an update, *Educational Evaluation and Policy Analysis*, Vol. 19, no. 2, pp. 141–64.

Hoy, W. K. and Miskel, C. G. (1989) Schools and their external environments, in R. Glatter (ed.), *Educational Institutions and their Environments: Managing the Boundaries*, Milton Keynes, Open University Press.

Laine, R. D., Greenwald, R. and Hedges, L. V. (1996) Money does matter: a research synthesis of a new universe of education production function studies, in L. O. Picus and J. L. Wattenbarger (eds), *Where Does the Money Go? Resource Allocation in Elementary and Secondary Schools*, Thousand Oaks, CA, Corwin Press.

Levačić, R. and Glover, D. (1997) Value for money as a school improvement strategy: evidence from the new inspection system in England, *School Effectiveness and Improvement*, Vol. 8, no. 2, pp. 231–53.

Levačić, R. and Glover, D. (1998) The relationship between efficient resource management and school effectiveness: evidence from OFSTED secondary school inspections, *School Effectiveness and School Improvement*, Vol. 9, no. 1, pp. 95–122.

Mintzberg, H. (1979) *The Structuring of Organisations*, Englewood Cliffs, NJ, Prentice Hall.

OFSTED (1995a) *Guidance on the Inspection of Nursery and Primary Schools*, London, HMSO.

OFSTED (1995b) *Guidance on the Inspection of Secondary Schools*, London, HMSO.

OFSTED (1995c) *Guidance on the Inspection of Special Schools*, London, HMSO.

OFSTED (1999a) Primary Schools Panda Annex 1998 Data, London, March.

OFSTED (1999b) Secondary Schools Panda Annex 1998 Data, London, February.

Ousedale Governors (1997) Ousedale Governors' Report to Parents 1996, Milton Keynes, Ousedale School.

Scheerens, J. (1999) Concepts and theories of school effectiveness, in A. J. Visscher (ed.), *Managing Schools Towards High Performance*, Lisse, Swets and Zeitlinger.

Scott, W. R. (1987) *Organisations: Rational, Natural and Open Systems*, Englewood Cliffs, NJ, Prentice Hall.

Swanson, A. D. and King, R. A. (1997) *School Finance: Its Economics and Politics* (2nd edn), New York, Longman.

Weick, K. (1976) Education organisations as loosely coupled systems?, *Administrative Science Quarterly*, Vol, 21, no. 1, pp. 1–21.

Wyndham, D. M. and Chapman, D. W. (1990) *The Evaluation of Educational Efficiency: Constraints, Issues and Policies*, Greenwich, CT, JAI Press.

2

LOCAL MANAGEMENT AND LEARNING OUTCOMES: MAPPING THE LINKS IN THREE GENERATIONS OF INTERNATIONAL RESEARCH

Brian J. Caldwell

Local management or self-management is a feature of the school reform movement around the world. Caldwell and Spinks (1998) consider the building of systems of self-managing schools to be one of the three major 'tracks' of change, the others being an unrelenting focus on learning outcomes and the creation of schools for the knowledge society. Once established, local management appears irreversible, as evidenced in support among the three major political parties in the British election in 1997, and its extension under the Blair government to the extent that local education authorities are expected to decentralize a higher proportion of available funds than had been required under the Conservatives.

Decisions on resources are central to self-management, as illustrated in the definition of Caldwell and Spinks (1998) based on their earlier conceptualization (Caldwell and Spinks, 1988) and further refinement by Bullock and Thomas (1997):

> A self-managing school is a school in a system of education to which there has been decentralised a significant amount of authority and responsibility to make decisions about the allocation of resources within a centrally determined framework of goals, policies, standards and accountabilities. Resources are defined broadly to include knowledge, technology, power, materiél, people, time, assessment, information and finance.
>
> (Caldwell and Spinks, 1998, pp. 4–5)

After a decade of reform, it is fair to ask about the extent to which there has been an impact on outcomes for students. It is sobering to note the consistent finding in early research that there appear to be few if any direct links

24

between local management or school-based management and learning outcomes (Malen, Ogawa and Kranz, 1990; Summers and Johnson, 1996). Some researchers have noted that such gains are unlikely to be achieved in the absence of purposeful links between capacities associated with school reform, in this instance, local management, and what occurs in the classroom, in learning and teaching and the support of learning and teaching (see Bullock and Thomas, 1997; Cheng, 1996: Hanushek, 1996, 1997; Levačić, 1995; OECD, 1994; Smith, Scoll and Link, 1996).

New ground is broken in this chapter to the extent that research of the kind cited above can now be seen as constituting the first generation of studies of school-based management, and that second and third generations of studies are now discernible. It is in the third generation that the nature of the linkage between local management or self-management and learning outcomes can be mapped in a manner that can be trustworthy in policy and practice.

The primary purpose of this chapter is to report school-based evidence of links between local management and learning outcomes for students in the third generation of studies. By learning outcomes is meant student achievement of any kind for which there are outcome measures. The evidence from the third generation studies confirms the generally positive ratings of principals in second generation studies in systems of public education where all elements of a comprehensive reform programme have been in place for several years. Particular attention is given here to findings from a five-year longitudinal project in Victoria, Australia, where 90 per cent of the state's education budget has been decentralized to about 1,650 schools, the largest system of public education anywhere with this level of decentralization in funding. Links between local management and learning outcomes are modelled and mapped. The chapter concludes with implications for policy-makers and practitioners.

THE INCONCLUSIVE NATURE OF THE LINKAGE IN FIRST AND SECOND GENERATION STUDIES

The research that is the main focus of attention in this chapter is, in fact, from the third generation of studies on the broad phenomenon of school-based management. Two earlier generations are discernible, the first of which was concerned with the impact of school-based management, with most studies undertaken in the USA. The much cited work of Malen, Ogawa and Kranz (1990) falls in this category, with Summers and Johnson (1996) providing a meta-analysis of the first generation. They located 70 studies that purported to be evaluations of school-based management, but only 20 of these employed a systematic approach and just seven included a measure of student outcomes. They concluded that 'there is little evidence to support the notion that school-based management is effective in increasing student performance. There are very few quantitative studies, the studies are not statistically rigorous, and the evidence of positive results is either weak or non-existent' (Summers and Johnson, 1996, p. 80). Apart from the 'overwhelming obstacles' in the way of assessing the impact of school-based management, Summers and Johnson drew attention to the fact that few initiatives 'identify student achievement as a major objective. The focus is on organisational processes, with virtually no attention to how process changes may affect student performance' (Summers and Johnson, 1996, pp. 92–3).

For Hanushek, the findings are not surprising because of the absence of a purposeful link between school-based management and student performance. He noted the review of Summers and Johnson and observed that 'decentralisation of decision-making has little general appeal without such linkage and, indeed, could yield worse results with decentralised management pursuing its own objectives not necessarily related closely to student performance' (Hanushek, 1996, p. 45).

In a report on the effects of school resources on student achievement, Hanushek (1997, p. 156) drew attention to the finding 'that simply de-centralising decision-making is unlikely to work effectively unless there exist clear objectives and unless there is direct accountability'. It is the absence of this framework that characterizes the context for what are described here as first generation studies. School-based management in the USA was and, for the most part, continues to be a modest initiative compared to local management in England and Wales, or the self-managing schools of Victoria, Australia. On the decentralization side, few resources were shifted to the school level for local decision-making. On the centralization side, curriculum and standards frameworks and requirements for accountability were rudimentary in most instances. School-based management was for the most part a well-intentioned effort to empower teachers and, to a limited extent, the community, and there was little connection in expectation, process or outcome to student learning.

The second generation of studies has accompanied the more far-reaching reforms in local management and self-management, with most of the available budget in a school system decentralized to the local level within a comprehensive and centrally determined curriculum, standards and accountability framework, as in England and Wales, and in Victoria. In general, the findings have been as inconclusive as the first generation. Levačić (1995, p. 190) found that, of four criteria associated with intentions for the local management of schools in Britain (effectiveness, efficiency, equity and choice), 'cost-efficiency is the one for which there is most evidence that local management has achieved the aims set for it by government', especially through the opportunity it provides for schools to purchase at a lower cost for a given quality or quantity than in the past, and by allowing resource mixes that were not possible or readily attainable under previous more centralized arrangements. For effectiveness, she concluded that there is 'little evidence from this [case study] sample of schools of local management stimulating any significant changes in the way schools operate with respect to their core technology of teaching and learning' (Levačić, 1995, p. 105).

In Britain, as elsewhere, there was no research that endeavoured to map a cause-and-effect relationship between local management and discretionary use of resources, on the one hand, and improved learning outcomes for students on the other, building on the findings of studies that yielded strong opinion-based evidence that gains had been made (for example, Bullock and Thomas, 1994). Drawing predominantly on evidence from Britain (England and Wales) but referring also to outcomes elsewhere, Bullock and Thomas concluded that:

> It may be that the most convincing evidence of the impact of local management is on the opportunities which it has provided for managing the environment and resources for learning, both factors that can act to support the quality of learning in schools. What remains elusive, however, is clear-cut evidence of these leading through to direct benefits on learning, an essential component if we are to conclude that it is contributing to higher levels of efficiency.
>
> (Bullock and Thomas, 1997, p. 217)

Bullock and Thomas then went to the heart of the issue:

> If learning is at the heart of education, it must be central to our final discussion of decentralisation. It means asking whether, in their variety of guises, the changes characterised by decentralisation have washed over and around children in classrooms, leaving their day-to-day experiences largely untouched. In asking this question, we must begin by recognising that structural changes in governance, management and finance may leave largely untouched the daily interaction of pupils and teachers.
>
> (Bullock and Thomas, 1997, p. 219)

A review of reform in Australia, Britain and New Zealand, Sweden and the USA led Whitty, Power and Halpin (1998, p. 111) to conclude that 'there were insufficient grounds to claim that self-managing schools are currently enhancing student attainment'. While these authors fail to cite findings from third generation studies of the kind set out below, their conclusion is generally fair as far as findings in second generation studies are concerned.

ILLUMINATING THE LINKS IN THIRD GENERATION STUDIES

A third generation of studies emerged in the last two years of the 1990s. The policy context was the same as for the second generation, namely, local management in England and Wales and self-management in Victoria, with the emergence of more comprehensive and coherent systemic reform in the USA, as in Chicago. There are, however, three important differences to mark this generation of study. First, by the late 1990s, a substantial set of data on student achievement had been established as a result of system-wide tests that enabled change at the local level to be tracked over several years. Schools were also able to draw on an increasingly deep pool of other indicators. Second, the policy framework had become more explicit with respect to expectations for schools to make the link between elements in the school reform programme and learning outcomes for students. This reflected change on Track 2 ('an unrelenting focus on learning outcomes') in the classification of Caldwell and Spinks (1998). Third, researchers were utilizing an increasingly sophisticated array of techniques for analysis of data, including structural equation modelling and data envelope analysis[1] along with more focused approaches to case study.

Self-management, self-government and choice in England and Wales

Third generation research in England and Wales is at the cutting edge in assessing the impact of different levels of self-management on student achievement, especially under conditions where there are a choice of schools. There is conflicting evidence in this regard. On the one hand is a study at Lancaster University (Bradley, Johnes and Millington, 1999; see also related studies on school size reported in Bradley and Taylor, 1998, and Taylor and Bradley, 1999). Data envelope analysis was applied to four data sets: performance (student achievement and truancy rates); school characteristics (student–teacher ratio, school type and socio-economic circumstance of students); expenditure (teachers, books and materials); and local demographic conditions (unemployment rate, socio-economic composition). Data for all secondary schools in England over the period from 1993 to 1997 were analysed. They found that:

> the greater the degree of competition between schools, the more efficient the schools tend to become. Moreover, differentials in efficiency between the most and the least efficient schools appear to narrow in response to competition. These effects have strengthened over time, a finding which is consistent with the evolution of the quasi-market. Competition between schools is also found to be an important determinant of the change in relative efficiency over time.
>
> (Bradley, Johnes and Millington, 1999, p. 18)

One implication, according to the authors, is that 'policymakers should take care when deciding whether to close a particular school, since the gains from reduced public expenditure may be outweighed by the loss of efficiency in neighbouring schools because of the reduction in competition between schools' (ibid., p. 18).

On the other hand, a study at the Open University revealed that the provision of choice between grant maintained schools and locally managed schools had yielded no significant difference between examination results of students attending the two types of schools once students' social backgrounds are taken into account (Levačić and Hardman, 1999; Levačić, Hardman and Woods, 1998). Researchers compared results of students in secondary schools for 91 grant maintained schools and 206 locally managed schools. They noted that results in grant maintained schools increased faster in the early 1990s because their more flexible admissions policies meant that they were 'better placed to covertly select pupils by ability'. They also concluded that grant maintained schools have been 'poor value for money' and that the policy that led to their creation was 'yet another example of how additional expenditure on education does not of itself deliver concomitant improvements in learning' (cited by Budge, 1999, p. 26).

Comprehensive reform in Chicago

An increasing number of school districts in the USA are establishing local management on the scale now evident in England and Wales, but these are still a small minority among the 15,000 jurisdictions in that nation. The public school district in Chicago is one such system with a comprehensive and relatively coherent set of reforms dating from 1988. The stated goal of the Chicago School Reform Act was to raise the level of student achievement to match national norms. According to Hess (1999, p. 67) the chief mechanism to achieve this goal is a system of school-based decision-making, with school councils and local responsibility for school improvement planning, budget allocation and selection of staff within a framework of system-wide standards and tests.

There is promising but contested evidence of the impact of school-based decision-making and learning outcomes in Chicago. Reading scores in 1990 were compared with those achieved in 1997. Nearly half of the schools included in the study posted impressive gains, with Donald R. Moore, Executive Director of Designs for Change that conducted the study, reporting 'strong evidence that the schools that have taken the greatest advantage of that decision-making opportunity [under decentralization] are improving student achievement' (cited by Lawson, 1997, p. 3), with the most improved schools having higher ratings of a school council focus on improvement, principals, teacher influence, teacher–parent relationships, safety, co-operative teacher effort and learning. While the researchers included controls on student backgrounds in their analysis, other researchers not involved in the study questioned whether sufficient account had been taken of change in student demographics on a school-by-school basis.

The most powerful evidence of linkage between self-management and learning outcomes in Chicago, arguably in any jurisdiction, has emerged in the longitudinal studies of the Consortium on Chicago School Research (Bryk, 1998; Bryk *et al.*, 1998). Value-added measures of student achievement over a number of years were included in the design of an innovative productivity index. A model of direct and indirect effects, including a capacity for self-management, was derived. As with the study reported in the preceding paragraph, this evidence is contested. Hess (1999) reported mixed experience in the analysis of longitudinal achievement data over a ten-year period and detailed case studies of experience in 14 schools. His conclusion on the importance of resources is striking:

> budget analyses . . . and interview comments from principals show that discretionary funds were important to schools in their efforts to change. Principals said over and over that these funds were the engine that allowed them to make changes in their schools. We found, however, that their efforts were compromised to the extent that they were forced to siphon off resources to maintain programs cut by the board of education to balance the budget each year. Further, we have seen that some schools spent a lot of new discretionary money without much to show for those expenditures in terms of effective use of funds to foster improved student learning. More money was crucial to improvement in the schools where improvement was taking place. But more money did not automatically translate into better student outcomes. How the money was used does appear to matter.
>
> (Hess, 1999, p. 81)

Research in Victoria, Australia, helps explain how money may be used in efforts to achieve improvements in learning outcomes for students.

Self-managing schools in Victoria

Education in Australia is constitutionally the responsibility of state/territory governments rather than the Commonwealth (national) government. The six states and two territories vary in the extent to which systems of self-managing schools have been established in the public sector since 1970. Particular attention is given in this section of the chapter to the processes and outcomes of the most recent wave of reform in the state of Victoria, which has occurred since early 1993 under the rubric of Schools of the Future, so almost 90 per cent of the state's budget for public education has been decentralized to schools for local decision-making within a curriculum and standards framework in eight key learning areas. Schools have a capacity to select their own staff, who remain employed by the central authority, with provision for annual and triennial reports to the local community and the state Department of Education, Employment and Training on a range of indicators.

The objectives and purposes of the reform ranged over educational ('to enhance student learning outcomes', 'actively foster the attributes of good schools'); professional ('recognise teachers as true professionals', 'allow principals to be true leaders'); community ('to determine the destiny of the school, its character and ethos') and accountability ('for the progress of the school and the achievement of its students') (Hayward, 1993).

Findings cited here are drawn from several research projects. The primary source is the Cooperative Research Project, a joint endeavour of the former Education Department, the state agency with responsibility for public education, the Victorian Association of State Secondary Principals, the Victorian Primary Principals Association and the University of Melbourne. The project began in mid-1993 and concluded in mid-1998, completing on schedule a planned five-year longitudinal study of the processes and outcomes of the reform. Seven state-wide surveys of representative samples of principals were conducted and these covered virtually every aspect of the reform, including its impact on learning outcomes for students (Cooperative Research Project 1994; 1995a; 1995b; 1996; 1997; 1998). Seventeen investigations, including two reported here (Hillier, 1999; Wee, 1999a; 1999b) focused on discrete elements, including leadership, professional development, new workplace practices, resource allocation and school improvement.

More recent work, including the studies of Hillier and Wee, extended the work of the Cooperative Research Project in an international collaborative effort, pooling research from Australia (University of Melbourne), Britain (Open University) and the USA (University of Wisconsin at Madison). There were two purposes of this larger effort, which was supported by the Australian Research Council: first, the development of models for funding that transcend national boundaries (see findings in Ross and Levačić, 1999) and, second, investigation of the impact of school-based decisions about resource allocation on learning outcomes for students.

Successive surveys in the Cooperative Research Project consistently found that principals believed there had been moderate to high level of realization of the expected benefit in respect of improved learning outcomes for students. In the final survey in 1997, 84 per cent gave a rating of 3 or more on the 5-point scale (1 is 'low' and 5 is 'high').

As in the first generation of studies, such findings do not illuminate the issue of the extent to which the capacities fostered by the reform impact on learning outcomes. Structural equation modelling using LISREL 8 (Jöreskog and Sörbom, 1993) was employed in the analysis of data in the 1995, 1996 and 1997 surveys. The model reported here derives from the 1997 survey (Cooperative Research Project, 1998). This survey was of a truly representative sample of school heads, classified according to school type, school size and urban/rural setting.

The first step was to create seven clusters of related survey items and to treat these as constructs. These constructs were formed from 45 survey items concerned with attitudes to the reform ('Confidence in the Attainment of Schools of the Future Objectives'), support ('Curriculum and Standards Framework Curriculum Support'), and outcomes ('Curriculum and Learning Benefits', 'Curriculum Improvement due to the Curriculum and Standards Framework', 'Planning and Resource Allocation Benefits', 'School and Community Benefits', 'Personnel and Professional Benefits').

Figure 2.1 contains the explanatory regression model that shows the interdependent effects among variables (in this instance, latent variables that represent the constructs) on the variable 'Curriculum and Learning Benefits', which is the object of interest in this section of the chapter. Standardized path coefficients are shown, representing the direct effects (all paths are statistically significant beyond the $p < 0.05$ level by univariate two-tailed test). The fit between the data and model is very good indeed, with an Adjusted Goodness of Fit Index of 0.969, indicating that almost all (96.9 per cent) of the variances and co-variances in the data are accounted for by the model.

The path coefficients may be interpreted in this manner. The direct effect of 'Personnel and Professional Benefits' on 'Curriculum and Learning Benefits' is indicated by a path coefficient of 0.299. This indicates that an

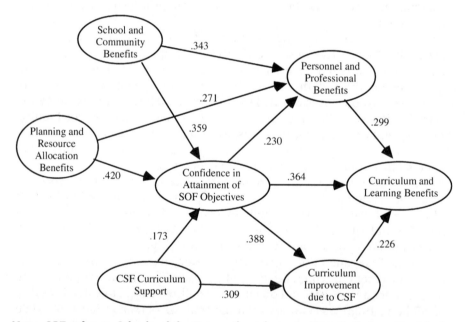

Notes: SOF refers to Schools of the Future, the reforms in Victoria that are roughly the equivalent to those that followed the 1998 Education Reform Act in Britain.
CSF refers to Curriculum and Standards Framework, roughly equivalent to the second version of the National Curriculum in Britain.

Figure 2.1 Explanatory regression model showing interdependent effects among factors influencing perceived 'Curriculum and Learning Benefits'
Source: Cooperative Research Project (1998)

increase in the measure of 'Personnel and Professional Benefits' of 1 standard deviation, as reflected in ratings of principals, produces an increase in the measure of 'Curriculum and Learning Benefits' of 0.299 of a standard deviation.

The model shows that three variables have a direct effect on 'Curriculum and Learning Benefits', which includes improved learning outcomes for students. These are 'Personnel and Professional Benefits' (which reflects ratings for realization of the expected benefits of better personnel management, enhanced professional development, shared decision-making, improved staff performance, more effective organization following restructure, increased staff satisfaction and an enhanced capacity to attract staff); 'Curriculum Improvement due to CSF' (which reflects ratings for improvement of capacity for planning the curriculum, establishing levels and standards for students, moving to a curriculum based on learning outcomes and meeting the needs of students); and 'Confidence in Attainment of SOF Objectives'.

Noteworthy are the pathways of indirect effects, illustrated for 'Planning and Resource Allocation Benefits', which is mediated in respect of its effect on 'Curriculum and Learning Benefits' through 'Personnel and Professional Benefits' and 'Confidence in Attainment of SOF Objectives'. Expressed another way, realizing the expected benefits of better resource management, clearer sense of direction, increased accountability and responsibility, greater financial and administrative flexibility, and improved long-term planning, will have no direct effect on 'Curriculum and Learning Benefits' but will have an indirect effect to the extent they impact on 'Personnel and Professional Benefits' which in turn have a direct effect on 'Curriculum and Learning Benefits'.

Also noteworthy are the constructs that have direct effects on 'Confidence in Attainment of SOF Objectives'. High ratings of confidence were associated with high ratings for the achievement of 'Planning and Resource Allocation Benefits', 'School and Community Benefits' and 'CSF Curriculum Support'. The likely explanation is that unless principals experience benefits in these last three domains, they are unlikely to have confidence in the reform.

The findings in these surveys are limited to the extent that they are based on the perceptions of principals rather than measures of student achievement. This has been a concern in most efforts to determine the impact of reform in recent years. In the case of the Cooperative Research Project, there was no system-wide baseline data on student achievement when the reform was implemented, and efforts to compare achievement in schools in the pilot phase with that in schools that had not entered at the outset were thwarted by a union ban on the collection of data.

Principals were asked to indicate the basis for their rating of the extent to which the expected benefit of improved student learning had been realized. They rated the importance of certain achievement measures and indicators of attendance, time allocations in curriculum, participation rates, exit/

destination data, parent opinion, staff opinion and level of professional development (23 indicators were provided). Most principals indicated moderate to high importance for these indicators in arriving at their ratings. In the
absence of direct access to student achievement data that would put the
matter beyond doubt, one way or the other, a high level of trustworthiness
ought be attached to these findings, given consistency in ratings, the stability
of the model over three years of surveys, and declarations by principals that
they took account of a range of indicators in forming their judgements.

MAPPING THE LINKS

Two sets of case studies in Victoria (Hillier, 1999; Wee, 1999a; 1999b) help
illuminate the links illustrated in the model in Figure 2.1 under conditions
where principals report improved learning outcomes. Are the linkages evident in the model confirmed in deep on-site investigations in particular
schools where improvement is claimed? The research design in both
studies thus started with schools where principals made such a claim. The
first task was to test the validity of these claims, drawing on evidence in the
particular schools selected for study. The second task was to seek explanations for how such improvement occurred and then to match it against
the linkages or pathways that are shown in the model in Figure 2.1.

A case study approach was adopted. The studies differed in one important respect. Hillier's was conducted in two stages, with one round of data
collected in 1996, soon after each element of the reform was in place and
the pool of indicators was in the early stages of implementation. The second stage occurred in 1998, when Hillier returned to the three schools to
assess progress since 1996.

Wee's study reported in detail here was conducted in late 1997, when the
pool of indicators was well developed and a substantial body of evidence
was available to test claims of improved learning outcomes. A feature of her
study was the relentless probing for evidence and an extended pursuit of
explanations to account for improvement where this was found. The research was carried out in four primary schools in the Western Metropolitan
Region in Melbourne. Eight primary schools that expressed a willingness to
participate in case studies following the survey of principals in 1996 were
invited to name up to three areas of the curriculum where improvement in
student learning had occurred and where they believed evidence was available to substantiate their claim. Four schools were selected, reflecting
diversity in size, setting and curriculum area where evidence of improvement was claimed. A wide range of curriculum areas was covered.

Findings revealed that schools could cite evidence that their efforts have
led to improved outcomes for students. They drew on many sources of data
in recognizing improved student learning in their schools. This illustrated
the capacity being developed in the system to gather information about the
performance of schools. It was noted above in connection with the findings

in the final survey of principals in the Cooperative Research Project that most respondents had been able to draw on up to 23 indicators in making their judgement of the extent to which there had been improvement in learning outcomes for students.

Maps of direct and indirect links were prepared by Wee for each school using the rigorous approach to data collection, data display and data reduction for qualitative research proposed by Miles and Huberman (1994). These maps show how school capacity associated with being a School of the Future had led to improved outcomes for students. A synthesis of maps from the four schools is contained in Figure 2.2.

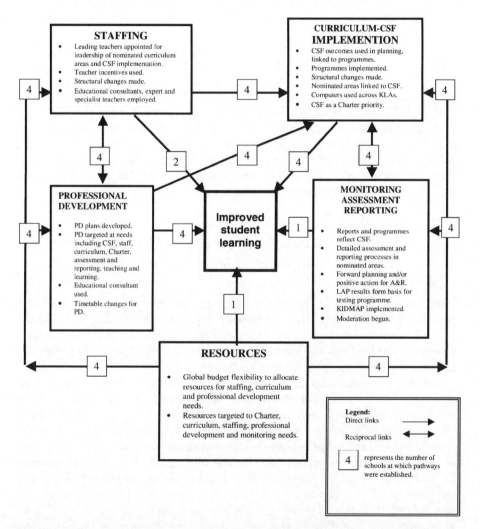

Figure 2.2 Synthesis of maps from four schools showing direct and indirect links between elements of the reform and learning outcomes for students
Source: Wee (1999a; 1999b)

Actions at the school level that have had a direct impact on student learning are in the domains of professional development, implementation of the curriculum and standards framework and monitoring. The impact of resource allocation is indirect.

These maps are consistent with the explanatory model based on survey findings (Figure 2.1). Each of the direct and indirect links illustrated in Figure 2.2 is a manifestation of links in Figure 2.1, with the exception of the impact of monitoring, including assessment and reporting (A&R), which is not contained in the explanatory model. Developing a capacity at the school level for developing and utilizing a wide range of techniques for monitoring student progress has impacted directly on improvement in student learning and on the way staff have implemented the curriculum and standards framework.

Evidence from the four schools suggests that there have been important changes in the 'core technology of teaching and learning' which was not apparent in the case study research of Levačić in the earlier days of local management in Britain (Levačić, 1995, p. 105).

The pool of indicators in schools in Victoria has now become quite deep. Principals and their colleagues have an unprecedented amount of data to monitor developments in their schools, including levels of student achievement and other learning outcomes. Clearly, the next stage in this third generation of studies is to undertake more broadly based research across a representative sample of schools that draws on these data.

IMPLICATIONS FOR POLICY-MAKERS AND PRACTITIONERS

The research in Victoria suggests that structural rearrangements are but a precondition. Whether there is impact depends on making links across several levels to reach the classroom and the student, so that 'the changes characterised by decentralisation have washed over and around children in classrooms' (Bullock and Thomas, 1997, p. 219).

The implications for policy-makers and practitioners are relatively clear. These may be expressed in the form of strategic intentions, along the lines proposed by Caldwell and Spinks (1998) who derived a set of 100 from their review of developments on the three tracks for change around the world. The following reflect the findings reported in this chapter. Each may be prefaced by an action statement for the system or school. For (1) this may be 'In Metropolitan Education Authority, it is recognized that the primary purpose of self-management is . . .' or 'In Local Secondary College, it is recognized that the primary purpose of self-management is . . .', with appropriate amendment in the subsequent text. Each such intention can form the basis of more detailed planning or the design and delivery of professional development programmes.

1) The primary purpose of self-management is to make a contribution to learning, so schools that aspire to success in this domain will make an unrelenting effort to utilize all the capacities that accrue with self-management to achieve that end.

2) There will be clear, explicit and planned links, either direct or indirect, between each of the capacities that come with self-management and activities in the school that relate to learning and teaching and the support of learning and teaching.

3) There is a strong association between the mix and capacities of staff and success in addressing needs and priorities in learning, so schools will develop a capacity to optimally select staff, taking account of these needs and priorities.

4) There is a strong association between the knowledge and skills of staff and learning outcomes for students, so schools will employ their capacity for self-management to design, select, implement or utilize professional development programmes to help ensure these outcomes.

5) A feature of staff selection and professional development will be the building of high performing teams whose work is needs based and data driven, underpinned by a culture that values quality, effectiveness, equity and efficiency.

6) Schools will have a capacity for 'backward mapping' in the design and implementation of programmes for learning, starting from goals, objectives, needs and desired outcomes, and working backwards to determine courses of action that will achieve success, utilizing where possible and appropriate the capacities that accrue with self-management.

7) A key task for principals and other school leaders is to help make effective the links between capacities for self-management and learning outcomes, and to ensure that support is available when these links break down or prove ineffective.

While there is much that is still uncertain about the nature and impact of school reform, it is evident that the means are at hand to create a system of public schools that will provide a high quality of education for all students and that will be professionally rewarding for teachers and other professionals. The challenge is how to put the pieces together. Making effective the linkage between local management and learning outcomes is a promising start.

NOTE

1 Data envelope analysis refers to the analysis of data from very large numbers of subjects, in this instance, all secondary schools in Britain, with many variables in several domains, each of which may be considered an 'envelope'.

REFERENCES

Bradley, S., Johnes, G. and Millington, J. (1999) School choice, competition and the efficiency of secondary schools in England. Unpublished paper. Centre for Research in the Economics of Education, Department of Economics, Management School, Lancaster University.

Bradley, S. and Taylor, J. (1998) The effect of school size on exam performance in secondary schools, *Oxford Bulletin of Economics and Statistics*, Vol. 60, no. 3, pp. 291–322.

Bryk, A. S. (1998) Chicago school reform: linkages between local control, educational supports and student achievement. Presentations with colleagues in the Consortium on Chicago School Research in a Symposium at the Annual Meeting of the American Educational Research Association, San Diego, April.

Bryk, A. S., Sebring, P. B., Kerbow, D., Rollow, S. and Easton, J. Q. (1998) *Charting Chicago School Reform: Democratic Localism as a Lever for Change*, Boulder, CO, Westview Press.

Budge, D. (1999) OU study scotches myth of excellence, *Times Educational Supplement*, 23 April, p. 26.

Bullock, A. and Thomas, H. (1994) *The Impact of Local Management in Schools: Final Report*, Birmingham, University of Birmingham and National Association of Head Teachers.

Bullock, A. and Thomas, H. (1997) *Schools at the Centre: A Study of Decentralisation*, London, Routledge.

Caldwell, B. J. and Spinks, J. M. (1988) *The Self-Managing School*, London, Falmer Press.

Caldwell, B. J. and Spinks, J. M. (1998) *Beyond the Self-Managing School*, London, Falmer Press.

Cheng, Y. C. (1996) *School Effectiveness and School-Based Management: A Mechanism for Development*, London, Falmer Press.

Cooperative Research Project (1994), *Base-Line Survey*, report of the Cooperative Research Project on 'Leading Victoria's Schools of the Future', Directorate of School Education, Victorian Association of State Secondary Principals, Victorian Primary Principals Association, The University of Melbourne (Fay Thomas, Chair), available from Department of Education, Employment and Training.

Cooperative Research Project (1995a) *One Year Later*, report of the Cooperative Research Project on 'Leading Victoria's Schools of the Future', Directorate of School Education, Victorian Association of State Secondary Principals, Victorian Primary Principals Association, The University of Melbourne (Fay Thomas, Chair), available from Department of Education, Employment and Training.

Cooperative Research Project (1995b) *Taking Stock*, report of the Cooperative Research Project on 'Leading Victoria's Schools of the Future', Directorate of School Education, Victorian Association of State Secondary Principals, Victorian Primary Principals Association, The University of Melbourne (Fay Thomas, Chair), available from Department of Education, Employment and Training.

Coperative Research Project (1996) *Three Year Report Card*, report of the Cooperative Research Project on 'Leading Victoria's Schools of the Future', Directorate of School Education, Victorian Association of State Secondary Principals, Victorian Primary Principals Association, The University of Melbourne (Fay Thomas, Chair), available from Department of Education, Employment and Training.

Cooperative Research Project (1997) *Still More Work to be Done But . . . No Turning Back*, report of the Cooperative Research Project on 'Leading Victoria's Schools of the Future', Department of School Education, Victorian Association of State Secondary Principals, Victorian Primary Principals Association, The University of Melbourne (Fay Thomas, Chair), available from Department of Education, Employment and Training.

Cooperative Research Project (1998) *Assessing the Outcomes*, report of the Cooperative Research Project on 'Leading Victoria's Schools of the Future', Department of Education, Victorian Association of State Secondary Principals, Victorian Primary Principals Association, The University of Melbourne (Fay Thomas, Chair), available from Department of Education, Employment and Training.

Hanushek, E. A. (1996) Outcomes, costs, and incentives in schools, in E. A. Hanushek and D. W. Jorgenson (eds.), *Improving America's Schools: The Role of Incentives*, Washington, DC, National Academy Press.

Hanushek, E. A. (1997) Assessing the effects of school resources on student performance: an update, *Educational Evaluation and Policy Analysis*, Vol. 19, no. 2, pp. 141–64.

Hayward, D. (1993) *Schools of the Future: Preliminary Paper*, Melbourne, Directorate of School Education.

Hess, G. A. (1999) Understanding achievement (and other) changes under Chicago school reform, *Educational Evaluation and Policy Analysis*, Vol. 21, no. 1, pp. 67–83.

Hillier, N. (1999) Educational reform and school improvement in Victorian primary schools 1993–1999. Unpublished thesis for the degree of Doctor of Education, University of Melbourne.

Jöreskog, K. G. and Sörbom, D. (1993) *LISREL 8: User's Reference Guide*, Chicago, Scientific Software, Inc.

Lawton, M. (1997) Chicago study credits school-based reforms, *Education Week*, 5 November, p. 3.

Levačić, R. (1995) *Local Management of Schools: Analysis and Practice*, Buckingham, Open University Press.

Levačić, R. and Hardman, J. (1999) The performance of grant-maintained schools in England: an experiment in school autonomy, *Journal of Educational Policy* (forthcoming).

Levačić, R., Hardman, J. and Woods, P. (1998) Competition as a spur to improvement? Differential improvement in GCSE results. Paper presented at the International Congress for School Effectiveness and School Improvement, Manchester, January.

Malen, B., Ogawa, R. T. and Kranz, J. (1990) What do we know about site-based management: a case study of the literature – a call for research, in W. Clune and J. Witte (eds), *Choice and Control in American Education Volume 2: The Practice of Choice, Decentralisation and School Restructuring*, London, Falmer Press.

Miles, M. B. and Huberman, A. M. (1994) *Qualitative Data Analysis: An Expanded Sourcebook* (2nd edn), Thousand Oaks, CA, Sage Publications.

OECD, Directorate of Education, Employment, Labour and Social Affairs, Education Committee (1994) *Effectiveness of Schooling and of Educational Resource Management: Synthesis of Country Studies*, points 22 and 23, Paris, OECD.

Ross, K. N. and Levačić, R. (eds.) (1999) *Needs-Based Resource Allocation in Education via Formula Funding of Schools*, Paris, UNESCO, International Institute for Educational Planning.

Smith, M. S., Scoll, B. W. and Link, J. (1996) Research-based school reform: the Clinton Administration's agenda, in E. A. Hanushek and D. W. Jorgenson (eds), *Improving America's Schools: The Role of Incentives*, Washington, DC, National Academy Press.

Summers, A. A. and Johnson, A. W. (1996) The effects of school-based management plans, in E. A. Hanushek and D. W. Jorgenson (eds), *Improving America's Schools: The Role of Incentives*, Washington, DC, National Academy Press.

Taylor, J. and Bradley, S. (1999) Resource utilisation and economies of scale in secondary schools. Unpublished paper based on research funded by the Economic and Social Research Council, Department of Economics, Management School, Lancaster University.

Wee, J. (1999a) Improved student learning and leadership in self-managed schools. Unpublished thesis for the degree of Doctor of Education, The University of Melbourne.

Wee, J. (1999b) *Making Links in Self-Managed Schools: Improved Student Learning and Leadership*, no. 3 in a Series on Excellence in Education, School Effectiveness and Continuous Improvement Unit, Department of Education, Melbourne, available from The Department of Education, Employment and Training, GPO Box 4367, Melbourne, 3000.

Whitty, G., Power, S. and Halpin, D. (1998) *Devolution and Choice in Education: The School, the State and the Market*, Buckingham, Open University Press.

3

THE MOVE TOWARDS ENTREPRENEURIALISM

Lesley Anderson

INTRODUCTION

The restructuring of public education systems across the globe over the past decade is well documented (for example, Ball, 1994; Bullock and Thomas, 1997; Smyth, 1993). In a bid to be more internationally competitive (Levačić, 1995, p. 2), various governments have focused on improving educational standards and accountability (Dimmock, 1993) through the creation of devolved systems that provide various degrees of institutional autonomy. In many cases, these changes have been linked to enhanced parental choice and often are characterized by the introduction of a 'market' element into the provision of educational services (Whitty, Power and Halpin, 1998, p. 3). In this 'new', market-orientated educational world, where inability to attract sufficient students can result in closure, schools and colleges are affected by the external environment more than ever before (Foskett, 1999, p. 33). There is an imperative to work with the community because, as Coleman, Bush and Glover (1994, p. 2) comment: 'satisfying the client is (now) the most important determinant of income'.

Inevitably, in their attempts to ensure client satisfaction, schools and colleges are concerned with improvement which, according to Hopkins, Ainscow and West (1997, p. 270) 'is not about the implementation of centralised reforms in a more effective way . . . [but] . . . is . . . more to do with how schools can use the impetus of external reforms to "improve" or "develop" themselves'. Hence, since the early 1990s, the innovative management of change and external relations has become a vital activity for effective headteachers, principals and other managers and, for some of these people, the experiences have brought to light hitherto un-discovered or, possibly, frustrated abilities and skills of innovation and

41

entrepreneurialism. Thus, both a new term has been introduced into educational language – the entrepreneurial leader – and a new attribute associated with effective educational leaders. Indeed, Boyett and Finlay (1993a, p. 114) highlight 'the premium now attached to those heads who are able to recognise entrepreneurial opportunities'. However, before exploring how these school and college managers demonstrate their new found skills and abilities, it is pertinent to consider what it means to be entrepreneurial – the question which is addressed in the next section.

DEFINING ENTREPRENEURIALISM

To begin with there is a difficulty over which form of the term is correct. There is a question over whether the noun is 'entrepreneurialism' or 'entrepreneurship'. Or do these two words describe different but similar concepts? Consulting various dictionaries provides little conclusive advice. Thus, for the purpose of this discussion, the term 'entrepreneurialism' is used on the basis that this word describes a concept that is approaching that of 'entrepreneurship'. However, inevitably there is overlap and lack of clarity about the interpretation attached to the words by other writers as exemplified throughout the chapter.

In line with many other innovations in education in recent years (Gunter, 1997, p. 7), the concept of entrepreneurialism/entrepreneurship is borrowed from the business world. According to Binks and Vale (1989, cited by Boyett and Finlay, 1993b), 'the essence of entrepreneurship is to perceive worthwhile opportunities and to act upon them'. They stress the importance of both parts of this twin identity – alertness and action. Kirzner (1973) and Stevenson, Roberts and Grousbeck (1994) provide similar definitions although the second group of writers add the proviso that 'the active search for possibilities [is] unrestricted by resources'. This, in turn, begs the question of how such an approach is achieved. More realistically perhaps, Casson (1982, cited by Boyett and Finlay, 1993b) defines an entrepreneur as 'someone who specialises in taking judgmental decisions about the co-ordination of *scarce* resources' (my italics).

Drucker (1985, cited by Fullan, 1992, p. 19) characterizes entrepreneurs as 'exploiting innovation', an approach which has been used previously by Schumpeter (1934) who emphasized the innovative role of the entrepreneur which arises out of discovery of new markets, products, processes and structures. Liebenstein (1968) takes a different view and regards the entrepreneur primarily as a gap filler, reducing an organization's 'slacks' by identifying unexplored gaps in process or product markets. However, according to Huuskonen (1992, cited by Lahdeniemi, 1997, pp. 174–5), the know-how and expertise attributed to entrepreneurs are insufficient in themselves to differentiate them from the rest of the population. He suggests: 'The entrepreneur is a person who simultaneously a) bears overall responsibility for managing the company; b) is an investor in the venture capital of the company; c) exercises the supreme right of decision; and d) is the source of ultimate authority in the company.'

Although none of these definitions state it explicitly, there is an implication, within each of them, of an element of risk associated with entrepreneurialism. This is confirmed by standard texts on economics. For example, in Maunder *et al.*'s (1987, p. 3) definition of entrepreneurship, they assert that 'it encompasses taking risks (possibly losing large sums of wealth on new ventures)'. Later, they state 'The entrepreneur is the person who takes the chances' (ibid., p. 313), who 'is a risk taker' (ibid., p. 539).

But what, then, is an educational entrepreneur? Boyett and Finlay (1993a, p. 115) draw on empirical data from interviews with headteachers. From the range of definitions provided by the interviewees, these writers quote three of them:

> A teacher (usually a headteacher) who grasps the opportunities offered by Local Management of Schools to promote and develop the resources of the institution with the object of achieving better provision for students and raising standards. The educational entrepreneur believes that promotion (including marketing) and fundraising can have a positive effect on morale of teachers, students, parents and the local community.

> One who is always seeking to create improvements within the working environment for the benefit of both staff and students. This includes constantly looking for new opportunities to enhance the premises; improving the quality of tuition provided; and increasing the range and quality of teaching materials available.

> Someone who intends to change long established practices to enable the future of the institution itself and not simply be external factors.

Boyett and Finlay suggest that these statements 'reflect, in detail, what entrepreneurship writers have described in general over the past 50 years or so' and they go on to comment: 'What is particularly interesting is that, thrust into this "quasi"-free market situation, the educational managers have produced for themselves a descriptive model of the educational entrepreneur, which shows little differentiation from that described by the entrepreneurial theorists in relation to the business organization' (Boyett and Finlay, 1993a, p. 115).

In discussing what is worth fighting for in headship, Fullan (1992, pp. 19–32) defines headteachers as middle managers and, as such, is troubled by the expectation that they take the lead in the implementation of new policies, programmes and procedures which they, themselves, have had no part in developing (Fullan, with Stiegelbauer, 1991). He suggests that a new conception of headship is needed and draws heavily on the work of Block (1987) who, in turn, talks about the development of the 'entrepreneurial spirit' in innovative organizations. Block explains that 'this spirit is typified by responsibility, public accountability, interactive professionalism, and the recognition that playing positive politics is essential, possible and the key to effectiveness'. He goes on to use the concepts of the entrepreneurial spirit and positive political skills to argue convincingly that 'it is possible for middle managers to shape, if not create, organisations that they believe in, even in the midst of the nonrational world' (Fullan, 1991, p. 20).

Finally, the entrepreneurial school is described by Campbell and Crowther (1991, p. 13). They see it as 'one in which there exists a passionate commitment to use all available resources to create new ideas and actions that will enrich the quality of education, and life generally, within the school and its community'.

ENTREPRENEURSHIP, MANAGEMENT AND LEADERSHIP

If some educational managers display the characteristics of the entrepreneur, what is the connection between management and entrepreneurialism in schools and colleges? Boyett and Finlay (1993b, p. 3) suggest entrepreneurship is a special type of management although they then go on to state that, 'contextually, there is fluidity between each . . . [they] can be displayed by a continuum with entrepreneurship and management at extreme poles'. Hence, it seems that there is confusion about whether entrepreneurship/entrepreneurialism is a style of management or a characteristic of leadership.

Smyth (1993, p. 7) also links entrepreneurialism and management when he talks about the move towards self-managing schools which has occurred in many countries. His argument is that self-management is a way of introducing 'greater discipline and control' over schools and colleges through 'a cultural shift from education to management and other forms of entrepreneurialism'. In Smyth's view, the entrepreneurial, industrial model is 'largely discredited' and he asks why educationalists would want to 'emulate this derelict model that failed so demonstrably as evidenced by the corporate excesses of the 1980s'. However, putting aside this question, it is evident that Smyth equates management and entrepreneurialism to the extent that he regards them as the same side of the 'self-management' coin.

Discussing cultural leadership, Caldwell and Spinks argue that entrepreneurialism is a requirement for successful leadership of self-managing schools. They assert that:

> [the] strategies available . . . are not only workable but also eminently desirable to the extent that they have educational integrity. The intention is to enhance the quality of education. The processes involved should enrich the work of educational leaders and create opportunities for educational leadership. They should pervade in the self-managing school.
>
> (Caldwell and Spinks, 1992, p. 79)

However, they also offer a word of caution about the assumption suggested by Smyth (1993) above, that is 'a shift to self-management implies a re-focusing of the work of teachers to replace funds which formerly came from government' (Caldwell and Spinks, 1992, p. 83). Caldwell and Spinks assert that the link between the restructuring of schools along the lines of self-management and the reductions in resource allocation to them is unrelated and coincidental. They conclude by suggesting that marketing and other entrepreneurial aspects of management can be carried out with the 'highest educational integrity, maintaining a focus on the central purposes of schooling' (ibid., p. 83).

In their later book, *Beyond the Self-Managing School*, Caldwell and Spinks (1998) discuss strategic leadership and management in the turbulent times at the end of the second millennium, and draw on Boisot's (1995) classification of management responses in the exercise of strategic leadership. Boisot (1995) introduces intrapreneurship, a version of entrepreneurship that is internal to the organization. Intrapreneurship occurs when there is high turbulence in the organization's environment as well as poor capacity to extract and process useful information, in other words, low understanding. Like entrepreneurship, intrapreneurship is an approach to management that 'encourages individual initiative when it is not possible to formulate a coherent and integrated organisational response . . . For schools, intrapreneurship may be appropriate, for example, for some developments in information technology' (Caldwell and Spinks, 1998, p. 199).

Boyett and Finlay (1993a) acknowledge that not all educational managers are comfortable in the role of innovator and, indeed, from their research into entrepreneurship in education, they identify a dichotomy between control and innovation. When headteachers were asked to prioritize a list of attributes of importance to the educational entrepreneur since the changes introduced by the 1988 Education Reform Act, 'making use of structures' was the attribute they considered to be most important. Structures suggest control and minimization of risks while, in contrast,

> risk is the opportunity cost of innovation. The more adverse to risk an institution is, the greater their reluctance to innovate. Hindrances and constraint to entrepreneurship can be viewed as an element of the judgmental and, hence, risk-taking decision-making process. Policies aimed at reducing entrepreneurial constraints improve the risk-taking, innovative behaviour of schools.
>
> (Boyett and Finlay, 1993a, p. 118)

CREATING AN ENTREPRENEURIAL CULTURE

The importance and influence of the school or college culture is well documented (Hopkins, Ainscow and West, 1994; Stoll and Fink, 1996). Indeed, according to Schein (1985, p. 2), 'the only thing of real importance that leaders do is to create and manage the culture'. So, it follows that the effective entrepreneurial headteacher or college principal sets out to create a culture that supports and encourages an entrepreneurial approach. The headteacher of The Garibaldi School in Mansfield, Sir Bob Salisbury, provides an excellent example of this. (Sir Bob was awarded a knighthood in 1998 for services to education.)

Boyett and Finlay (1993b; 1995) highlight the cultural changes brought about by Bob's appointment as headteacher of the school in their accounts of 'The Garibaldi Story'. As they explain, when Bob Salisbury was appointed as headteacher of the school in 1989, it was in a very poor state. Its regard in the community was very low, staff were demoralized and there was an acute lack of resources. Alongside this, the culture was one that did not encourage initiative. In Bob's words: 'The public image and the reputation was demoralising in itself, but much more important than that, the lid had never been lifted from these people. There was a culture that meant that people would not have a cup of tea without asking for permission' (Boyett and Finlay, 1993b, p. 2).

One of Bob's first tasks was to bring about change, in both the culture and reputation of the school. He went about the former by a process of delegating responsibility to staff and developing them to use their initiative. Furthermore, he took advantage of community links through members of the school's governing body. The outcome of these changes is that the school has become a thriving centre for entrepreneurial activities, some examples of which are described later in this chapter.

So how can the degree of success in changing the culture be measured? It could be argued that one way is by the fact that, in 1993, The Garibaldi School was awarded the title of the East Midland Company of the Year. Another is by the knighthood awarded to the headteacher. But these measures still beg the question about relevance and applicability to the school situation. Sir Bob Salisbury's answer is found in the projects, financed through entrepreneurial activities, which have had a direct impact on the learning and teaching in the school. As well as hugely improved facilities for pupils and staff, pupils' attendance has increased dramatically, most parents now attend parents' meetings, there is no vandalism at the school thus enabling more of the budget to be spent directly on pupils' learning, there has been a significant increase in pupils' recruitment in both Years 7 and 12 and, last but not least, examination results have improved dramatically.

However, against this success, there are opportunity costs in that managing and actually carrying out entrepreneurial activities takes time and money that could be used in different ways. Kirby (1992, p. 1) highlights this point: 'generating income through fundraising and other related activities is an option which a school either chooses for positive reasons, or else rejects with a clear understanding of what opportunities it is foregoing'. Similarly, Salisbury (undated, p. 3) argues that 'one-off activities are not generally effective'. He advocates arrangements that operate year after year with minimal administration.

In contrast, Richard Parker, headteacher of Lodge Park School, Corby and well known in the Northamptonshire area for entrepreneurial activities, is confident that his efforts in this area only take up a small part of his time. This is despite also talking about developing a culture that reflects such an approach and having an impressive record of obtaining sponsorship and other funding. Richard expressed this view during an opportunistic interview specially undertaken in preparation for this chapter. He went on to state that he did not want to be described as an 'entrepreneur'; for him, 'it's the human touch that is important'. 'If you show passion, if you show you care, it does work', he added. Richard's passion was evident. He explained that he was determined to 'rise above my principles in order to access additional funding for the kids in this schools. I will do anything'. His examples of 'doing anything' included nurturing civil servants from the Funding Agency for Schools (now abolished) by inviting them to visit the school regularly because, as he said, 'they like to get out and about' and keeping in touch with the local Member of Parliament. His strategy certainly pays off as will be demonstrated later in this chapter.

Kirby (1992, p. 1) is also concerned about the ethics involved when schools focus on fund-raising, or entrepreneurial, activities which are just about making money. He argues that,

> the values which motivate and sustain a school community must always be educational rather than commercial. Ideally, a fundraising project should involve:
>
> • both the giving of entertainment and/or service to the community
> • the taking back into the school of not only revenue, but also a rich vein of new ideas and experiences with many potential uses and benefits.
>
> (Kirby, 1992, p. 1)

Likewise, the issue of ethics is raised by Kingham (1993, p. 99) who acknowledges that 'some readers may be horrified at a teacher pursing (entrepreneurial) tactics'. In his defence, he describes himself as 'a realist' because, although the government should provide sufficient funding for schools, he knows this does not happen. Kingham is motivated to generate additional income through entrepreneurial methods because he wants the best for the students he works with.

Moreover, there is no doubt that entrepreneurial events can have benefits over and above the income generated. For example, a well-planned event can attract a lot of useful publicity for a school or college as well as providing an opportunity to develop stronger links with the community. It can also bring together groups such as staff and governors in a different way. Furthermore, for a member of a fund-raising team, there can be useful staff development experience. Finally, the activity itself can be used to enhance learning and teaching, particularly in terms of developing economic and industrial understanding as well as fostering entrepreneurial skills among pupils and students. For example, aspects of an activity can be linked with different areas of the curriculum; the production of publicity material for an event can form part of an English lesson; a business studies group can monitor the accounts; in the case of a themed event such as a Victorian fair, background research can be carried out in a history lesson.

ENTREPRENEURIAL APPROACHES TO FINANCING LEARNING AND TEACHING[1]

Fund-raising

Fund-raising through one-off activities such as fêtes, raffles and social events is probably the most traditional way in which schools and colleges generate income. The aim is usually to create additional revenue for school or college funds which is then used to support 'special' or 'extra' activities. Sometimes, fund-raising projects are set up with a specific outcome intended, for example, the acquisition of a particular piece of equipment for use in the school or college.

Enterprise

In addition to one-off fund-raising activities, schools and colleges can set up their own ongoing businesses that generate revenue for the institution on a regular basis. For example, the lettings, trading and services included in Table 3.1 can be classified in this way. Such enterprise is evident in developing countries. Bush, Qiang and Fang (1998, p. 139) point out that 'school-run businesses is a particular feature of Chinese education and relates in part to the emphatic view that education and work must be closely linked if China is to sustain its economic growth'. Fouts and Chan (1997) connect the growth of school businesses in China to the strategic decision to direct a large proportion of the public funding available into key schools. As they explain:

> The result of this action was that a very large majority of the schools [had] to see to their own financial welfare. The limited funding available to most schools in China meant that the school factories and resulting profits became more and more important as a second source of income.
>
> (Fouts and Chan, 1997, p. 36)

Table 3.1 Fund-raising activities used by schools and colleges

Trading	School/college shops, customized products e.g. sweatshirts, stationery, pens, sportswear with school/college logo
Entertainment/social events	Dramatic and musical events, barn dances, discos
Gambling	Raffles, lotteries
Services	Training, photocopying, catering, translations
Waste collection	Newspapers, aluminium cans
Lettings	Use of premises for evening classes, weddings, other large gatherings, car-boot sales, sports fixtures
Collecting wrappers etc.	Crisp packets with associated offers, supermarket vouchers
Sponsored events	Various activities according to the age/interests of pupils/students

Examples of Chinese enterprise in education are quoted in the literature. These include a school in Guangdong province that receives about a third of its operating budget from its factories (Fouts and Chan, 1997) and others in Shaanxi province that generate significant extra income through running or letting farms, shops and a restaurant (Bush, Coleman and Si, 1998).

Evidence of similar activities was found by the author when researching educational management in schools in South Africa prior to writing this chapter. Some schools, particularly those that had formerly been black but which were not at the extreme end of the deprivation continuum, were raising additional income in order to enhance learning and teaching through enterprises such as operating a tuck shop and selling the produce produced through farming school land.

Support from companies

There are a number of ways in which commercial companies can, and do, provide support to schools and colleges (Coleman, 1999). Marsden (1997, pp. 169–70) lists a range of reasons why a company will get involved as well as providing another list of why it may not support an appeal. Adapted and extended versions of the lists are given below:

Reasons companies support schools and colleges:
- It conforms to their policy of local community support.
- It conforms to their current advertising/marketing strategy.
- There is an existing close connection with the school or college.
- Many employees have children at the school or college.
- Key personnel in the company are former pupils/parents/former parents.

- It benefits the work environment.
- It benefits recruitment of workers.
- It benefits staff development.
- It demonstrates a commitment to equal opportunities.
- It helps them to clinch a commercial deal with the school or college.
- It gives them a competitive advantage over their competitors.
- They are obliged to support because they are school or college suppliers.
- The chairman/managing director is keen to support the school or college.

Reasons companies do not support school or college appeals:
- The company does not want to be seen to support one particular school or college rather than others or charities in the area.
- The company is concerned that an association with the school or college could embarrass its staff or shareholders. The clients or customers could be offended if the company appears to favour one school or college rather than others or local charities.
- The publicity offered by the school or college is not of any real value to the company.
- The school or college is unable to provide the benefits the company wants in return for its support.
- The company does not want to be seen to be giving money to a school or college when it is cutting back on other costs.
- The company cannot afford to contribute to the appeal.

Sometimes companies are willing to help in kind rather than giving actual money. For example, Kingham (1993, pp. 98–9) describes how he obtained free advice on the design aspect of his project from the building trade as well as benefiting from goods and other services at cost. However, Salisbury (undated, p. 2) realistically points out 'there are few fairy godmothers around . . . most sponsorship requires some return'. Sponsorship is considered next.

Sponsorship

Sponsorship implies benefits to the company in return for financial outlay. Marsden (1997, p. 172) provides examples of the benefits which can be negotiated by a company offering to fund a school or college sports hall:

- staff to use the facilities at a reduced cost at certain times each week;
- the company to be acknowledged as sponsor on a large plaque in the entrance foyer;
- the company to be able to display leaflets for its products in the foyer;
- the company to be acknowledged each year in the school magazine;
- the company's managing director to be invited as a guest of honour to speech days and other major events;
- the company's chairman to present the sports day prizes each year.

As mentioned earlier, over the past five years, Lodge Park School in Corby has benefited from considerable building and site development, much of it paid for with monies raised from sponsorship. For example, the site has a new sports hall and leisure centre, including a floodlit hard area and various new teaching suites. At the time of writing, the school is engaged in a millennium project that involves the development of a training suite and cyber café. The headteacher, Richard Parker, prioritizes the school's links with business and industry as well as personally nurturing local community connections. He talked about 'reading' local business people in order to ensure his approach was sensitive and attractive to their individual and company interests and needs. He mentioned one local contact who did not like to be taken for granted as far as sponsorship was concerned. The school demonstrates its gratitude to the sponsors by naming rooms and suites after the benefactors.

Salisbury (undated, p. 3) also raises the 'WIIFM' factor or 'What's in it for me?' His experience at The Garibaldi School shows that the most successful projects, particularly in terms of those which survive and develop over time, have mutual benefit in that, as well as providing resources for the school or college, they generate new profit for the company. He lists the following examples of 'mutually beneficial' schemes that have been successful:

- Trialling products – this involves the school providing expert consultation and feedback on equipment in return for the use of the product.
- Showroom idea – companies are invited to build showrooms on site in the school or college so that potential customers can visit and observe the products in use.
- Ticket agency – the school or college markets and sells tickets for activities of interest to its students, for example, theme parks.
- Franchising courses – schools and colleges of further education working in collaboration.
- Lettings – to groups within the local community but especially to companies.

Fozard and Meek (1990/91) report on their experience of fund-raising in connection with a computer project for the physically handicapped child. They found success by approaching local, high profile companies because, generally, such companies preferred to be associated with appeals from the locality. They report that, as well as the benefit to the school, the companies' interests were enhanced through publicity in the local press or their house magazine. Reporters and photographers were frequently invited to attend visits and presentations to the extent that the writers recommend the availability of a press release to ensure appropriate coverage (ibid., p. 27).

However, if a company supports a project in a tax-effective way by covenant or gift aid then there can be no reciprocal benefits to the company other than an acknowledgement.

Benefactors

Parents, former students and other individuals are also a source of funding to schools and colleges through donations. As well as supporting fund-raising events, some parents are willing to sign a deed of covenant as a way of supporting the school or college, or make a one-off contribution. Both these types of donations are tax-effective in that they attract tax relief: the payment is made net of tax, and an equal amount of tax can be reclaimed by the school or college (Rosenberg, 1998, p. 112). Similarly, former pupils or students can be encouraged to retain an interest in, and commitment to, their school or college through an alumni or former pupils association. For example, one of the case study schools referred to in Chapter 13 of this volume, Northampton School for Boys, has recently benefited from a large donation for a building from an old boy. The benefactor has remained actively involved in the school and, in fact, chaired its Grammar School Foundation. However, as in the case of relationships with other external groups, such associations have to be managed and nurtured in order to maximize the benefits to the school or college which, in itself, has an associated cost.

Salisbury (undated, p. 3) highlights the fact that 'people give to other people'. Hence, it is advisable to turn 'appeals for provision into appeals for people'. For example, rather than setting up a straightforward appeal to fund a new sports hall, he advises that it is contextualized by arguing that crime-, drugs- and drink-related incidents can be reduced by the provision of the new sports hall (Salisbury, undated, p. 3).

Furthermore, parents, former students and friends are more likely to support a project that is also receiving money from another source, for example, from the government or the National Lottery (Marsden, 1997, p. 11). Turner (1990, p. 27) describes a situation where, after an appeal for donations to a school fund-raising project, a local millionaire offered first to double any parental contributions up to a limit of £50,000, then challenged the school to raise another £50,000 in two years on the understanding that he would double it to £100,000 within a ten-year period. As Turner goes on to explain, 'everyone could now see a real purpose in raising money and the target of £50,000 from parents, pupils and friends of the school was finally passed with a few thousand pounds and a few days to spare' (ibid., p. 27).

Partnership

The long-term relationships mentioned earlier are likely to stem from the establishment of a partnership between a company and a school or college. Schools and colleges that develop such relationships are usually the most forward-looking (Marsden, 1997, p. 173) and have considerable expertise in managing their external relations.

The value of a partnership is that, over time, trust and understanding of each partner's strategies and culture can be achieved which, in turn, makes it more likely that ways can be found for them to work together to mutual benefit or, indeed, for the company to support the school or college through donations. Salisbury (undated, p. 2) warns that talking about sponsorship or finance at an initial meeting with a company representative frequently results in the communication ending at that contact. He suggests the following approaches as effective:

- Building up long-term communications rather than 'cold calling'; establishing personal communication with the managing director or equivalent.
- Using existing networks and communications in order to blur the edges between the world of commerce and education; for example, schools and colleges joining the local chamber of commerce.
- Loaning personnel with particular skills which is easy to arrange and is a form of sponsorship.
- Encouraging companies to give surplus or obsolete equipment and superfluous materials to schools and colleges.

UK's private funding initiative

A particular form of partnership between companies and schools and colleges was introduced by the Conservative government in 1992 and is known as the Private Funding Initiative (PFI).

In recent times, both Conservative and Labour governments in the UK have turned to the private sector in a bid to seek additional funding for public education. According to Gillian Shepherd, Secretary of State for Education at the time, PFI was introduced as one part of the government's 'radical policies to raise standards achieved by pupils and students; and to promote efficient management of schools and college' (Shephard, 1994, p. 1). She explained it as a mechanism for broadening the 'base of capital investment in education and to introduce skills, ideas and management practices from the private sector' (Shephard, 1994, p. 1) based on a commercial partnership. Notwithstanding the stated intention, the fact remains that the strategy represented another move to 'privatize' education.

As part of its 'Third Way' politics (Blair, 1998), New Labour relaunched the initiative in 1998 under the name Public Private Partnerships (PPP) (DfEE, 1998a; 1998b; FEFC, 1998) and even set up a Private Finance Division within the Department for Education and Employment with a view to promoting opportunities to encourage the private sector to work with education. Despite different political rhetoric, the approach of this government is, in many ways, similar to that of the previous one: 'through public private partnerships, any organisation, large and small, with interests in construction, facilities, management, services provision or finance, could take up commercial opportunities in what is a large and relatively untapped market' (DfEE, 1998a, second page).

At the time of writing, a number of projects involving colleges of further education, LEAs, schools and the private sector have been set up under the various categories within the PPP; further projects are awaiting approval (see DfEE [undated]). One such example is the development of sports and leisure facilities at Wyggeston and Queen Elizabeth 1 College in Leicester, the background to which was investigated in preparation for this chapter. The college is located in an urban area that is served by five post-compulsory education colleges. Although there is a demand for places, competition between the different institutions is great and, in order to survive as a self-managing unit, the college needed to increase its student numbers. Furthermore, prior to incorporation in 1993, there had been little investment in its buildings. Thus, the college fixed on a growth strategy that included investment in specialist sports teaching. However, it was evident that it was not going to achieve the sort of facilities it required without private investment and so, in line with government policy and the encouragement of the Further Education Funding Council, the college sought a private partner. A few years later, with limited investment of its own resources, the college now boasts a purpose-built sports and leisure centre.

Bidding

More than a decade ago, the introduction of a mechanism for distributing funding which triggered an image of wafting honeypot odours stirring slumbering bears into salivating activity prompted the use of a new phrase: 'honeypot management'. Under honeypot management a donor, which may be an organization, a group or an individual, invites bidders (other organizations, groups or individuals) to bid for funding with submissions designed to achieve the donor's objectives. Thus, the bidders who are awarded funding become the instruments of change and bring about the implementation of the donor's desired policies (Knight, 1987, p. 204).

Honeypot management is essentially about achieving change and, in more recent times, has regularly been used in education, for example, the technology college programme, education action zones. Central government or a government quango, a local education authority (LEA) or school or college managers may act as donors while LEAs, schools and colleges, groups within them or even individuals may be the bidders. Knight (1987, pp. 209–10) discussed the advantages and disadvantages of honeypot management and concluded:

'Honeypot Management' is a very powerful device for using allocation of finance to effect change in education. Used intelligently, sparingly, and sensitively, it could be used to create speedier, better directed and more effective change, and encourage innovation and local variation to meet local needs. Used thoughtlessly, extensively, or crudely, it could encourage centralism, distort priorities, weaken morale, and create rapidly diminishing returns.

(ibid., p. 212)

Alongside honeypot management, there are a variety of other sources of external funding and grant aid which schools and colleges can access. Examples include the National Lottery, the European Union, the United Nations and the World Bank as well as various trusts and foundations. Relevant advice for schools is set out in the Funding Agency for Schools' (FAS) booklet, *Bidding for Funds: A Guide to Accessing Additional Sources of Funding for Schools* (FAS, 1997).

Using professional fund-raisers

In this era of educational entrepreneurialism, one option available to schools and colleges wishing to generate additional finance and resources is to employ a professional fund-raiser, either as a consultant or, although less likely, on a permanent basis. Carnie (1996, p. 9) highlights the 'hundreds of questions to which you need answers in your quest for raising income', a task requiring expertise as well as time. Thus, a school or college may decide that an effective and efficient use of resources can be obtained by employing a professional fund-raiser.

Various sources of advice about selecting and working with a fund-raising consultant are available (Carnie, 1996, p. 10; Marsden, 1997, pp. 95–109; Rosenberg, 1998, pp. 272–8); additionally, professional associations for fund-raisers and researchers provide further guidance and credibility (see Carnie, 1996; Marsden, 1997; Roberts, 1993).

SUMMARY

In considering the move to entrepreneurialism in education in recent times, this chapter has explored what it means to be entrepreneurial, its relationship with leadership and management and the concept of creating an entrepreneurial culture in a school or college. Although schools and colleges have always been involved in fund-raising, there remains a tension between the extent to which school and college managers adopt the role of the entrepreneur and their position as professional leader. Furthermore, being entrepreneurial is not a requirement for effective educational management nor do all managers find it comfortable or easy. Indeed, Boyett and Finlay's (1993a) survey identified a variety of constraints that restrain full entrepreneurial development, however aware headteachers and principals are about the opportunities available for their schools.

Nevertheless, it seems that both the present and former governments endorse, as well as actively encourage, such an approach through competition and self-management. It is likely that the educational entrepreneur will continue to be held in high esteem because as Boyett and Finlay (1993a, p. 121) advise: 'Accepting this approach can effectively reduce the cost of managing change, whilst simultaneously encouraging a more positive approach to innovation and the increase of quality levels in the UK educational system.'

NOTE

1 A note on terminology: a variety of terms are used to describe the different approaches to generate funding and resources that are not necessarily mutually exclusive. In the following sections I have attempted to represent the main areas of activity using appropriate classification although I am aware that there are overlaps as well as omissions.

REFERENCES

Ball, S. J. (1994) *Education Reform: A Critical and Post-Structural Approach*, Buckingham, Open University Press.

Binks, M. and Vale, P. (1989) *Entrepreneurship and Economic Change*, London, McGraw Hill.

Blair, T. (1998) *The Third Way: New Politics for the New Century*, Fabian Pamphlet 588, London, The Fabian Society.

Block, P. (1987) *The Empowered Manager*, San Francisco, Jossey-Bass.

Boisot, M. (1995) Preparing for turbulence: the changing relationship between strategy and management development in the learning organization, in B. Garrett (ed.), *Developing Strategic Thought: Rediscovering the Art of Direction-Giving*, London, McGraw-Hill.

Boyett, I. and Finlay, D. (1993a) The emergence of the educational entrepreneur, *Long Range Planning*, Vol. 26, no. 3, pp. 114–22.

Boyett, I. and Finlay, D. (1993b) The Garibaldi Story. Unpublished paper.

Boyett, I. and Finlay, D. (1995) An English case of educational entrepreneurship, *International Studies in Educational Administration*, Vol. 23, no. 2, pp. 52–64.

Bullock, A. and Thomas, H. (1997) *Schools at the Centre?* London, Routledge.

Bush, T., Coleman, M. and Si, X. (1998) Managing secondary schools in China, *Compare*, Vol. 28, no. 2, pp. 183–95.

Bush, T., Qiang, H. and Fang, J. (1998) Educational management in China: an overview, *Compare*, Vol. 28, no. 2, pp. 133–40.

Caldwell, B. and Spinks, J. (1992) *Leading the Self-Managing School*, London, Falmer Press.

Caldwell, B. and Spinks, J. (1998) *Beyond the Self-Managing School*, London, Falmer Press.

Campbell, D. and Crowther, F. (1991) What is an entrepreneurial school? in F. Crowther and B. Caldwell (eds), *The Entrepreneurial School*, Sydney, Ashton Scholastic.

Carnie, C. (1996) Finders keepers, *Education Marketing*, Vol. 4, pp. 9–10.

Casson, M. (1982) *The Entrepreneur: An Economic Theory*, Oxford, Robertson.

Coleman, M. (1999) Working with employers and business, in J. Lumby and N. Foskett (eds), *Managing External Relations in Schools and Colleges*, London, Paul Chapman.

Coleman, M., Bush, T. and Glover, D. (1994) *Managing Finance and External Relations*, Harlow, Longman.

DfEE (Department for Education and Employment) (undated) Private Finance Division: PFI/PPP project listings.

DfEE (Department for Education and Employment) (1998a) *Investing for Excellence: Business Opportunities in Education and Employment*, London, DfEE.

DfEE (Department for Education and Employment) (1998b) *Investing in Excellence: Guide to the Structure and Financing of Education and Employment Sectors*, London, DfEE.

Dimmock, C. (ed.) (1993) *School-Based Management and School Effectiveness*, London, Routledge.

Drucker, P. (1985) *Innovation and Entrepreneurship*, New York, Harper and Row.

FAS (Funding Agency for Schools) (1997) *Bidding for Funds: A Guide to Accessing Additional Sources of Funding for Schools*, York, FAS.

FEFC (The Further Education Funding Council) (1998) *Public Private Partnership: Prospects in Further Education*, Coventry, FEFC.

Foskett, N. (1999) Strategy, external relations and marketing, in J. Lumby and N. Foskett (eds), *Managing External Relations in Schools and Colleges*, London, Paul Chapman.

Fouts, J. and Chan, J. (1997) The development of work-study and school enterprises in China's schools, *Journal of Curriculum Studies*, Vol. 29, no. 1, pp. 31–46.

Fozard, B. and Meek, L. (1990/91) Fundraising for a computer project for the physically handicapped child, *Headteachers Review*, Winter, pp. 26–7.

Fullan, M. (1992) *What's Worth Fighting for in Headship?* Buckingham, Open University Press.

Fullan, M., with Stiegelbauer, S. (1991) *The Meaning of Educational Change* (2nd edn), London, Cassell.

Gunter, H. (1997) *Rethinking Education*, London, Cassell.

Hopkins, D., Ainscow, M. and West, M. (1994) *School Improvement in an Era of Change*, London, Cassell.

Hopkins, D., Ainscow, M. and West, M. (1997) School improvement – propositions for actions, in A. Harris, N. Bennett and M. Preedy (eds), *Organizational Effectiveness and Improvement in Education*, Buckingham, Open University Press.

Huuskonen, V. (1992) *Yrittajaksi ryhtyminen* (*To be an entrepreneur*), Turku School of Economics and Business, Series A-2, Raision Painopojat Oy.

Kingham, P. (1993) Something for nothing: every school's dream, *School Librarian*, Vol. 41, no. 3, pp. 98–9.

Kirby, M. (1992) *Generating Income: Fundraising*, Cambridge, Pearson.

Kirzner, I. (1973) *Competition and Entrepreneurship*, Chicago, University of Chicago Press.

Knight, B. (1987) Managing the honeypots, in H. Thomas and T. Simkins (eds), *Economics and the Management of Education: Emerging Themes*, London, Falmer Press.

Lahdeniemi, T. (1997) Entrepreneurial education and its potential: a view from Finland, *Industry and Higher Education*, Vol. 11, no. 3, pp. 174–5.

Levačić, R. (1995) *Local Management of Schools*, Buckingham, Open University Press.

Liebenstein, H. (1968) Entrepreneurship and development, *American Economic Review*, Vol. 58, n.p.

Marsden, S. (1997) *Capital Fundraising for Schools*, London, Pitman.

Maunder, P., Myers, D., Wall, N. and LeRoy Miller, R. (1987) *Economics Explained*, London, Collins Educational.

Roberts, J. (1993) How to obtain funding, *Training Officer*, April, Vol. 23, no. 3, pp. 79–81.

Rosenberg, H. (1998) *A Handbook of School Fundraising*, London, Kogan Page.

Salisbury, R. (undated) Alternative Funding. Unpublished notes, Mansfield, The Garibaldi School.

Schein, E. (1985) *Organizational Culture and Leadership: A Dynamic View*, San Francisco, Jossey-Bass.

Schumpter, J. (1934) *The Theory of Economic Development*, Cambridge, MA, Harvard University Press.

Shephard, G. (1994) Forward by the Secretary of State, in *Education Means Business: Private Finance in Education*, London, Department for Education.

Smyth, J. (ed.) (1993) *A Socially Critical View of the Self-Managing School*, London, Falmer Press.

Stevenson, H., Roberts, M. and Grousbeck, H. (1994) *New Business Ventures and the Entrepreneur* (4th edn), Chicago, Richard D. Irwin, Inc.

Stoll, L. and Fink, D. (1996) *Changing our Schools*, Buckingham, Open University Press.

Turner, A. (1990) Making your first million, *School Governor*, April, pp. 25–7.

Whitty, G., Power, S. and Halpin, D. (1998) *Devolution and Choice in Education: The School, the State and the Market*, Buckingham, Open University Press.

4

FINANCING SCHOOL-BASED EDUCATION IN ENGLAND: PRINCIPLES AND PROBLEMS

Anne West, Hazel Pennell, Robert West and Tony Travers

INTRODUCTION

This chapter examines the way in which funds for education in England are distributed from central to local government and from local government to schools. It also explores the ways in which money notionally intended for 'special' or 'additional' educational needs is used at school level. A number of problems with the current system are discussed. Some of these are of fundamental importance and suggest that the distribution of resources from central to local government is not being adequately targeted on need. A number of alternative mechanisms are proposed to allocate money to local authorities.

Whilst this study focuses on the situation in the UK, there are a number of issues we discuss that are relevant to the financing of education in an international context:

1) It is possible for a financing system that is basically redistributive to be used by central government to distribute resources to local government, and at the same time to combine it with a system of demand-side financing at the school level. Within the Education Standard Spending Assessment (SSA) (used to distribute funds to local authorities) the element for additional educational needs is clearly specified and given a fixed value. However, at the local level, the element for additional educational or special educational needs is not specified. It is up to each local education authority (LEA) to determine how it takes account of different needs in its funding formula for schools. Thus within an LEA, where there are pockets of disadvantage, the local funding formula will not necessarily benefit such schools.

2) Democratically elected bodies such as local councils will act in ways that maximize their own chances of re-election. This is in line with

public choice theory and needs to be borne in mind by policy-makers. The fact that authorities that were the least deprived and historically the lowest spenders opted to spend comparatively more money on education in the mid-1990s may at first sight seem paradoxical, but the overall political context meant that a reduction in expenditure would have affected their chances of re-election. The electorate had become increasingly informed about educational issues as a result of government reforms designed to increase parental involvement in schools.

3) The use of varying types of statistical indicators is a matter of concern. In the quasi-market that now exists in England, there is a range of financial incentives that are open to manipulation at school level. For example, additional funds are frequently associated with deprivation or with special or additional educational needs. What is important from a policy perspective is that there is now an awareness that such indicators are open to manipulation and that there may be perverse effects as a result.

This chapter highlights a number of important issues concerned with the financing of school-based education in England. The process is complex. We explore the mechanisms that are used by central and local government to fund schools and the strategies used to meet the varying needs of pupils. Local financial management has provided scope for the innovative use of funds, but we still know little about the strategies used by schools to meet the varying needs of pupils and how these are linked to pupils' outcomes. There is clearly a need to find out more about how the use of resources affects outcomes for pupils with different types of needs.

The second section of this chapter describes the national funding context and the mechanisms used by central government to distribute funds to local authorities. The third section explores the way in which the education budget is determined at a local level and the role played by different directorates/departments within local authorities and by central government. The fourth section focuses on the distribution of resources by the local authority to schools with specific reference to funding special educational needs and additional educational needs. The fifth section looks at the way in which schools use money intended for pupils with 'additional educational needs'. The penultimate section examines some of the problems associated with the financing of school-based education and proposes three alternative models that could be used to distribute funds to local authorities that would offer greater transparency. The final section summarizes the key issues to emerge and discusses their broader implications.

DISTRIBUTION OF RESOURCES FROM CENTRAL TO LOCAL GOVERNMENT

The responsibility for expenditure on school-based education is divided between two government departments, the Department for Education and

Employment (DfEE) and the Department of the Environment, Transport and the Regions (DETR). The DfEE is responsible for central government's direct expenditure on education, as well as expenditure made available for specific grants (these support expenditure on initiatives and training) and credit approvals for capital expenditure. The DETR provides finance for local authorities' expenditure on education through the Revenue Support Grant (RSG). The RSG is not hypothecated, which means that local authorities are not forced to spend a specific amount on education. It is also important to stress that money for education comes primarily from central government (around 80 per cent). The remaining 20 per cent is obtained through Council Tax (a local property tax).

All state-maintained (i.e. not independent) schools are now funded by local authorities. Each year the government's view of the 'appropriate' amount of revenue expenditure for all local authorities is set out in the RSG settlement. This gives the Total Standard Spending (TSS) which is the total amount of revenue expenditure of local authorities (net of specific grants). The TSS is made up of 'control' totals for each service area (education, personal and social services, police, fire and civil defence, highway maintenance, all other services, and capital financing). The government calculates the share each authority should have of the control total for each service for which it is responsible: the sum of these service areas is the total SSA for each authority (see Audit Commission, 1993a, for more details). The view of the government is that: 'An SSA represents the Government's view of the amount of revenue expenditure which it would be appropriate for an authority to incur to provide a standard level of services consistent with the Secretary of State's view of the appropriate amount of revenue expenditure for all authorities' (Department of the Environment, 1990, p. 1).

Whilst local authorities are able to spend above or below their Education SSA, the evidence suggests that Education SSAs have constrained expenditure within narrow limits (see West *et al.*, 1999a). It is also important to stress that the government has reserve powers to prevent what it considers to be 'excessive' increases in Council Tax. (At the time the research was carried out, the mechanism used to prevent such increases was known as 'capping'.)

The Education SSA is split into five service sub-blocks:

- primary (pupils aged 5 to 10);
- secondary (pupils aged 11 to 15);
- post-16 (pupils aged 16 or more for whose education the authority is responsible);
- under 5s (the population of children aged up to 4);
- a category of 'other' (the population of those aged 11 or more, with added weighting for those aged 16 to 24 years).

A local authority's Education SSA is mainly based on the school population in the relevant age group, but calculations for each LEA are modified to allow for differences in social needs, costs etc. The following components are used:

- the number of pupils/residents;
- additional educational needs;
- population sparsity;
- the area cost adjustment;
- free school meals.

For the primary and secondary sub-blocks of the Education SSA, all components are used, whilst for the others, fewer components are used (for example, there is no allowance for free school meals in the 'other' service block).

The number of children plays the most important role in determining the Education SSA and is based on an estimate of the number of pupils in schools maintained by the local authority. It represents more than 70 per cent of the total. That central government should direct its assistance where needs are greatest or resources least has been part of the political consensus for many years (Audit Commission, 1993a) and an 'Additional Educational Needs' (AEN) component recognizes that the cost of providing a standard quality of education is greater in the case of some children than others. In general, children from deprived backgrounds or who come from minority ethnic groups are believed to require extra resources. Rather than attempting to identify these children individually, the current system uses a set of surrogate or 'proxy' indicators whose value is calculated on an authority-wide basis. These are:

- the proportion of children aged under 18 in private households containing a lone-parent family;
- the proportion of dependent children of claimants receiving income support;
- the proportion of children aged under 16 in private households who were born outside the UK, Ireland, the USA or Old Commonwealth, or whose head of household was born outside these areas.

These indicators are combined in a simple equation to produce a single score. The weightings given to each indicator vary: 'This is to maintain a balance between factors measuring "general" social disadvantage and the ethnic factor which measures more specific language and cultural difficulties' (Department of the Environment, 1990, p. 11). To determine the proportion of money that will be allocated on the basis of additional educational needs, the slope of the function relating the AEN index to past expenditure is calculated. In the early 1990s, the weighting given to the AEN index was reduced from 21 per cent to 16 per cent for primary and secondary sub-blocks (see West, West and Pennell, 1995), with the result that local authorities with high levels of need suffered a reduction of resources.

Population sparsity is another issue addressed in the Education SSA. There is clear evidence that school size and home-to-school transport costs are linked to sparseness of the population (see Department of the Environment, 1990). In addition, small schools are subject to diseconomies of scale and wider catchment areas mean higher costs because there is more home-to-school travel. Both small school size and home-to-school transport thus result in higher unit costs of provision. The population sparsity indicator addresses this issue using data gathered from the census. There is also an 'Area Cost Adjustment'. This indicator is designed to 'reflect . . . the differences in labour costs between London and the rest of the country' (Department of the Environment, 1990, p. 12) and uses information from the New Earnings Survey which is an annual 1 per cent random survey of people in employment. It covers employees in all occupations in all types and sizes of business in all industries.

Finally, pupils whose families receive income support are entitled to free school meals and milk. The additional costs associated with this entitlement are allowed for in the primary and secondary sub-blocks by allocating around 2 per cent of each control total based on the proportion of children of income support claimants in the LEA.

HOW THE EDUCATION BUDGET IS DETERMINED AT A LOCAL LEVEL

Given that the amount of money that local authorities spend on the services for which they are responsible is not hypothecated, local authorities have to decide, each year, how much they are going to spend on education. In this section, we examine the process by which the education budget is determined.

In order to gain an overview of the budget-setting process, six English local authorities were selected as case studies (Table 4.1). Two were inner London authorities, one was an outer London local authority, one was a northern metropolitan authority and two were shire authorities – one in the East Midlands and one in the West Midlands. The authorities also differed in terms of size, historical spending levels and socio-economic profiles. All were budgeted to spend at or above SSA in 1996/97. In the two inner London local authorities the education budget (according to DETR figures)

Table 4.1 Political complexion of case study local authorities

Local authority	Political complexion 1996
Inner London	Labour
Inner London	Conservative
Outer London	Conservative
Northern Metropolitan	Labour
East Midlands shire county	Labour
West Midlands shire county	Labour-Liberal Democrat

was 11 per cent and 14 per cent respectively over Education SSA. In contrast the shires were spending 1 per cent and 2 per cent above their Education SSA.

Whilst all authorities budgeted to spend at least at the level of the Education SSA, historically, the two shire counties spent below Education SSA. This is an important point to bear in mind in the discussion that follows.

Setting the overall and education budgets

Two specific issues were addressed in the context of setting the education budget. First, information was gathered on how the overall budget was set within different authorities. Second, information was sought on the way in which the education budget was determined.

Local authorities used different processes to determine their overall budgets. The two Conservative authorities had both adopted an overtly 'corporate approach' with officers playing a key role in determining the overall budget and also the education budget. In both cases, the Chief Executive and the Director of Finance were reported to be key players in the budget-setting process. But, as stated by one Director of Education: 'On a corporate basis I would say that everybody is equal . . . in reality some individuals are stronger than others'. In both authorities, there was a three-year budget-planning process (this was not a characteristic of any of the other local authorities). The Assistant Borough Treasurer in one of the authorities said: 'We have been consistently encouraging members to take a longer term view when managing the council's finances.'

The London and Metropolitan Labour-controlled authorities differed in that politicians were more integrally involved in the budget-setting process. Indeed, the Leader in one of the authorities felt that the members were more involved in decision-making on the budget than in other councils: 'There has always been a tradition here, all members – backbenchers – have a say at two stages. Once through their committee areas and second as members of the administration group [the members of the governing party]. The Labour Group is the body that in the end takes all the important decisions.'

In this London authority, the key players were the Chief Executive and the Leader of the Council. In the Metropolitan authority, the Chief Executive, Director of Finance, the Director of Education and Leisure and the Director of Social Services were all considered to be highly influential in setting the overall budget. However, the Director of Education reported that 'proposals for budget changes are put through a politically-driven process'. In both shire counties the Director of Finance was perceived as being the most influential director, with a key role being played by the Chief Executive.

Decisions about education expenditure

It is also important to stress that in these authorities, different pressures affected the way in which decisions about how much to spend on education were made. In the two Conservative authorities the desire to keep Council Tax low was an overriding concern. In one, financial prudence is an issue for politicians. The authority traditionally sets a low Council Tax and that is 'a major driver'. There is a history of slimming down as an authority and it has 'externalized enormously' (for example, salary payments and some council services). One of the consequences of contracting out services was noted by a senior politician: 'Oddly enough, when you have things out to contract, you can't cut them back in the way that you can otherwise' (Chair of Education). Thus an attempt at an efficiency saving – in terms of minimizing inputs in relation to outputs – was preventing cuts in expenditure taking place. In the other Conservative authority, Council Tax was reported to be the key issue politically: 'We are keen to keep Council Tax at the lowest possible rate. If we can still keep a low Council Tax and still subsidize education and social services in the way we do by making savings elsewhere we think that is running an efficient ship' (Chair of Education).

In all other authorities, the situation was different. Certainly, there were concerns about the finances, but the desire to keep Council Tax low was not paramount. Rather there were concerns about the levels of government funding and the capping limit. All four were spending at the capping limit: 'Council Tax is irrelevant. We set a [low Council Tax] and we are not allowed to choose whether it would be appropriate for it to be a little higher' (Leader, Shire); 'we budget at whatever the capping level is and the Council Tax is a consequence of just that' (Chief Executive, inner London).

Thus, in all the non-Conservative authorities, external financial constraints affected the education budget – in general, the prospect of capping. In the Conservative authorities, the desire to keep Council Tax low was an overriding concern with this being seen as part of a desire to be 'efficient' in terms of service provision.

Equity issues

There was considerable variation between the authorities in terms of the emphasis given to equity issues. What is particularly interesting is the fact that a focus on equity issues did not split according to party political lines.

In two of our case study local authorities (both long established and Labour controlled) high priority was given to equity issues. In the inner London Labour LEA, for example, school meals were seen as having an anti-poverty focus both for pupils and for school meals staff (where there was a minimum earnings guarantee). As noted by the Chief Executive: 'In some areas there would be a real choice between providing school meals in-house or ploughing the money into teachers . . . that is not an area of discussion.' In the metropolitan authority, school meals were also a priority.

In addition, one of the two shire counties had recently become Labour controlled and the reintroduction of hot school meals had been a manifesto commitment. Another initiative involved targeting expenditure on the most deprived areas within the county.

However, in the Conservative inner London local authority, equity issues also had a high profile. In particular, the council chooses to 'top up' the Education SSA because of the needs in the area. The Director of Education reported that the education priorities reflected the needs of the area: 'very mobile, large numbers whose first language is not English, relatively high SEN [special educational needs], some areas of social disadvantage'.

Thus, in spite of a desire to keep Council Tax low, a requirement to focus on the needs of the area was recognized. The similarity between the two London local authorities, even though of different political complexions, is clear. They both served populations which were high in needs of various kinds and both adopted a similar strategy of targeting their resources on these needs. Both had been part of the former Inner London Education Authority with its historically high levels of expenditure.

Relationship between Education SSA and education budget

As local authorities are not obliged to spend the amount that the government allocates for education through the Education SSA, analyses were conducted to examine the relationship between Education SSAs and local authority education expenditure (for details see West *et al.*, 1999a). Across England there was a consistent difference between the LEA types over the years 1994 to 1997, with shires (rural local authorities) tending to spend furthest above their SSA than other LEA types and outer London spending least. The correlation between education spending and the Education SSA remained fairly constant over the time period. However, there was evidence that different types of local authority showed different time trends. The shires showed an increase and then a large decrease in spending relative to SSA. Outer London showed a slight increase, inner London showed a slight increase and the metropolitan authorities a slight decrease. During this period, the Conservative government was committed to cuts in public expenditure, but at a local level the shire councils chose to increase expenditure markedly relative to Education SSA in the mid-1990s when there was a poor local government settlement. What appears to have happened is that authorities chose to maintain real spending levels while SSA fell, thus widening the gap between SSA and spending.

Using public choice theory (see Le Grand and Winter, 1987), it would appear that decisions were taken at a local level to try to ensure that education, a service used more than other local services by the middle-classes, was saved from severe cuts imposed by central government. Traditionally low spending shires thus 'overspent' (relative to Education SSA) at even higher levels than previously. Perhaps of even greater significance is that new political awareness, generated by local management of schools, the introduction of grant maintained schools (see West and Pennell, 1997, for further details) and increasingly well-informed governors and well-educated parents, made cuts impossible. The way in which authorities responded can be seen as rational behaviour, designed to maximize the opportunities for re-election.

DISTRIBUTION OF RESOURCES TO SCHOOLS BY LEAs

The Education Reform Act 1988 has had a major impact on the way in which resources are allocated to schools by local authorities under local management of schools (LMS). The process is described in detail elsewhere (e.g. Levačić, 1993), but in essence there has been a 'quasi-voucher' mechanism in place, whereby 80 per cent of funds for schools are allocated by LEAs on the basis of pupil numbers (see West and Pennell, 1997). Local management of schools has been perceived as one of the major success stories of the Conservative education reforms, and the headteachers interviewed in the case studies provide added support.

At the time of the interviews the six LEAs were delegating between 89 per cent and 93 per cent of the potential schools budget to schools. In one case the amount delegated to secondary and middle schools was effectively 98 per cent. This 'extended LMS' had been introduced in the wake of the threat of schools opting out of local authority control and according to the officer responsible for LMS: 'in order that schools could stay within the LEA partnership and yet have the same freedom of action as [grant-maintained] schools had'.

Our interviews revealed that headteachers welcomed the freedom that LMS gave them to manage their school effectively and to focus their expenditure on determined priorities. One headteacher commented: 'I don't think of LMS in purely financial terms. It's about managing your own school and taking the decisions which are pertinent to your own school so you can adjust whatever is happening to suit your own needs.'

The benefits of LMS in increasing value for money and the accountability of schools was another issue highlighted, as indicated by the following headteachers: 'Schools have become far more careful and precise about how they manage . . . resources and are far more focused on value for money.' 'If I am held accountable for what goes on in this school and local management does that then clearly I am going to be far more focused in what I am doing. With accountability goes responsibility'.

Although headteachers were generally very positive about LMS, several problems were identified. The failure to pay *actual* teaching staff costs was seen as a particular difficulty as it drove 'down the quality of the teaching force because there is pressure to look for the cheapest rather than the best'. Other issues of concern were the disparity in funding between primary and secondary schools and the difficulty of managing resources in schools with fluctuating rolls.

In April 1999, a new approach to the distribution of funds to schools by local authorities was introduced by central government. This is called 'Fair Funding'. In essence, it is a rationalization of LMS, with expenditure on central education services being strictly regulated. The proposals involve a significant increase in the level of financial delegation to schools. Under Fair Funding, the LEA can retain funds centrally to support its role in four key areas:

- strategic management;
- access (planning of school places, admissions, transport, etc.);
- school improvement;
- special educational provision.

The main services for which schools could expect to receive additional delegated funding include:

- building repairs and maintenance;
- school meals;
- management support (payroll, etc.);
- curriculum advisory services;
- supply teacher cover.

The new recurrent funding framework applies to all state-funded schools (including former grant maintained schools that were more autonomous than others) and as a result of the tightening up of regulations the government has already published league tables on LEA central planned expenditure, to compare LEAs. There is a Local Schools Budget (LSB) and an Individual Schools Budget (ISB). This is a simplification of the previous situation. For primary and secondary schools 80 per cent of their total share of the ISB is allocated on a pupil-led basis. The model has a menu-type approach to enable LEAs to allocate funds. This allows them largely to replicate their previous LMS formulae.

The 'menu' includes:

- pupil numbers weighted in accordance with pupils' assessed special educational need;
- provision of adjustments to take account of actual teaching salary costs;
- payments based on social deprivation indicators (e.g. entitlement to free school meals);
- payments to reflect size of buildings or grounds;
- lump sum payments to all schools or to all schools of specified size;
- payments to schools whose budget shares would otherwise be reduced year-on-year by more than a percentage amount.

It is also interesting to note that output-related funding is also possible with provision being made for funding school sixth forms using approaches linked to recruitment, participation and achievement.

Under Fair Funding there is a considerable extension in the amount of delegation to schools in respect of building work, the school meals service, some central support services, ancillary services, and curriculum, advisory and training services. Interestingly, the headteachers in our study (carried out before the introduction of Fair Funding), with one exception, did not want any more responsibilities delegated to them; in fact, two actually wanted less delegated. In the main, headteachers valued the services provided centrally and were concerned that more delegation would lead to deteriorating services (Pennell and West, 1998).

Primary headteachers valued in particular the expertise the LEA could provide over health and safety matters, building regulations, legal advice, training and transport:

> I'd hate to get stuck . . . with school buses . . . I'm happy that they take over similar sorts of administrative issues . . . I don't want to deal with people's contracts – I am happy to do the appointments then send it off to the LEA to sort out the paperwork. Structural maintenance – I don't want that.

> The bit that worries me is things like building regulations.

The areas that they particularly did not want to take over were transport and, in some cases, buildings. Headteachers also showed no enthusiasm for taking over the school meals service. In general, the headteachers valued backup, expert advice, inspection and advisory services and training. Following the introduction of LMS, some headteachers noted that the time LEA officers could spend on building matters and legal advice had been reduced.

It seems that the new system of Fair Funding may not be welcomed by all headteachers. Whether the reforms introduced by Fair Funding will be as well received as those introduced by LMS remains to be seen.

Funding special and additional educational needs

Our research had a particular focus on the ways in which local authorities funded special and additional educational needs. We are using two different concepts here. Pupils with *special educational needs* have been identified as having learning difficulties of one type or another. There is a Code of Practice in relation to SEN (Department for Education, 1994). Within schools and local authorities, pupils may be at one of five stages of SEN. At stage 5, a pupil will have a 'statement of special educational need' and attached to that will be financial resources over and above those provided to the school under local management. Lower stages require support to be provided either by the school alone or by the school and the local authority. Specifically excluded from the official definition of special educational needs are English language needs unless these are accompanied by learning difficulties above and beyond the language needs. *Additional educational needs* is an overarching concept. This concept has been used in other research studies (West and Sammons, 1996) and includes a variety of needs – for example, special educational needs, English language needs and social disadvantage.

The LEAs in our research used a range of different indices to distribute funds to schools. The formulae also ranged in their level of sophistication. Whilst in several cases entitlement to free school meals was used as a proxy for the differences between schools in the number of SEN or AEN pupils, in others the formulae were more complex. The most complex consisted of an AEN weighted formula made up of a number of indicators (eligibility for free meals, pupils from large families/one-parent families, first language/ years in UK education, homelessness, children in care, pupil mobility and excluded pupils). Two authorities used a moderated SEN audit to distribute funds for non-statemented SEN.

Thirteen headteachers of primary and secondary schools in six local authority areas were interviewed. In these schools the levels of social disadvantage and/or the number of pupils with special educational needs were higher than the LEA average. Headteachers raised a number of issues of concern about the indicators used for the distribution of funds to schools for SEN/AEN. Where free school meals entitlement was used as a single measure for AEN or SEN, some headteachers were concerned that it did not adequately reflect the needs of the pupils in their schools. For example, a primary headteacher where free school meals was used as a proxy for SEN considered that:

> Free school meals do go with social disadvantage but that is not the only disadvantage a child can suffer. A huge proportion come from one-parent families, there are a lot of refuges around here so there are a lot of them where the mother has been battered or the child has been battered – enormous social problems.

A headteacher of a secondary school where free school meals was the major component of funding for AEN noted: 'I don't think it's a very sophisticated formula . . . We've noticed this year . . . there's going to be a drop in numbers of students on free school meals . . . but we haven't noticed a drop in the needs of students.'

Indeed, it is likely, particularly at secondary level, that parents may not complete the relevant forms as their children do not choose to eat school dinners. As the pupil is no longer identified as being eligible for free school meals, the additional funding attached to that pupil is lost to the school. But the problem is not confined to secondary schools as is indicated by the following comment from a headteacher of a primary school in a shire county: 'We have quite a few families who are entitled to free school meals but don't claim because they prefer not to. So that figure is very arbitrary.'

In contrast, headteachers appeared to appreciate the efforts made by some LEAs to design more sophisticated formulae to meet the characteristics of their school population.

Some headteachers, whose school populations were more disadvantaged than the majority of the schools in the LEA, were concerned at the level of funding they received. A secondary headteacher from one of the shire counties commented:

> There are . . . issues of social disadvantage in pockets [of the LEA] . . . where I think perhaps the resources that one needs and the expertise that one needs are slightly different to the norm . . . But the increased delegation to schools means that the LEA isn't quite in the position that it used to be to be able to do that . . . When you look at the statistics overall for [the LEA] the needs for ethnic [minority] pupils because they are such a small percentage of the overall figure – it's not so meaningful to people in other parts of the county.

There is clearly a lack of transparency for at least some headteachers in terms of the process of local financial management.

HOW SCHOOLS USE MONEY ALLOCATED FOR SPECIAL AND ADDITIONAL EDUCATIONAL NEED

The headteachers of the 13 case study schools were asked how they used resources for those with SEN or other needs (social disadvantage, English as an additional language (EAL)). As expected, headteachers directed most of their resources to staffing. In particular, resources were directed to employing a special educational needs co-ordinator (SENCO) and additional staff (either teachers or classroom support staff). Each of the schools had a SENCO in post at the time of the interview.

The seniority of the member of staff employed as a SENCO and the time allocated for the role varied considerably between schools. In a small outer London primary school the SENCO was a full-time classroom teacher who was given a responsibility point and was relieved of teaching for half a day per week by the headteacher who took his class. The headteacher was concerned at the level of resourcing but considered that was all that could be afforded within the very constrained budget. The other primary schools tended to be more generous in their staffing with classroom support staff in post as well as the SENCO and in one school a 0.5 full-time equivalent (FTE) teacher was also employed to work on an intensive reading recovery programme (partially funded by the LEA). In one primary school the SENCO was the deputy headteacher.

Secondary schools in the main employed more staff to work with SEN pupils. In a well-resourced inner London secondary school, with a high proportion of pupils on the special educational needs register, a member of the school's senior management team was employed as the SENCO. The headteacher considered that the appointment: 'Both raised the profile of learning support and the importance of it, and provided somebody who had access to management at the most senior level within the school.'

In this school the headteacher had put together a specialist team which dealt with both SEN and EAL issues consisting of the SENCO and seven FTE teachers. This school had the advantage of a rapidly increasing roll and a young teaching staff who were comparatively inexpensive to employ.

The other inner London secondary school was in a somewhat different position. The headteacher who had taken over two years previously when the school was in very difficult circumstances explained:

> Because I had a choice . . . the money goes globally into our budget but the question is what does least damage. The extra SEN money . . . and much of the social disadvantage money went into maintaining reasonable class sizes rather than specialist SEN support. Now that is a decision I would stand by.

The school employed a SENCO at 0.4 FTE and two other teachers at 1.7 FTE. The headteacher was aware that this was inadequate for the needs of the school and said that he would invest more in SEN as soon as the budget improved.

Another resourcing question raised by headteachers was who to employ to support the SENCO: teachers or classroom assistants. In a few cases headteachers felt that they were not in a position to make a choice. One primary headteacher in a shire county who employed classroom assistants explained: 'You don't get enough to do anything else.'

However, where headteachers were in a position to choose they did not always feel that it was necessarily the best use of their resources to employ trained teachers rather than classroom assistants. In one secondary school, for example, a decision had been made to reorganize SEN and to make an existing member of the teaching staff redundant and replace her with four classroom support assistants to support the SENCO. The headteacher explained that the change was made: 'Because we were basically using expensive teachers to support in the classroom and they were doing a job . . . which was lower than the level of a professional teacher. By changing we feel we can provide support to more children'.

In contrast to SEN, resources for pupils with EAL were generally supplied by the LEA as a centrally run service using joint government-LEA funds. In three LEAs, English as an Additional Language was a component factor in the LMS formula but in only one case was the funding separately identified.

Headteachers did not appear to separately target resources on pupils who came from socially disadvantaged backgrounds. The headteacher of an outer London secondary school explained: 'There isn't any money that's designated for social disadvantage but in any case we have so many children that would fit into that it would be a ridiculous thing to try and sort out.' However, given the nature of the intake into their schools a number of headteachers felt it was important to use part of their resourcing to maintain a good pupil–teacher ratio at least where needs were greatest. One secondary headteacher explained: 'We have smaller class sizes in certain areas – with setting arrangements – particularly for English and maths. We put more into literacy and numeracy and less into science.'

PROBLEMS WITH THE FINANCING OF EDUCATION

There are a number of intractable problems to do with the financing of school-based education. This section will examine in turn problems related to the distribution of resources from central to local government and perceptions of problems at a local level. It will then examine possible alternatives to the funding of schools at a national level.

Distribution of funds by central government to local government

Determining the standard level of service

The description of SSAs refers to a 'standard' level of service. This term is not defined. However, it implies that the system should be in some sense fair, but this still leaves considerable room for interpretation (Audit Commission, 1993b, p. 23): 'It could mean equalising inputs (teachers per pupil, perhaps adjusted for need) or outcomes (e.g. attainment or improvement) each of which could lead to different distributions of resources.'

Use of census data for the indicator proxies

There are problems with the use of census data to determine key elements in the AEN index – the lone-parent and the ethnicity indicators (see West, West and Pennell, 1995):

1) The census is carried out at ten-yearly intervals and is therefore not responsive to shorter-term demographic fluctuations.
2) In the most recent (1991) census there was under-recording of the population and particularly amongst those in greater need through homelessness or poverty.
3) Census data may not show accurately the level of need in schools in local authorities where significant proportions of the population choose to educate their children privately.
4) The census takes no account of pupils attending schools in LEAs where they are not resident.

Use of past spending to determine weightings

The weighting given to the AEN index in the Education SSA is largely determined by a statistical technique called multiple regression. This examines the relationship between values of the index and past expenditure on the assumption that past expenditure reflects the resource needs associated with that index. However, there is good evidence to show that spending constraints imposed by central government are paramount and that some LEAs are spending less than they would wish to on education because they need the money for even higher priorities, such as obeying a statutory requirement to repay capital debt.

Basis for the area cost adjustment

There is considerable concern about the Area Cost Adjustment (ACA), whereby additional resources go to certain local authorities outside London but not to others. Teachers' salaries are only higher in London, not in the South East generally (which is the region benefiting from the ACA). On the basis of a survey of LEAs, Hale and Travers (1993) reported that one local authority in the South East, and therefore in receipt of the adjustment, accepted that the argument for retaining the Area Cost Adjustment for the counties around London was weak.

Use of proxy indicators in the additional educational needs index

The AEN index is intended to cover costs associated with both social disadvantage and ethnicity. There are problems with the index. First, ethnicity in itself is not an indicator of need – indeed, the differing examination performance of various ethnic minority groups lends support to this notion. Lack of fluency in English is undoubtedly a factor, but is not measured in the AEN index. Second, Hale and Travers (1993) question the relevance of composite indicators such as the AEN, when the factors used are highly associated with one another.

Our research explored the relationships between the indicators that are used to construct the AEN (together with some that are not used) and national test results at the age of 7 and examination results at the age of 16 (see also West *et al.*, 1999a; 1999b). Our analyses show that there are some very strong negative relationships at the level of the LEA between indicators of need and educational performance.

In particular, at the LEA level, there was a very close and highly significant *negative* relationship between the proportion of children dependent on income support recipients and Key Stage 1 results and between the proportion of children dependent on income support recipients and GCSE results. Moreover, once the proportion of children dependent on income support claimants had been entered into a regression equation predicting Key Stage 1 and GCSE results, we found that no other variable added consistently and significantly to the prediction of achievement. Clearly, the relationship between poverty and low academic attainment is extremely high. Indeed, the relationship is closer than the current AEN index to which this indicator contributes.

Interestingly, there was no relationship at the LEA level between the proportion of children with statements of special educational needs and outcomes at either Key Stage 1 or at the GCSE level. The correlations for the proportion of children with or without statements and outcomes were similarly low.

Perceptions of problems at a local level

National funding issues were a major concern to headteachers. In most cases, there was a fairly high level of awareness of national funding issues and how local authorities were funded by government.

The interviews with headteachers of schools in six local education authorities revealed widespread dissatisfaction with the amount of money they received. Respondents were asked whether they considered that the amount of money they received from their LEA was adequate to meet the needs of their school. The following examples illustrate the concerns felt:

> I think that the temptation must be to say 'no' . . . Formulas find it difficult to work out the interaction between the different factors . . . There is an answer, it's basically make the cake bigger.
> (Inner London LEA secondary headteacher)

> I think the fault lies with the standard spending limit [*sic*] that is imposed by government. It is quite noticeable that in [this LEA] our standard spending limit is far lower than in any of the authorities around us . . . It goes back to when the Conservatives had control of the council they kept the spending limits low.
> (Shire LEA primary headteacher)

Only in one inner London LEA were resources felt to be adequate. The local authority in this case had a sophisticated formula for funding additional educational needs:

> Everybody would say they need more resources . . . I suppose I would have to admit that the resources we have in the school are adequate to meet needs . . . We are a school with a rapidly increasing roll . . . At the same time we have got a very young staff . . . They're cheap and therefore there is a lot of flexibility . . . I also think that this authority spends well on education.
> (Inner London LEA secondary headteacher)

Headteachers in LEAs outside the South East were concerned about the ACA and in traditionally low spending authorities about the level of funding available to schools: 'Having taught in [an LEA in the South East] I feel even more incensed, I think. I can understand why some metropolitan areas . . . and inner city areas might receive more funding but I cannot understand why schools can't be funded on a fairer common funding formula.'

The failure of the previous Conservative government to fully fund the teachers' pay award was another issue of general concern. Finally, the general shortage of funds for education is highlighted by the substitution of private money for public money for schools: 'One of the ways in which we are doubly disadvantaged is that schools in affluent areas [of the LEA] are often heavily subsidized by their Parent Teacher Associations' (Outer London LEA primary headteacher).

The interview data suggest that the major problem with the overall education budget for schools in England is the 'size of the cake'. Even in comparatively well-resourced LEAs in London and the Metropolitan LEA, at school level, there were perceived to be unmet needs. The situation for the shire counties was compounded by historically low levels of expenditure by former Conservative administrations.

Other methods to distribute funds to local authorities

Given the problems identified above, is there a 'better method' of funding education at a national level? During 1998, the Labour government reviewed the way in which money is allocated to local authorities. Many options were considered but a government working group paper (DETR, 1998a) suggested that most or all of these would have resulted in a redistribution away from areas of higher need towards those with less need. In the event, no changes were made:

> It would not have been right to take decisions on Area Cost Adjustment and Additional Educational Needs now, when it was clear that there were unresolved issues raised by local government which need further work during the period of SSA stability . . .
> We also need to look at the case for more radical reform, to produce something which is clearer and more robust than the existing system. We need a system which is more easily understood by the voter, and accepted as fair and stable.
>
> (DETR, 1998b, p. 6)

The method used in the government's review was the same as that used previously – namely, multiple regression, indicators being regressed against expenditure, which the government assumes to be a measure of 'need'.

Given the problems identified in relation to the mechanism used to distribute money from national to local government, it is important to examine possible alternative methods. These could include a staffing driven model and needs-based approaches.

Activity-led staffing

A number of local authorities have found an activity-led staffing (ALS) approach to be a useful tool to distribute money to schools within the local authority within the overall framework of LMS. Work on ALS has been carried out in a number of local education authorities, for example, Cambridgeshire, Stockport, Essex and Leeds. The overall aim of such an approach is to identify the curriculum and management activities within schools and to quantify the resources required to carry out these activities.

In an activity-led approach, teachers' activities could be drawn up on the basis of the 'School Teachers' Pay and Conditions' documents produced by the DfEE. For non-teaching staff and for other costs, a 'needs-driven' approach could be used. For example, in certain subject areas, technicians will be required. In all schools, there is a need for textbooks and library books to be purchased and for computer hardware and software to be purchased and upgraded. An ALS model could be used for generating education budgets for local authorities (with spreadsheets being drawn up and models tested out). To accompany an ALS approach, there are varying kinds of social and educational need that might be included: children with special educational needs (statemented and unstatemented); children with a need for English language teaching; and children eligible for free school meals (see West, West and Pennell, 1994).

Unfortunately, the special educational needs indicators have been shown to be flawed in that they do not relate in any consistent way to educational outcomes and it appears likely that success in obtaining a statement may be related to other factors (see West *et al.*, 1999a).

> There was no great correlation between 'pure' deprivation factors (unemployment, poor housing etc.) and children with special educational needs . . . [and] there was no correlation between measures of health and special educational needs which might be expected to provide a greater degree of correlation. . . . It was suggested that the willingness or otherwise of parents in different areas to ask schools to identify any special educational needs they may have might be affecting the apparent level of needs in different areas. A child who might be deemed to have SEN when compared with other children in a particular school/authority might not always be deemed to have SEN when compared with other children in a different school/LEA.
>
> (DETR, 1998a, para 2.1.14–2.1.15)

Needs-based approach focusing on attainment

Another proposal would be to use an approach that does not depend so much on teachers but on pupil characteristics. In order to distribute funds using this approach, costs associated with teaching pupils with different attainment levels and those with behavioural difficulties could be estimated on the basis of research or expert judgement. Funds would be distributed to LEAs on the basis of the characteristics of the *intake* to their schools so as not to be seen to 'reward' poor attainment. There would be a problem with such an approach, namely that there are no national baseline tests and the national test results at the age of 11 are not currently held by the DfEE at the level of individual *secondary* schools.

One possibility is for a fully moderated baseline assessment (preferably a *national* baseline assessment) to be considered as the basis for funding primary schools. Key Stage 2 national test data could be used as the means for funding secondary schools if collated appropriately. The lower a given pupil's national curriculum levels in these tests, the greater the amount of money that would follow the pupil. These tests are national and externally marked. They are thus robust measures that would be difficult – if not impossible – to manipulate at school level. The results of these tests would be valuable for funding a wide variety of SEN – and in some cases may obviate the need for statements (which vary enormously across the country and do not appear to be related entirely to need – see West *et al.*, 1999a). Some types of complex needs (visual impairment, hearing impairment, Down's syndrome) and severe behaviour problems would clearly require additional funding. An alternative, less radical approach would be to use well-moderated SEN audits that could provide models for funding pupils with non-statemented special educational needs.

Needs-based approach focusing on poverty

A second needs-based approach that would be much simpler to operate would be to provide additional funds to LEAs on the basis of the degree of poverty in the LEA (e.g. proportion of children dependent on income support recipients). This is because there is a very high correlation between poverty and later attainment. This is stronger than any other relationship tested. Using this approach, LEAs would not be 'rewarded' for poor attainments, but would be seen to be receiving funds to reduce social exclusion or perhaps to compensate for the adverse effects of poverty on educational attainment. Such an approach might involve analysing the additional cost incurred at school (and LEA) level as the proportion of children from disadvantaged backgrounds increases. It is clear from the case studies that reducing class size is one way in which schools with disadvantaged intakes target their additional resources; this and other methods could be explored further and associated costs examined.

However, it would be important not to use school-based indicators; problems associated with the use of free school meals eligibility were identified by one headteacher in our study and reinforce the notion that school-based indicators may have perverse incentives:

> We don't have people telling the truth about free school meals. Middle-class schools . . . once again have 72 per cent – the same as us [a school with a high level of need within the LEA]. Well, they are just measuring it in a different way or telling lies as we call it . . . I think the whole system is corrupt.

There is a 'window of opportunity' to replace what is seen by many to be a system that is open to political manipulation by one that is fairer and more transparent.

ACKNOWLEDGEMENTS

The support of the Economic and Social Research Council (ESRC) is gratefully acknowledged. The work was funded by ESRC award number R000236559. We would like to thank all those who made this research possible in the DfEE, the DETR, LEAs and schools. We would also like to thank Audrey Hind for computing assistance and John Wilkes for administrative support. The views expressed are the authors' own.

REFERENCES

Audit Commission (1993a) *Passing the Bucks: The Impact of Standard Spending Assessments on Economy, Efficiency and Effectiveness*, Vol. 1, London, HMSO.

Audit Commission (1993b) *Passing the Bucks: The Impact of Standard Spending Assessments on Economy, Efficiency and Effectiveness*, Vol. 2. London, HMSO.

Department for Education (1994) *Code of Practice on the Identification and Assessment of Special Educational Needs*, London, Department for Education.

Department of the Environment (1990) *Standard Spending Assessments: Background and Underlying Methodology*, London, Department of the Environment.

Department of the Environment, Transport and the Regions (1998a) Chapter 2: Education SSA at http://www.local.doe.gov.uk/finance/ssa/9900/subgroup/ch2.pdf., para 2.1.14–2.1.15.

Department of the Environment, Transport and the Regions (1998b) Prescott delivers good deal for local government, press release, 2 December, at http://195.44.11.137/coi/coipress.nsf.

Hale, R. and Travers, T. (1993) *£36 Billion and Rising? A Study of Standard Spending Assessments*, London, CIPFA.

Le Grand, J. and Winter, D. (1987) The middle classes and the welfare state under Conservative and Labour governments, *Journal of Public Policy*, Vol. 6, pp. 399–430.

Levačić, R. (1993) Assessing the impact of formula funding on schools, *Oxford Review of Education*, Vol. 19, no. 4, pp. 435–57.

Pennell, H. and West, A. (1998) *Comments on the Consultative Paper Fair Funding: Improving Delegation to Schools*, London, CER.

West, A. and Pennell, H. (1997) Educational reform and school choice in England and Wales, *Education Economics*, Vol. 5, no. 3, pp. 285–305.

West, A. and Sammons, P. (1996) Children with and without 'additional educational needs' at Key Stage One in six inner city schools – teaching and learning processes and policy implications, *British Educational Research Journal*, Vol. 22, no. 1, pp. 113–27.

West, A., West, R. and Pennell, H. (1994) *A Better Cake: Towards a Rational Approach for Financing Education*, Leicester, Secondary Heads Association.

West, A., West, R. and Pennell, H. (1995) The financing of school-based education: changing the additional educational needs allowance, *Education Economics*, Vol. 3, no. 3, pp. 265–75.

West, A., Pennell, H., West, R. and Travers, T. (1999a) The financing of school-based education: main findings, *Clare Market Papers*, no. 15, Centre for Educational Research, LSE, London.

West, A., West, R., Pennell, H. and Travers, T. (1999b) Financing schools in England: expenditure, poverty and outcomes, Centre for Educational Research, London School of Economics, London.

5

FUNDING LEARNING IN FURTHER EDUCATION

Jacky Lumby

INTRODUCTION

Vocational education is currently a live issue internationally. Governments consider it particularly suitable as a vehicle for social engineering and a means of solving multiple economic and social ills, such as general levels of educational underachievement, youth unemployment and skill short-ages (Psacharopolous, 1997). Funding is the lever used by governments to drive the direction and pace of change to achieve their political goals. The UK provides an example of this political leverage in action and its impact on learning. Consideration of the management of finance inevitably in-volves reference to the detail of the relevant national system. This chapter is grounded in specific UK systems and issues, but in exploring the man-agement of reducing funds and changing culture to enhance the quantity and quality of vocational education, it is hoped that food for reflection will be provided for those managing vocational education in other environments.

In 1993, colleges of further education in the UK were incorporated, achieving autonomy from their previous controllers, the local education authorities (LEAs). Shortly after, both the level and methodology of fund-ing changed explicitly to achieve a political steer (FEFC, 1992). The fund-ing methodology was intended to refocus colleges on becoming more efficient, recruiting more students and raising the quality of achievement, all through a quasi-market mechanism that directly linked numbers of students and their success to income.

The situation prior to 1993 undoubtedly required national action. The disparity in funding made available to colleges through the LEAs was seen as unjustifiable and detrimental to students. The method of funding provided little incentive to colleges to concern themselves with the process of learning after recruitment: ' "bums on seats" and as many as possible . . . The fact that you were losing students and had poor retention was no bother really' (Burton, 1994, p. 399).

The Audit Commission (1993) estimated that typically 30–40 per cent of students starting a course did not achieve their qualifications. As Gorringe (1994) indicates, the seminal FEFC document on the new methodology was pointedly entitled *Funding Learning* (FEFC, 1992, my emphasis), to indicate an end to the previous system of funding merely on the basis of numbers of students. From this time forward, not only the numbers enrolled but also students' process of learning and their final achievement counted. As Gorringe (1994, p. 68) asserts, 'the methodology is the message'. The emphasis on funding learning, not teaching, was certainly there but, in the funds made available for growth, to a degree the message was still 'bums on seats' and enrolments grew from 900,000 full-time equivalent enrolments in 1992/93 to 13 million in 1996/97 (FEDA, 1998). This was achieved by a range of tactics, including reducing contact hours between the student and lecturer and replacing some teaching with resource-based learning, so that the same number of lecturers could support a larger number of students. Students were also encouraged to take additional qualifications so that where previously a student may have had one major qualification aim, they might now have several, each counting as an enrolment. The system of franchising, that is, selling on funded units to other organizations who would deliver the training and be paid part of the college income generated, was also a major route to more students on roll. However, despite a focus on increasing the numbers entering the system, retention and achievement also became critical in attracting funds. A review carried out by the FEFC concluded that 'the methodology works' (FEFC, 1997, p. 7).

Inevitably, the new system has attracted both champions and detractors. The number and range of objectives the funding was planned to achieve, the methodology and the level of funding, have all drawn both opprobrium and approval (Betts, 1994). The debate on the intended and unintended, positive and negative effects, which has continued since 1993, has been confused by the difficulty of distinguishing the impact of lower overall levels of funding and the methodology itself. There has been a significant decline in both recurrent and capital funds made available to the sector up to 1998/99, though that trend was reversed to a degree in 1999/2000 (FEFC, 1999). There is also concern about the coherence and effectiveness of the funding methodology, for example, doubt as to whether long-term strategic aims such as widening participation can be achieved through a system which deliberately created the free for all of a quasi-market (Billett, 1998).

A fundamental review (Kennedy, 1997) acknowledged a number of problems that had resulted from the funding system. The issues in question were also reflected in the findings of the limited research undertaken to that date. Concerns expressed by colleges themselves and the FEFC, supported by research findings and Kennedy (1997), coincided with a change of government and led to a sea change which had been anticipated by college managers (Lumby, 1998). The aggressive competitive market encouraged from 1993 to 1998 in phase I of the history of newly incorporated colleges was superseded by phase II as the funding methodology was adjusted in 1999–2000. Previous orthodoxies such as market freedom, competition and transparent, equal funding for all colleges were replaced by a thrust towards nationally controlled growth, collaboration and some differential funding related to geographical and social disadvantage. The replacement of the FEFC and Training and Enterprise Councils (TECs) with a Learning and Skills Council from 2001 heralds unabated change in systems and culture.

Since 1993, research has largely focused on the overall impact of the new funding methodology and resulting national policy issues. The internal management of funding within each college has received scant attention. The experience of managers of finance who have had the unenviable task of dealing with the reduction in funding levels and a rapidly changing culture has not been widely explored. The rising number of colleges in category C, that is, colleges with weak financial positions (see Table 5.1), indicates that many colleges and finance managers have found themselves operating in sight of the abyss of financial disaster.

Table 5.1   College financial health groups

	1994	1995	1996	1997	1998
Group A (reasonably robust)	309 (70%)	257 (57%)	206 (46%)	197 (44%)	213 (49%)
Group B (financially vulnerable)	106 (24%)	135 (30%)	148 (33%)	151 (34%)	142 (33%)
Group C (financially weak)	25 (6%)	60 (13%)	93 (21%)	96 (22%)	80 (18%)

Note: Table indicates numbers of colleges in financial health categories A–C, 1994–98.
Source: Provided by the Further Education Funding Council, July 1999.

Table 5.1 indicates a possible reversal of the trend of growing numbers of colleges in financial difficulties in 1998, but also the extent of the struggle which the sector has faced, with almost a quarter of colleges in a financially weak position in 1997.

RESEARCHING THE EXPERIENCE OF FINANCE MANAGERS

This chapter reviews the context in which colleges have had to work and reports on the perspective of managers of finance in 11 of the 217 general further education colleges (FEFC, 1998). It reviews what they believe to be the impact on their own college and how they have sought to work with the system to promote learning and to ensure survival. The opportunity sample includes colleges located in six of the nine regions within England. Five of the colleges were noted for outstanding achievement in management in the Chief Inspector's annual report for 1997–98 (FEFC, 1998). The managers interviewed cannot be representative of the great diversity of experience within the sector, but do offer a snapshot of the developing management of finance within colleges and, in some cases, in colleges which are notably successful in the view of the inspectorate. Managers are identified by a letter to preserve anonymity.

PRINCIPLES OF THE UK FUNDING SYSTEM

The FEFC (1997) made explicit the aims and method of its 1993–98 funding. The system was designed to achieve a means of steering policy, a framework for change with some degree of stability, encouragement for colleges to be responsive, an increase in quality and growth of provision and, finally, promotion of accountability and value for money. To achieve this agenda, colleges were paid in a currency of 'units', so many units being available per student for the enrolment and induction period (entry), for the actual programme of learning itself (on-programme), and for accreditation (achievement). The units earned varied according to the programme of learning, the number of units available being listed in a tariff table. The value of each unit varied from college to college, depending on a calculation taking into account historical levels of funding. Consequently, while this provided some stability for colleges which had previously been generously funded, it also provided a cause of complaint for colleges whose unit value, or average level of funding (ALF), was lower than other colleges, particularly where such disparity existed between colleges in close proximity. The FEFC planned to move towards a convergence of funding where the unit value is standard, to the advantage or disadvantage of each college, depending on its current ALF.

The context for financial management was consequently extremely challenging. Managers had to acquire skills in dealing not only with multi-million pound budgets but with a hugely detailed bureaucratic system for requesting, accounting for and often repaying monies, 'an apparently inexorable tide of bureaucratisation' (Graham, 1997, p. 549). The resulting overriding compulsion to focus on funding was difficult to resist (Lumby, 1996). A rapidly deepening divide in perspective and culture between managers and lecturing staff resulted: 'Employers for their part, are promoting the issues of flexibility and responsiveness whereas the staff side are concerned over exploitation and worsening of quality of delivery. There appears to be no common ground at all' (Graham, 1997, p. 553).

This is not to suggest that managers were not concerned with the quality of learning, or lecturers did not understand the demands of the new funding system, but rather that they saw things differently. Managers were faced with not only leading an often divided staff, but one that was frequently hostile given the level of redundancies and the increasing replacement of full-time permanent posts with part-time staff (Ainley and Bailey, 1997). Some colleges, whether through preference or through financial need, manipulated the funding system to achieve the maximum number of units rather than the learning most appropriate to their area by 'tariff farming', i.e. increasing provision in the area where it is easiest to make income, and by franchising provision, often with organizations far from the locality, raising concern that: 'the new ethos has encouraged colleges not just to be businesslike but to perform as if they were businesses' (Kennedy, 1997, p. 3).

This concern led to the adjustment of the funding system to return to something closer to the original LEA system. Colleges were directed to focus on their local community and to collaborate. Although plans for the unit value to converge remained, additional funding was provided for London colleges and for provision for students resident in postal areas which met criteria of deprivation. Franchising was confined to the locality of each college and was no longer so lucrative (FEFC, 1999). The freedom for colleges to grow was restricted. Those who manage finance in colleges faced yet another change, not just in funding method, but in culture.

MANAGING IN COLLEGES

The Finance Managers interviewed reflected a range of experience and views but they held in common the experience of attempting to contribute to an internal culture change. Decisions on how to manage finance were in all cases an important element of the attempt to influence the direction of change. Certain issues emerged as vital, most critically how to enrol staff in understanding and co-operating with the management of finance, how to harness information and how to allocate funds internally. Actions in all these areas were explicitly or implicitly designed to attempt the double achievement of both surviving financially and supporting teaching and learning

The first hurdle was that to make any sort of decision about what income to expect and how to distribute it internally, good information was required. Managers emphasized how important it was to have accurate information on which to plan and against which to measure how far the college was on course or otherwise. This is easy to acknowledge but extremely difficult to achieve. One manager explained: 'We must hold a million pieces of data per year and they need to be put on to the computer, added to databases and they need to be reported. That's an enormous burden' (Finance Manager C).

The technical aspects of managing the inputting and storage of data, huge task though this is, is only the tip of the iceberg. Having accurate data from staff to input is even more problematic. Asked how far staff were aware of administrative procedures, one manager felt:

> It will differ across the college even now. There are one or two faculties which have done a good job. There are one or two faculties which have not done as well and if you go into those faculties and ask people simple questions like 'Where does our money come from?' you will get a surprised reply, and as for knowing the procedure to enrol or withdraw a student, some of them still don't know.
>
> My job is very dependant on people playing the game. So in that sense, there has been a shift in administration awareness and there has been resistance to it which you can understand, not necessarily sympathize with, but you can understand when people come into FE [further education] to lecture and teach and they have to spend some of their time doing these administrative tasks.
>
> (Finance Manager K)

Whereas leadership for most managers in further education in pre-incorporation days may have involved primarily curricular issues, the objectives of the manager have widened and must include enrolling staff in an information-gathering process which they do not automatically see as valuable and almost certainly see as secondary to their main role of teaching. In one sense, of course, it is secondary, but if lack of accurate information hinders the process of making curricular decisions, or even threatens the finances and therefore survival of the college or subunits of the college, then information cannot be seen simply as a secondary and less relevant process.

Another issue was justifying the investment needed to achieve the required information levels:

> In order to be able to provide decent management information which the academic managers want and should have, we have got to invest quite a bit of money in non-educational activity. We would have to put a lot of money into internal computer systems, so you are going to spend tens of thousands to be able to make decisions about hundreds of pounds. There is a certain irony about it. I am afraid that is the route that we are going to have to go.
>
> (Finance Manager A)

Information was seen as needed to make educational decisions, not just financial ones, but the task of persuading staff that information on finance could not be divorced from curriculum management was not easy and not yet universally achieved. This task was seen as not just relevant to senior managers, but to all those with a management role from principal to course team leader. Assuming that information could be gathered and stored, the interpretation of a million or more pieces of data to achieve a format which was usable by academic managers was another landmark target which was still some distance off. The synergy of different sorts of information to support the process of decision-making was destabilized by the differences in perspective.

DECISION-MAKING

All but one of the managers acknowledged that maximizing income had been a strong driver in their college and that the funding system had led to practice (not necessarily in their own college) which was questionable: 'The policy steer that the FEFC were trying to create went a bit pear shaped because they unleashed this monster which they could no longer control' (Finance Manager F).

The resulting practice was perfectly allowable within the regulations but, as one manager explained, analogous to tax avoidance rather than tax evasion, legal but dubious. One manager felt that the post-incorporation period could be characterized as 'stack'em high and teach'em cheap', with units being brokered through franchising. Units worth £11 were sold on at £5, the resulting profit remaining with the college. In no case was it suggested that the purpose of such practice was accruing funds for its own sake. Rather colleges franchised programmes because they saw this as the only means of generating additional income to ensure financial survival or to subsidize provision for the local community, which was their primary aim. Nevertheless, once caught in 'the morass of making sure that we maximize our activity to meet our targets', retaining educational values was difficult:

> Ultimately, because the unit levels are capped and because there is no real room to manoeuvre around that cap, we are always trying to maximize our units and minimize the cost of those units so it is very much a numbers game. Any sort of education or social policy which underpins this tends to get lost.
>
> (Finance Manager A)

One manager's experience was different. His college was highly successful in financial terms and yet: 'I feel that the influences of the market and the demand for learning have been a more important and felt trend than anything related to finance' (Finance Manager I).

This college took as its starting-point the learning needs of existing and potential students and attempted to attach funding to activities to meet those needs. There was, however, no sentiment. It was a hard-nosed attitude towards decisions which were apparently educationally based, but actually reflected a producer perspective, as such a stance was not tenable in the highly competitive location within which they worked: 'There are eight other colleges in the locality so you cannot think "well I am going to carry on running my GCSE in Sanskrit for the sake of the three members of staff who can teach it and screw the rest of the world". You just cannot do that' (Finance Manager I). However, where the need was consumer led, the college was working on ways of manipulating resources to meet that need:

> When there is a course with an uneconomic number of people, be-cause of the economic climate we have to close it. We are looking at that as a major issue and trying to look at ways of replacing it by some sort of information technology alternative whereby people can study using terminals having fewer class contacts. If an economic number for a class was 15 and we had three students wanting to study some-thing, if they met once every five weeks, economically it is the same as if there were 15 students who met every week, so if you could provide them with all the materials to keep going for four weeks, and they meet once every five weeks for a tutorial, as in the Open University, then maybe you can respond to that need.
>
> (Finance Manager I)

A number of colleges reported similar experimentation. Additionally, col-leges seemed to be emerging from a period of feeling they were being driven by the numbers game to seeing decisions as Janus-like, reflecting both fi-nancial considerations and educational values as two sides of the same coin. One manager explained that training in the area of construction had to be flexible because of the flexible employment patterns. Even if they were successful in recruiting those working in construction, if provision was not flexible enough, then they would not stay. Innovative flexible practices were needed both to meet educational needs and to remain finan-cially viable: 'The way I look at things you can't de-couple them. It actually comes down to the same thing at the end of the day' (Finance Manager B).

No manager indicated a willingness to run loss-making programmes in the long term, but where there were temporary shortfalls in income match-ing expenditure due to market vagaries, the issue of cross-subsidy from areas which generated surplus income arose. There was a diversity of prac-tice in internal budgeting to tackle this and other issues.

BUDGETING

Simkins (1998) suggests that the types of thinking required for strategic rational management of resources include:

- organisation-wide thinking;
- zero-based thinking;
- longer-term thinking.

These modes of thought are allied to a process which aims to achieve effectiveness, not just efficiency. In other words, the aim is not just to deliver learning at the cheapest unit cost, but to ensure that the overall objectives of the organization are achieved. The range, quality and amount of learning must be right. Kedney and Davies (1995) concluded that colleges had generally not achieved such thinking. Practice has developed since 1993, but the environment changes constantly. Roberts (1999, p. 25) believes that thinking must develop even further, beyond the organization to reflect the new partnership approach: 'Education funding will not be provided from the new sources to support a narrow view of education; new funding will support a wider strategy in which education is seen as a key player.' Thinking must therefore go beyond the organization to encompass a local and regional perspective.

Managers in further education parallel the position of national government; they too employ resources as a major tool to shape activity and the course of change. They must use funds to meet the short-term need to offer quality learning to current students, but must also use it to meet the longer-term need to shape organizational development. All of the finance managers interviewed were aware of this, but had chosen varying means to achieve their aims. Of the 11 colleges, six were using a method of distributing funds internally in a way which was not decided by mathematical formulae. They did not start from a zero base and calculate the funds generated by organizational units of the colleges as a starting-point for distributing the college's income relative to how much each unit had earned. Nor did they start from a zero base and calculate the resource needs of the units to achieve the teaching and learning which had been planned. Instead the method employed may have been *ad hoc*, with a range of factors taken into account on a different basis for different units or at different times. Alternatively, the process may have been one of negotiation between the senior management team and heads of school/faculty. These methods were therefore micropolitical in approach, with outcomes to a degree dependent on the priorities, power and persuasiveness of the participants. The relationship between income generated and income gained by any subunit of the college was loosely coupled.

In contrast, five of the colleges were using a formula to calculate income for subunits, though some degree of negotiation and historical data were also involved. In these five colleges, the relationship between income generated and income earned by subunits was much more tightly coupled, though not necessarily to the point where failure to generate the projected income would automatically spell redundancies or closure of a course or of the subunit. Strategic plans to retain a certain breadth of curriculum meant that senior management would look at the factors causing shortfalls in income and might protect areas which were losing money, at least on a short-term basis. Nevertheless, the use of formulae to calculate the distribution of income made any such protection much more apparent. Weick (1976) argues that one advantage of loose coupling is that subunits in difficulty can be isolated and helped. It may be easier to offer financial protection for subunits facing difficulties through negotiation than through a transparent system where any deviation from the formula becomes immediately apparent. Such transparency risks provoking resistance or resentment from those sub-units whose financial success has provided the means to subsidize those in trouble. The chosen method of distribution of funds therefore gave particular messages about the culture of the organization, how much the culture depended on human calculation or financial calculation. Those taking a more hard-nosed approach might argue that such an approach has student need at its heart, as there is little point in continuing to offer programmes which few people want. Those protecting minority interests also justify their attitude as being centred on students and the need to retain a broad and rich curriculum. Neither has a monopoly on being right, but the values of the institution are mediated through the debate on how to distribute funds.

All the colleges faced the overriding aim of ensuring costs, particularly staff costs, were kept to a minimum, but there were other cultural issues such as encouraging:

- flexibility in mode and place of delivery;
- team rather than competitive approach between subunits;
- acceptance of the need to support non-income generating services.

The use of an *ad hoc* or negotiated process was a positive choice in some cases. One college had tried funding programme areas on the basis of units earned and by a bidding system. Both had proved unsatisfactory. The former resulted in perceived inequities in funding. The latter induced competition and disappointment. The issue of competition within the college was felt particularly acutely by three of the colleges. Asked how budgeting was undertaken, one manager explained:

> Largely it has been a very ineffective and inefficient way around historical budgets to be honest. We have got nothing sophisticated about linking resources to units or an internal competitive market. We have got a strong management team that all pulls and works together. There is not 'we are going to cut your department, your pay' whatever. Everybody shares. It is the *Titanic* that is sailing along. Moving the deckchairs around is not going to make any difference. If you are going to avoid the iceberg you have got to move the ship.
>
> (Finance Manager I)

The lack of 'sophistication' is used positively to achieve the primary goal of leadership, focusing everybody on the same goal and working together to achieve it. Another manager working in a small college also saw avoidance of destructive competition as the key. Eschewing mechanistic approaches to budgeting had allowed them to achieve that. As well as the diminution of competition, the negotiated approach gave freedom to move funds around freely, supporting areas of development without the need to justify stepping outside a formula.

Other colleges had moved to a formula or costing-based approach:

> We have developed what we call a contribution model. What that does is to take the funding units by course and any other sources of income, and then, based upon that, every course is required to make a minimum 40 per cent return into central costs . . . The income from all courses will be taken on the credit side as it were and then the indirect course costs of supporting that, which would include the manager, any administrative support, any technician support, any equipment and consumables are all delegated down and that is one element of cost. The other element of cost is the direct professional teaching hours to deliver that programme or instructor hours. When those costs are deducted from the income the remainder must be 40 per cent of the total income that has gone into that section.
>
> (Finance Manager F)

In this way, sections were encouraged to see the need to generate sufficient income to cover central services. Another college had a similar system:

> Broadly, 40 per cent of our income goes on overheads, 60 per cent on the academic provision so we take 60 per cent of our income and then we take the total number of 'on-programme' units that we are going to earn that year, divide one into the other and that gives us the rate per unit that will be allocated to the academic areas. That rate hasn't really changed much over the last few years. It's been about £10.40 and it's always just 'on-programme' because that gives the best weighting between areas because if you use entry and remission and things like that it distorts the allocation.
>
> (Finance Manager C)

In both cases, sections could calculate the income required and what they were likely to retain. There was, therefore, a direct relationship between what they earned and what they kept. In both colleges, courses which were not able to make a 40 per cent contribution could run at the discretion of the section. If one course was generating a contribution of 45 per cent then another could run while only making 35 per cent. Cross-subsidy of this kind was easy within schools but problematic across different schools. This may be one of the disadvantages of the formula approach.

Two colleges had adopted an approach using costing: 'We've gone back this year to zero-based budget particularly with course costing methodology so that the budget will be built up from the course costing process' (Finance Manager H). The second college used teaching costs as part of a negotiated process. The costs were calculated on historical data:

We have looked at the actual data for a particular year so we know what the actual staff costs are, we know the number of taught hours going against each of the programmes. We will identify servicing going on between different schools and one or two other minor issues and from that say for this particular school the cost per taught hour is whatever.

(Finance Manager B)

Discussion involves consideration of the business plan, self-assessment, staffing requirements and the overall costs of each school. Schools are also charged an hourly accommodation rate, which varies according to day and time. Weekend and evening charges are lower. In this way there is a financial incentive to move outside the peak daytime hours and be more flexible.

It would in theory be possible to transfer all FEFC income generated by the subunit of a college directly to that subunit, if sufficient additional income could be generated to cover central costs. This is unlikely to be achievable in practice. Consequently, colleges are experimenting with ways of distributing income to achieve a balance between motivation and equity. Educational aims would be supported at a financial loss if necessary, but within fairly stringent parameters. If, as in the case of FEFC funding, 'the methodology is the message' then the internal distribution of funds within each college is also the message, communicating whether the college was a whole ship or a convoy of fairly independent boats, whether loss-making educational activity could be accommodated and under what circumstances and finally how learning itself can be shaped and developed with the resources available. The concept of loose and tight coupling may be helpful as a theoretical underpinning for further research and analysis of colleges' approach (Weick, 1976). Some colleges saw a very tight coupling between the external and internal methodologies as encouraging a focus on learning. Others saw a much looser coupling, with the internal distribution of income independent of the external methodology as more effective. Far too little is yet known about the impact of different forms of budgeting upon culture and upon learning and teaching. More research is needed on the aims of those involved and the outcomes of different approaches.

CHANGING CULTURE

Overall, the colleges demonstrated significant change and no change. The idea that incorporation in 1993 was some sort of apocalypse after which colleges behaved totally differently was not the case:

The college actually wanted to deliver customer care and quality before those weasel words came out. We delivered that customer care before it became called customer care. It's always been seen as a caring college trying to, wherever possible, meet identified needs in the community. In that sense we've continued very well.

(Finance Manager G)

At the same time several of the colleges felt there had been a shift in culture. They saw the pre-1993 period as 'cosy' where lecturers focused on their teaching with little concern for demand, the cost of what they were doing, or the need to stay within a budget and deliver value for money. That had changed in part. In several colleges lecturers who did not wish to or could not change their attitudes had left. For the majority of those who had stayed, the initial disbelief at changed expectations, for example, at the level of detail required for audit purposes, had changed. People were far more aware of the resource base within which they worked and the need to see resource management as part of their duty to provide a service to students:

Our culture has changed quite radically. I would say we have got a teaching staff where easily 95 per cent are very much orientated towards the college and the requirements of the students. We have got 5 per cent who will just never be there but we can live with that. Of that 95 per cent, 75 per cent have a clear understanding of the link between where the money comes from and where their resources come from. The other 20 per cent are the dedicated teachers who feel 'I come here to teach and to help my students. Do not bother me about finance'. We can live with them as well. Their hearts are in the right place. They are not in the Luddite community.

(Finance Manager I)

Managers had changed also. They had got 'more streetwise, more savvy'. They recognized their dependence on the co-operation of all and acknowledged the dedication of the majority. Where financial problems arose, there was more likelihood of all managers getting together to find a college solution. Nevertheless, differences in approach still exist. One finance manager felt that he had to take decisions because academic managers were too soft and avoided hard choices. Another felt that such decisions were nothing to do with him as curricular decisions were the remit of academic managers. One finance manager recognized the hostility to his role which existed prior to taking up his post: 'The fact that the organization is appointing a Director of Finance for the first time doesn't exactly have everybody jumping and up and down in glee' (Finance Manager B). Nevertheless, the value of his contribution and the fact that 'finance' was not engraved on his heart had come to be recognized:

Hopefully it [the staff] got the perspective that I am not here just to look at what I would do if I were trying to deliver maximum value to shareholders or anything of that sort, but it's looking at the culture and ethos of the organization, what it's trying to achieve and looking at that from a financial perspective.

(Finance Manager B)

The overall impression from the finance mangers was that an accommodation had been reached. The majority of lecturers had shifted to appreciate the importance of financial management in ensuring that planned teaching and learning could take place, and financial managers had emerged from the often survival-driven priority given to finance above all else. In this sense, the culture change in colleges may have reached a point where internal partnership creates the environment where partnership with external organizations can now move forward.

THE FUTURE

Financial stringency was not a thing of the past for all the colleges. There were concerns particularly about where investment funds were to be acquired to deal with outdated buildings and the need for ICT development. Further efficiencies were anticipated: 'We've got to be lean machines. That's for sure' (Finance Manager H).

Not all staff had developed to the same point of understanding and co-operation. There is still a need to improve systems of costing and budgeting further. Collaboration will not replace competition overnight. Such a culture change needs time. Some colleges will continue to struggle to put the curriculum first when buildings are crumbling and there is little room for financial manoeuvre. All were attempting to achieve a larger percentage of their income from sources other than the FEFC, to gain a measure of freedom and security from the impact of policy changes. The strain on all staff in further education should not be underestimated. The 'efficiencies' exacted by the government have borne a heavy cost for those who work in the sector. Despite these challenges, the overall note was optimistic, largely because of a belief in the worth of what the colleges offered:

Management Team Meetings are not isolated conversations about finance or management or whatever. They are about where are we going? What is the driver? The driver in this college is always the curriculum. My job is to let the curriculum guys identify their needs and requirements and, hopefully, get enough resources for them to deliver those requirements.

(Finance Manager I)

Colleges have survived the five years following incorporation when levels of funding have fallen in real terms by 26 per cent (FEFC, 1998). They have adapted to a system which to date has funded them less generously than it has funded either schools or higher education. With all that has been achieved, there is still everything to play for.

REFERENCES

Ainley, P. and Bailey, B. (1997) *The Business of Learning*, London, Cassell.

Audit Commission (1993) *Unfinished Business: Full Time Educational Courses for 16–19 Year Olds*, London, OFSTED.

Betts, D. (1994) Funds for FE: a guide, *NATFHE Journal*, Summer, pp. 18–21.

Billett, S. (1998) Enterprises and vocational education and training: expenditure and expected returns, *Journal of Vocational Education and Training*, Vol. 50, no. 3, pp. 387–402.

Burton, S. (1994) Factors affecting quality in the new FE – principals' views, *Coombe Lodge Report*, Vol. 24, no. 5, pp. 349–439.

FEDA (1998) Online at www. feda.ac.uk/funding/commentaries/1.asp

FEFC (1992) *Funding Learning*, Coventry, FEFC.

FEFC (1997) *Fundamental Review of the Funding Methodology*, Coventry, FEFC.

FEFC (1998) *Quality and Standards in Further Education in England, 1997–98*, Coventry, FEFC.

FEFC (1999) *Funding Guidance 1999–2000*, Coventry, FEFC.

Gorringe, R. (1994) Devising a new funding methodology for further education – the funding learning approach, in C. Flint and M. Austin (eds), *Going Further*, Blagdon, The Staff College in association with the Association for Colleges.

Graham, I. (1997) Principals' response to incorporation and the new funding regime, *Journal of Vocational Education and Training*, Vol. 49, no. 4, pp. 545–62.

Kedney, B. and Davies, T. (1995) Cost reduction and value for money, *Coombe Lodge Report*, Vol. 24, no. 6, pp. 441–524.

Kennedy, H. (1997) *Learning Works: Widening Participation in Further Education*, Coventry, FEFC.

Lumby, J. (1996) Managing the curriculum in further education, *Vocational Aspect of Education*, Vol. 48, no. 4, pp. 333–48.

Lumby, J. (1998) Restraining the further education market: closing Pandora's box, *Education and Training*, Vol. 40, no. 2, pp. 57–62.

Psacharopolous, G. (1997) Vocational education and training today: challenges and responses, *Journal of Vocational Education and Training*, Vol. 49, no. 3, pp. 385–94.

Roberts, T. (1999) *The Funding Revolution: New Routes to Project Fundraising*, London, Falmer.

Simkins, T. (1998) Autonomy, restraint and the strategic management of resources, in D. Middlewood and J. Lumby (eds), *Strategic Management in Schools and Colleges*, London, Paul Chapman.

Weick, K. (1976) Educational organisations as loosely coupled systems, *Administrative Science Quarterly*, Vol. 21, no. 1, pp. 1–19.

Part II: Within the School and College

6

MANAGEMENT STYLES: IMPACT ON FINANCE AND RESOURCES

Tony Bush

INTRODUCTION: THE CONTEXT FOR INTERNAL RESOURCE ALLOCATION

Internal resource allocation is not simply a routine administrative process; it is a means of expressing and making operational the values of the institution, or perhaps of dominant groups and individuals within it. Spending decisions reflect the priorities of the decision-makers and often represent the outcome of a complex process of deliberation and review. The resource allocation process is an important aspect of strategic management.

Resource allocation has become more important in many countries as educational organizations have been accorded more autonomy. In England and Wales, this trend is represented by Local Management of Schools (LMS) and by incorporation of colleges. A parallel development in Hong Kong is the School Management Initiative (SMI) while Singapore has introduced a small number of independent and autonomous schools. Similar initiatives are evident in New Zealand and parts of the USA and Australia.

The shift to self-management in educational institutions has radically changed the context of resource allocation and also heightened the importance of this process. Because schools and colleges, in England and elsewhere, have a high degree of autonomy, they have a greater measure of control over the resource allocation process. Many schools now manage multimillion-pound budgets and spending decisions can and do have a powerful impact on their effectiveness and on the quality of teaching and learning. The principle underpinning the international trend to self-management is a belief that those 'close to the action' are more likely to make appropriate spending decisions than local or national politicians or officials, however well-intentioned they may be. The specific needs of pupils and students can be assessed better by those inside schools and colleges than those remote from the institution: 'The improvement of efficiency, quality and standards is best achieved by a reliance on micro-level decision-making through which relevant decisions about resource deployment are located as close to the point of delivery as possible, that is to say, within institutions' (Simkins, 1998, p. 64).

Devolved financial management is underpinned by the philosophy that decisions should be more efficient and effective if they are made by site managers who understand their impact on students and pupils. This argument can also be used to justify internal devolution by principals and governors to middle managers and other staff. Self-management provides the potential to empower staff because schools have much more control over financial and real resources: 'Certain groups of people in the community now have the opportunity to influence the course of events in the life of the school to a greater extent than in the past' (Caldwell and Spinks, 1992, p. 18).

Purkey and Smith (1985) argue that site management and collaborative decision-making are essential components of the framework for successful change: 'The staff of each school is given a considerable amount of responsibility and authority in determining the exact means by which they address the problem of increasing academic performance. This includes giving staffs more authority over curricular decisions and allocation of building resources' (Purkey and Smith, 1985, p. 358). If this view is accepted, devolution of power within schools is an important dimension if the potential benefits of devolved financial management are to be realized.

Effective resource management is likely to be even more important in periods of turbulence, such as that experienced by further education colleges in England and Wales in the 1990s. College incorporation, linked to independence from their local education authorities (LEAs), produced radical changes, not least in the funding regime introduced by the Further Education Funding Council (FEFC). One college principal explained the problems in her college:

> There were urgent reasons for reforms within resource management and more generally. These ranged from an inability to serve student and client needs adequately, to an increasing vulnerability for the college as a viable educational institution. The causes of these problems were deep and pervasive, and their removal was to require high-quality and long-term thinking. The direct barriers to effective resource management included . . . internal secrecy regarding allocations combined with a lack of feedback to spending areas.
>
> (Shackleton, 1994, p. 113).

MODELS OF EDUCATIONAL MANAGEMENT

Many writers on financial management in education (Bush, 1997; Coleman, Bush and Glover, 1994; Davies, 1994; Levačić, 1995; Simkins, 1989; 1998), draw on organizational theory to conceptualize and explain resource allocation in schools and colleges. Bush (1995) discusses six models of educational management which serve to explain events, situations and behaviour in educational institutions. Four of these have been cited in the financial management literature:

- rational models;
- collegial models;
- political models;
- ambiguity models.

The main features of these four models will be discussed in this section while their applicability to internal resource allocation will be considered later in the chapter.

Rational models

Bush (1995, p. 38) includes rational models within a broader discussion of bureaucracy and notes its emphasis on 'the process of decision-making':

The process of rational decision-making is thought to have the following sequence:

1) Perception of a problem or a choice opportunity.
2) Analysis of the problem, including data collection.
3) Formulation of alternative solutions or choices.
4) Choice of the most appropriate solution to the problem to meet the objectives of the organization.
5) Implementation of the chosen alternative.
6) Monitoring and evaluation of the effectiveness of the chosen strategy.

The process is essentially iterative in that the evaluation may lead to a redefinition of the problem or a search for an alternative solution.

This process is captured in Figure 6.1.

Rational models are normative in that they reflect views about how organizations and individuals ought to behave. They present an idealized view and have serious limitations as a portrayal of the decision-making process in education:

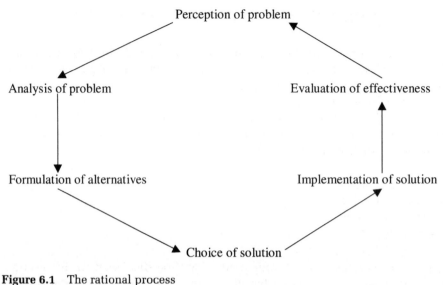

Figure 6.1   The rational process
Source: Bush (1995, p. 39)

- There may be dispute over objectives and the definition of the 'problem' is likely to be dependent on the particular standpoint of the individuals involved.
- Some of the data needed to make a decision may not be available.
- Most problematic of all is the assumption that the choice of solution can be detached and impartial. In practice, individuals and groups are likely to promote their own favoured solutions which in turn may reflect individual rather than organizational objectives.
- The perceived effectiveness of the chosen solution may also vary according to the preferences of the people concerned.

Collegial models

Collegial models emphasize the importance of participation in decision-making. Particularly in professional organizations, it is thought to be important for staff to be involved in those decisions which affect their working lives. Resource allocation is an important dimension of professional decision-making. The ability of teachers to perform well in the classroom is inevitably conditioned by the availability and quality of resources.

Bush (1995, pp. 53–5) sets out the main features of collegiality:

- Teachers have an *authority of expertise* which arises from their professional training and experience. This expertise, which is often based on specialist subject knowledge, gives teachers the right to take part in decision-making.

- Teachers have a *common set of values* arising from their training and early years of professional practice. These shared values guide the managerial activities of the school or college and provide the basis for a participatory approach to decision-making.
- Decisions are made by *consensus* rather than managerial decree or inter-group conflict. 'Consent' is regarded as an essential principle in school management.

Collegiality is an attractive model because it seems to provide for staff to engage in collaborative decision-making. In practice, though, it has certain limitations which are summarized by Bush (1995, pp. 67–9):

- Collegial decision-making tends to be *slow and cumbersome*, leading to frustration with the process.
- The notion of *consensual decision-making is flawed* and it is more likely that participants will represent sectional interests, leading to conflict rather than co-operation.
- Collegiality creates problems for principals who are *accountable* for decisions, even those which do not enjoy their personal support.
- Collegiality may fail because of the *apathy or hostility of staff*; it is wrong to assume that all staff want to participate.

Political models

Political models emphasize the prevalence of conflict in organizations. Interest groups form and pursue their interests at every opportunity. Decision-making involves bargaining and negotiation and the outcome is usually dependent on who has the most power. Bush (1995, pp. 74–7) sets out the main features of political models:

- Individuals have both personal and professional *interests* which they pursue within the organization. These coalesce so that interest groups form which may relate to subject specialism.
- The aims of different interest groups are likely to *conflict*.
- Decisions follow an often protracted process of *bargaining and negotiation*.
- Decisions are likely to be determined by the relative *power* of individuals and interest groups involved in the debate.

Political models are often regarded as realistic portrayals of decision-making in education. Teachers frequently recognize the applicability of these models to their professional settings. However, they may also overstate the prevalence of conflict in schools and colleges and underestimate the importance of both professional collaboration and routine bureaucratic processes.

Ambiguity models

Ambiguity models stress uncertainty and unpredictability in organizations. Ambiguity is regarded as a prevalent feature of complex organizations such as schools and colleges. Environmental and organizational turbulence combine to create a climate which is ill-suited to rational decision-making. Bush (1995, pp. 112–14) sets out the main features of ambiguity models:

- Lack of clarity about the *goals* of the organization.
- Schools and colleges are characterized by *fragmentation* and 'loose coupling' (Weick, 1976).
- There is *fluid participation* in decision-making, making the outcomes uncertain and unpredictable.
- There is an emphasis on *unplanned* rather than planned decisions.

Ambiguity models are valuable in countering the assumptions underpinning rational models but, in practice, schools and colleges operate with a mix of rational and ambiguous processes. The balance in individual institutions will depend on a whole range of organizational and environmental variables. These will certainly include the culture of the organization and the management style of its leaders, as Carr suggests in respect of colleges: 'Budget development is an organisational process which cannot be separated from the management style of the college senior management team. Management styles, whether autocratic, democratic, dictatorial or participative, influence the management process and so the manner in which the budget is built' (Carr, 1994, p. 29).

We turn now to examine the ways in which rational, collegial, political and ambiguity models impact on resource allocation in education. Rational models have been dominant in the academic and official literature on financial management, and they are given particular attention in this chapter.

RATIONAL MODELS OF RESOURCE ALLOCATION

The rational model of resource management is dominant in the literature and in official policy statements about financial resource allocation (Simkins, 1998, p. 65). The LMS policy in England and Wales was underpinned by assumptions of a rational approach to management. The government commissioned Coopers and Lybrand to prepare a report which has been influential and is clearly rational in orientation, as Levačić explains:

> The model of good management practice contained in the Coopers and Lybrand report is essentially a rational one. It advocates a system for allocating resources which is directed at the explicit achievement of institutional objectives. This requires clarity in the specification of objectives, gathering and analysing information on alternative ways of

attaining the objectives, evaluating the alternatives and selecting those actions judged most likely to maximize achievement of the objectives.

(Levačić, 1995, p. 62)

Simkins (1998, p. 66) shows that the rational model places a strong emphasis on 'value for money' and concepts of economy, efficiency and effectiveness. These are defined as follows:

1) *Economy.* The purchase of a given standard of good or service at lowest cost.
2) *Efficiency.* The achievement of given outcomes at least cost.
3) *Effectiveness.* The matching of results with objectives (Audit Commission, 1985).

Devolution of resource management to schools is based, in part, on the assumption that these objectives of economy, efficiency and effectiveness are more likely to be achieved by site managers than by those remote from the specific educational context.

The principles of rational management

The concept of rational management is underpinned by five core principles which include some overlapping elements:

1) *Aims and priorities.* Resource allocation should be informed by clearly articulated aims and by determining priorities among these objectives (Levačić, 1995, p. 62). Linked to this is the notion of output budgeting, where spending is related to objectives, rather than input budgeting, where the emphasis is on areas of spending such as staff, equipment and buildings (Davies, 1994, p. 346).
2) *Long-term planning.* Budgetary decisions should reflect an awareness of their long-term implications. This means going beyond the typical annual budget cycle to a consideration of the longer-term aims of the organization. Davies (1994, p. 347) refers to this as the 'multi-year-time-horizon' which 'is necessary if longer term financial planning and budgeting is to take place'.
    One of the reasons for the remarkable success of the Singapore economy has been the government's commitment to planning for the long term. 'Singapore's stable government means that, unlike most countries, it can and does adopt a long-term planning horizon which goes well beyond immediate economic and political imperatives' (Bush, 1999, p. 4).
3) *Evaluating alternatives.* There should be a thorough consideration of alternative patterns of expenditure based on evaluation of past actions

and assessment of the opportunity costs of different spending options. This process should involve environmental scanning to help in assessing the longer-term implications of expenditure (Levačić, 1995, p. 62; Simkins, 1989, p. 154).

4) *Zero-based budgeting.* Linked to a consideration of alternative spending options is the notion of 'zero-based' resource allocation. This involves taking a fresh look at all areas of expenditure rather than simply making incremental changes to previous spending patterns. In its purest form, this would mean that no previous activities would necessarily be funded in the future but would depend on a new justification of their relevance to institutional goals. In practice, it is likely to mean a more thorough scrutiny of current spending but not necessarily a fresh justification for all activities. Simkins (1989, p. 154) refers to this as 'some zero-basing'. We shall return to zero-based resource allocation later in this chapter.

5) *Selecting the most appropriate options.* Once the possible alternative spending patterns have been identified and scrutinized, with an element of zero-basing, rational models require a choice of the most appropriate option linked to organizational objectives. Levačić (1995, p. 62) refers to this as 'selection of the best set of actions which are judged to be most likely to maximise achievement of the objectives'.

Incremental budgeting

There are two main rational approaches to resource allocation; incremental and zero based. The incremental model treats the previous year's budget as the starting-point for the preparation of the new budget. There are marginal or 'incremental' changes but the budget remains largely unaltered from the previous year. Discussion is largely confined to the margin rather than focusing on the whole budget. An example of incremental budgeting would be a decision to increase departmental budgets by a fixed amount, say two per cent. Levačić reviews the merits and demerits of incremental budgeting:

> The attractions of incremental budgeting are that it requires far less information processing than zero-based or programme budgeting and is less likely to arouse micro-political activity as the status quo is not disturbed by groups and individuals being asked to justify their claim on resources. Its disadvantages are that the efficiency and effectiveness in resource use are not promoted by an unquestioning adherence to past patterns of resource allocation.
>
> (Levačić, 1995, p. 75)

Sutton (1996, p. 7) agrees that 'this "creeping incrementalist" approach is time-saving and low on conflict, but never challenges the status quo.' It is likely to be particularly inappropriate in times of dramatic change such as that impacting on further education in England and Wales in the 1990s, as

Shackleton (1994, p. 124) stresses: 'Those that have managed roll-forward budgets with little reflection will struggle with inappropriate definitions of efficiency and debilitating attempts at cost-cutting. In our case, paradigms and parameters were decisively changed.'

Zero-based budgeting

As we noted earlier, zero-based resource allocation begins with the assumption that all categories of spending should be scrutinized. Budget-holders must justify all expenditure, not just new initiatives or those at the margin of existing provision. Each area of expenditure is assessed against the organization's priorities and ranked in importance; funding then depends on the size of the budget. Cardiff High School, for example, changed its approach to internal resource allocation with the introduction of LMS. 'We decided to adopt a "needs" approach – "zero-based" in accountancy jargon – which in its simplest form requires the people who are to spend the money to bid for their share and justify their claim' (Hendricksen and Roberts, 1991, p. 5).

We noted earlier the importance of zero-based thinking at times of radical change. One such example was the introduction of grant maintained status at more than 1,100 schools in England in the 1990s. This sometimes led to a zero-based approach to resource allocation as the deputy head of Wold Newton, a small primary school, explains: 'The advent of GM status has led to a fundamental look at the school's budget. We have not simply been topping up previous budgets' (Bush, Coleman and Glover, 1993, p. 61). Carr takes up this theme in respect of English further education:

> In such circumstances colleges should consider the use of zero or priority based reviews as a means of establishing spending level options across discretionary budget areas. Without the use of priority based budget reviews colleges run a real risk of perpetual year on year incremental increases without the benefit of a fundamental appraisal.
>
> (Carr, 1994, p. 51)

Zero-based approaches have become popular in the literature, and in official reports on educational spending, but there is only limited evidence of their applicability in education. In practice, most educational programmes are not open to serious debate. Many countries have a compulsory curriculum, for example, and this reduces the scope for zero-basing in schools. Levačić (1995, p. 75) notes that 'it is time-consuming and potentially disturbing for staff who are made to feel insecure' and these disadvantages may outweigh the benefits except where schools and colleges are undergoing fundamental change.

A modified version of zero-basing is virement where managers move spending from one area of the budget to another. One of the main advantages of self-management is this ability to tailor spending to school priorities by viring expenditure from one area to another. This virement might involve spending more on one subject than another or varying the resource mix by increasing support staff or spending more on equipment rather than employing another teacher:

> The ability to vire between budget heads is the key to the flexibility in resource management which schools gain from LMS. The crucial issue is how that flexibility is to be exploited most effectively . . . Given the flexibility of virement, schools are responding by taking care over expenditure on utilities and getting better value for money for maintenance services.
>
> (Levačić, 1992, pp. 25–7)

Formula funding

Once areas of spending have been determined, using a zero-based or incremental model, organizations have to determine how to allocate budgets to subunits. An increasingly popular model, according to Thomas and Martin's research, is 'formula funding':

> The trend in funding departmental learning materials appears to be towards a 'formula' funded system based upon pupil numbers and timetable sessions for each subject, usually with a weighting allowance for practical subjects, such as science, which require increased funding for consumables. Such a system is perceived to be more equitable for allocating a basic allowance to each curriculum area. In School 17 for example, this was perceived as a more effective process by which staff can see how decisions on budgets are reached.
>
> (Thomas and Martin, 1996, pp. 76–7)

Sutton's (1996, p. 8) survey of 49 secondary and middle schools showed that 65 per cent 'used a formula based upon weighted student periods to allocate finance for educational resources'. Formula funding is an example of rational resource allocation in its implementation because the formula provides an 'objective' basis for decision-making. There is, however, plenty of scope for political activity in determining the weightings and we shall explore this prospect later.

COLLEGIAL MODELS OF RESOURCE ALLOCATION

The collegial model is popular in the educational management literature (Bush, 1995; Caldwell and Spinks, 1992; Campbell, 1985; Campbell and Southworth, 1993; Little, 1990; Wallace, 1989) but it has rarely been applied to budgeting or resource allocation. The implication of the rational model is that decisions will be made by the principal, 'the headteacher acting as the all powerful autocrat' (Sutton, 1996, p. 6), or by the senior management team. The assumption of the collegial model is that the rational process will involve the participation of a wider range of stakeholders.

> Budgetary decisions are likely to be made through a participative process involving many staff and all of the main groups, as well as senior staff and governors. This process should lead to wide accept-ance or 'ownership' of the decisions because it gives so many people the opportunity to take part.
>
> (Coleman, Bush and Glover, 1994, p. 17)

Davies summarizes the case for staff participation in financial management: 'The arguments for involving staff usually centre on the fact that staff want to be involved, decisions are better if staff are involved and that staff have to implement the changes decided upon' (Davies, 1990, p. 29).

Levačić's (1995, p. 89) study of LMS in one English county suggests that power is located with senior staff and governors: 'Headteachers derived their priorities from the general knowledge of the school and ad hoc discus-sion with staff.' Drawing on her work with 11 case study schools, Levačić summarizes the budgetary process:

> While there was considerable variation in the detailed practice of how priorities emerged and shaped the budget, a common core could be identified in all the schools. The priorities which informed budget-setting emerged from the strategic thinking of headteachers (and senior management teams in secondary schools). This involved discussions and negotiations with other staff, though the extent and nature of such consultation varied . . . In general, the budget reflecting such priorities was drawn up by the headteacher in the primary schools and by the senior budget manager and headteacher in the secondary schools.
>
> (Levačić, 1995, p. 90)

Levačić (1995, p. 97) attributes the limited degree of staff involvement, in part, to 'the problem of finding sufficient time' and concludes that LMS has had little impact on staff participation in financial management:

> Teacher involvement . . . had not changed significantly as a result of local management in most schools. This was particularly the case in the secondary schools where non-promoted teachers were not budget-holders. The situation of heads of department being budget-holders for departmental allocations had not changed. If anything there was a trend to less budgetary autonomy for heads of department due to

centralization of decision-making within the senior management team and a greater emphasis on addressing whole school priorities.

(Levačić, 1995, p. 128)

Thomas and Martin's (1996) research also emphasizes the importance of the head in financial matters. While the SMT also has a part to play, the head remains the key decision-maker: 'What emerges . . . is the pivotal role of the headteacher in giving shape and direction to developments in his or her school . . . In all schools, except one, the headteacher alone is mentioned as the decision-maker' (Thomas and Martin, 1996, p. 53).

The conclusion from the research reviewed in this section is that the potential benefits of teacher empowerment are not being realized because senior staff are retaining control in order to impose centrally determined school-wide priorities.

POLITICAL MODELS OF RESOURCE ALLOCATION

The main alternatives to rational resource allocation are the political models. The assumption here is that spending decisions depend on the interplay between interest groups, and the ultimate decisions owe more to the relative power of these groups than to rational considerations:

> 'Resource management is . . . a micropolitical process, providing an arena within which participants compete for the resources which will enable them to develop programmes of activity which embody their values, further their interests and help to provide legitimation for the activities in which they are engaged' (Simkins, 1998, p. 71).
>
> 'Resource allocation decisions are the outcome not of rational analysis but of the interplay of power, involving negotiation and bargaining. Thus the spending decisions represented in the budget are determined by the relative power and tactical stratagems of the different interest groups' (Levačić, 1995, p. 81).

Simkins (1989, p. 158) argues that the political model focuses on three variables which are relevant to an analysis of budgetary processes:

1) Differences in values and interests among individuals and groups. Such differences are most likely to result from different discipline groups. It is understandable that members of science or languages departments, for example, disagree about the relative importance of their subjects in the school or college curriculum.
2) The power that individuals and groups can bring to bear upon the decision-making process of the organization. Sources of power include the individual's formal position in the organization or their level of expertise. The power of groups may be influenced by their ability to mobilize

external resources and by their perceived centrality to the aims of the organization. For example, departments hosting core subjects within the English and Welsh National Curriculum are likely to hold more power than those responsible for the less significant foundation subjects.

3) The processes through which power is brought to bear on the decision-making situation. In budgeting, emphasis is likely to be on persuasion through the marshalling of expertise and the control of information, or upon the use of bargaining and exchange strategies to reach acceptable compromises on resource allocation.

Although there may be an elongated process of negotiation, resource allocation decisions ultimately depend on the relative power of participants in the bargaining process. Simkins (1998, p. 73) refers to 'an increasing centralisation of power over strategic choice' while research on grant maintained schools (Bush, Coleman and Glover, 1993; Thompson, 1992) shows that resource management is located overwhelmingly with headteachers. Wildavsky emphasizes that the resource allocation process is likely to have winners and losers:

> Since the budget represents conflicts over whose preferences should prevail, . . . one cannot speak of 'better budgeting' without considering who benefits and who loses or demonstrating that no-one loses. Just as the supposedly objective criterion of 'efficiency' has been shown to have normative implications, so a 'better budget' may well be a cloak for hidden policy preferences.
>
> (Wildavsky, 1974, pp. 132–3)

Bidding systems

Political processes may influence any modes of resource allocation. Formula funding may well involve political activity in determining the weightings, as we noted earlier. Similarly, autocratic budgeting may involve preliminary negotiations with interest groups to help ensure the acceptability of resource allocation decisions while incremental budgeting could lead to conflict, although this will probably be confined to the marginal activities under scrutiny. However, the type of resource allocation most likely to involve political activity is bidding.

A bidding system involves individuals or groups applying for resources to sustain or expand existing activities or to develop new initiatives. Bidding usually involves set criteria to enable bidders and decision-makers to assess priorities. This is a political exercise because applicants have to decide whether, and how much, to inflate bids while decision-makers have to assess the extent to which this has occurred as well as judge the relative merits of bids. The merit of this approach is that it does put pressure on curriculum leaders to justify and cost their requirements, and show how the proposed spending will impact on learning (Sutton, 1996, p. 7). Thomas and Martin illustrate the bidding system by giving examples from their case study schools:

> In School 5 each head of faculty made his or her case for the departmental budget requirements. This bid had to be based on curriculum need and justified in full. The process then required all information to be circulated prior to a meeting of all faculty heads at which the bids would be decided. The result of such a process is that some faculties would be more successful than others in 'winning' their funding. However, it was strongly felt that such an arrangement provided optimum use of the budget and it was accepted by staff that other faculties might have more pressing curriculum needs and that their own needs would be met appropriately. Such a needs-based system tended to follow National Curriculum demands.
>
> School 14 also organised a bid system. However, more of the school's budget was delegated to the departments and the type of bid therefore needed to be more comprehensive. This included consumables, including reprographics, curriculum maintenance and development, any special curriculum activities, ancillary support and furniture repairs. Each department was also required to forecast the future trend anticipated for three years ahead in order to give senior management a base from which to plan.
>
> (Thomas and Martin, 1996, pp. 77–8)

Thomas and Martin's (1996) research suggests that the bidding system was accepted by staff as an appropriate way of linking resourcing to curriculum needs but there is little doubt that bidding is likely to lead to political activity as Knight (1983, p. 118) suggests: 'This approach encourages departments to inflate their estimates . . . it tends to undervalue the modest and realistic departments against the pushy and wily ones; and it still leaves unsolved the problem of the final decision.'

The main merit of a political approach to resource allocation is that it is likely to satisfy a higher proportion of participants than many other methods, particularly those involving only the principal or a small number of senior staff. In this sense, it is likely to be preferable to a zero-based model which is designed to change the status quo and is bound to offend certain interest groups:

> It may be preferable to produce a budget that keeps the main interest groups and constituencies of the organisation happy rather than being involved in radical solutions which dissatisfy key stakeholders . . . an acceptable solution which satisfies the different goals and objectives in an organisation may be preferred to the most efficient one on rational grounds.
>
> (Davies, 1994, p. 350)

AMBIGUITY MODELS OF RESOURCE ALLOCATION

Ambiguity models challenge many of the assumptions of rational resource allocation. They suggest that there is little clarity over the goals of organizations, thus making problematic the notion of linking budgeting to aims. Because goals are unclear, it is difficult to determine priorities among competing alternatives and the concept of an optimum choice is also contentious. Budgetary decisions are likely to be characterized by a lack of clarity rather rationality. Levačić shows the impact of ambiguity on the rational model:

> The rational model is undermined by ambiguity, since it is so heavily dependent on the availability of information about relationships between inputs and outputs – between means and ends. If ambiguity prevails, then it is not possible for organizations to have clear aims and objectives. Reliable information about the relationships between different quantities and combinations of inputs and resulting outputs cannot be obtained, and so the second and third stages of the rational decision-making process cannot be carried out. This state of affairs would explain why decision-making, particularly in the public sector, does not in fact follow the rational model, but is characterized by incrementalism.
>
> (Levačić, 1995, p. 82)

Ambiguity damages the rational model which is based on the flawed assumption that there will always be sufficient information to make a clear choice among competing alternatives on objective criteria. In practice, and particularly at times of rapid and multiple change, there may always be sufficient ambiguity to make rational processes of resource allocation both imperfect and problematic.

CONCLUSION: INTEGRATING THE MODELS

The four models discussed in this chapter are all 'ideal types' and are not likely to appear in a pure form in any organization. Most schools and colleges will exemplify aspects of several models in their budgeting and resource allocation processes. The rational model is dominant in the official literature, but advocating a particular approach does not mean that this necessarily happens everywhere, or anywhere.

We noted earlier that zero-based budgeting, one of the rational models, was likely to be prevalent in organizations undergoing radical change. This has been the case in further education in England and Wales in the 1990s and Shackleton (1994) argues that a fundamental reappraisal of budgets is essential in this turbulent environment. Simkins (1998, p. 73) also notes that 'the severe funding pressures which are being placed on further education are causing the efficiency objective to dominate all others.' However, unpredictability also provides the breeding ground for ambiguity and the potential for damaging political activity.

Wildavsky (1974, p. 129) claims that only 'totalitarian regimes impose their normative theories of budgeting on others' but an inflexible commitment to rational models represents just such an imposition. He suggests that incremental budgeting is better because it helps in securing agreement and reduces the burden of calculation. Given the imperfections of the rational process in terms of inadequate information and unclear aims, it may be better to develop a modified form of rationality which recognizes the competing claims of collegial, political and ambiguity models. Simkins (1989) and Wildavsky both stress the benefits of linking rational and political models: 'Rationality must be built in to the budgetary process in ways which use organisational procedures to manage actively the political tensions which will almost inevitably be generated by difficult choices' (Simkins, 1989, p. 167); 'Economic rationality, however laudable in its own sphere, ought not to swallow up political rationality . . . economic rationality . . . might have bad consequences if it works as intended – indeed, if it can work at all' (Wildavsky, 1974, p. 194).

These suggestions for an accommodation between rational and political models can be extended to the other models considered in this chapter. Managers can improve the acceptability of resource allocation decisions by encouraging full participation by staff and other stakeholders. They should also recognize that planning must be flexible if is to be adapted to the rapid and multiple changes emanating from the external environment. Rational planning needs to be tempered by an explicit recognition that educational organizations are there to meet the needs of their pupils and students and that leaders do not have a monopoly in judging those needs. Conceptual pluralism, rather than adherence to one model, is likely to be a more effective approach to resource allocation.

REFERENCES

Audit Commission (1985) *Audit Commission Handbook: A Guide to Economy, Efficiency and Effectiveness*, London, HMSO.

Bush, T. (1995) *Theories of Educational Management: Second Edition*, London, Paul Chapman.

Bush, T. (1997) *Financial Management in Schools*, Leicester, University of Leicester.

Bush, T. (1999) Managing education in changing times. Paper given at Temasek Polytechnic, Singapore, May.

Bush, T., Coleman, M. and Glover, D. (1993) *Managing Autonomous Schools: The Grant-Maintained Experience*, London, Paul Chapman.

Caldwell, B. and Spinks, J. (1992) *Leading the Self-Managing School*, London, Falmer Press.

Campbell, J. (1985) *Developing the Primary Curriculum*, London, Holt, Rinehart and Winston.

Campbell, P. and Southworth, G. (1993) Rethinking collegiality: teachers' views, in N. Bennett, M. Crawford and C. Riches (eds), *Managing Change in Education: Individual and Organisational Perspectives*, London, Paul Chapman.

Carr, J. (1994) *Effective Financial Management in Further and Higher Education*, London, Chartered Association of Certified Accountants.

Coleman, M., Bush, T. and Glover, D. (1994) *Managing Finance and External Relations*, Harlow, Longman.

Davies, B. (1990) Participation in resource decision-making, *Management in Education*, Vol. 4, no.3, pp. 29–30.

Davies, B. (1994) Models of decision-making in resource allocation, in T. Bush and J. West-Burnham (eds), *The Principles of Educational Management*, Harlow, Longman.

Hendricksen, R. and Roberts, G. (1991) Participation in resource decision-making, *Management in Education*, Vol. 5, no. 4, pp. 5–9.

Knight, B. (1983) *Managing School Finance*, London, Heinemann.

Levačić, R. (1992) Local management of schools: aims, scope and impact, *Educational Management and Administration*, Vol. 20, no. 1, pp. 16–29.

Levačić, R. (1995) *Local Management of Schools: Analysis and Practice*, Buckingham, Open University Press.

Little, J. (1990) Teachers as colleagues, in A. Lieberman (ed.), *Schools as Collaborative Cultures: Creating the Future Now*, Basingstoke, Falmer Press.

Purkey, S. and Smith, M. (1985) School reform: the district policy implications of the effective schools literature, *Elementary School Journal*, Vol. 85, no. 3, pp. 353–89.

Shackleton, J. (1994) Achievement-based resourcing, in M. Crawford, L. Kydd and S. Parker (eds), *Educational Management in Action*, London, Paul Chapman.

Simkins, T. (1989) Budgeting as a political and organisational process in educational institutions, in R. Levačić (ed.), *Financial Management in Education*, Milton Keynes, Open University Press.

Simkins, T. (1998) Autonomy, constraint and the strategic management of resources, in D. Middlewood and J. Lumby (eds), *Strategic Management in Schools and Colleges*, London, Paul Chapman.

Sutton, M. (1996) Spending on educational resources in schools: who should decide? *Management in Education*, Vol. 10, no. 5, pp. 6–9.

Thomas, H. and Martin, J. (1996) *Managing Resources for School Improvement*, London, Routledge.

Thompson, M. (1992) The experience of going grant-maintained: the perceptions of AMMA teacher representatives, *Journal of Teacher Development*, Vol. 1, no. 3, pp. 133–40.

Wallace, M. (1989) Towards a collegiate approach to curriculum management in primary and middle schools, in M. Preedy (ed.), *Approaches to Curriculum Management*, Milton Keynes, Open University Press.

Weick, K. (1976) Educational organisations as loosely coupled systems, *Administrative Science Quarterly*, Vol. 21, no. 1, pp. 1–19.

Wildavsky, A. (1974) *The Politics of the Budgetary Process*, Boston, Little, Brown and Co.

7

FINANCIAL MANAGEMENT AND STRATEGIC PLANNING

Derek Glover

The aim of this chapter is to consider the ways in which financial and strategic planning are linked in school and college departments. Over the past decade there has been a major shift in the understanding by senior managers that resource management is an essential tool in achieving the aims of the school, college or department. The need for this understanding is now being extended to middle managers with an increasing emphasis on the acquisition of skills in the management of finance as part of subject leadership (Tompkins, 1997).

The links between financial and strategic practice have to be seen against the development of an 'official' model of good practice as shown by Coopers and Lybrand (1988), the Audit Commission (1993), the Teacher Training Agency (1997), and in the guidance for inspections set forward by OFSTED (1993; 1995a; 1995b). This model is essentially rational and urges that schools and colleges should be fully involved in an ongoing cyclic process which:

- establishes strategic aims for the organization;
- builds long- and medium-term plans which will enable the strategic aims to be met;
- produces an annual plan which is based upon the prioritization of objectives;
- establishes action plans which include details of objectives, resource needs, supervision, and criteria for success;
- monitors the progress of the action plans and outcomes from these;
- evaluates the contribution of these outcomes to the overall aims of the organization as a prelude to review and re-planning.

In this chapter we consider the elements of this cyclic process within a framework of rational approaches to resource allocation, and the implications of rational planning for middle managers.

In reality, because schools and colleges are dynamic organizations, such rationality may vary from the tightly technicist in which all resource allocation is strictly according to agreed plans, to the rather looser and more pragmatic approach in which the planning process has rationality only as a general guide which may be adapted as circumstance require. We are concerned with the way in which schools and colleges carry through this rational process and consider the impact of those factors which may lead to greater flexibility in financial management.

THE NATURE OF STRATEGIC PLANNING

One of the main functions of a leader is that he or she should know where the organization is going and how it is going to get there. The educational world now uses the term 'strategic' as shown in the frequent reference to strategic planning and evaluation in the assessment reports of the higher and further education quality assurance bodies and OFSTED and other inspection bodies for schools.

Mintzberg and Quinn (1996, p. 7) provide a starting-point for a working definition of strategy: 'A strategy is the pattern or plan that integrates an organization's major goals, policies, and action sequences into a cohesive whole.'

Ansoff (1987) gives a more commercially oriented process view but one which bears comparison with the world of education including the establishment of yardsticks by which present and future performance can be measured. However, and possibly arising from the application of strategic planning to the public services, Mintzberg (1994) later noted that:

- strategic planning had become an industry in itself and that this inhibited appreciation of the realities of life in the day-to-day practice of the organization;
- the so-called experts were using forecasting techniques which were based upon models which change from day to day;
- the staffing of organizations changes and brings with it differing viewpoints;
- the environment and context change within the period of forecasting.

Despite these cautions, Mintzberg argues that, on balance, some major framework for development is essential, although he accepts that the longer the planning period the greater the uncertainty that a plan will be achievable. This is a particular problem for those who seek to have a tight relationship between future planning and financial management – the reality is that annual financial allocations are only known a matter of months in advance.

In practice, Caldwell and Spinks (1992), having considered the particular needs of the self-managing school, see strategy at a local and more domestic level although they recognize that the national context affects planning. For them the leader has to understand the competitive position of the school or college, understand the major trends which will affect development, ensure that all stakeholders are aware of matters of strategic importance and ensure that evaluation and review are used to prevent the plans being of no value as soon as they are written. Bailey and Johnson (1997) have considered the ways in which strategies develop in organizations and these are likely to have implications for financial management:

- a logical, rational and totally intended planning perspective – financial plans are fully known;
- a logical but incrementalist perspective building year by year on 'where we are now' – incremental financial plans;
- a political perspective dependent upon the operation of internal and external pressures – financial plans subject to power dynamics;
- a cultural perspective in which planning is linked to the perpetuation of a set of shared values – financial plans linked to status quo;
- a visionary perspective in which organizational development is driven by a view of 'where we are going' – financial plans linked to the major objective;
- a natural selection perspective in which future direction is determined by the strength of the competition between other perspectives – financial planning is evolutionary but cannot be forecast.

THE PRACTICALITIES OF STRATEGIC PLANNING

Once again, whilst the framework for strategic development may be set out, a degree of uncertainty is implicit in the type of plan and, whilst strategic plans may exist, they may be little more than a guide to the future. Where plans are of this sort it is difficult to tie financial management to them – the link is tenuous and unplanned. However, where the link is made, more explicit financial resources can be used to optimum effect to achieve desired outcomes. Mintzberg (1994) referred to the former as emergent rather than planned strategies. For many schools and colleges the process works in an emergent way in response to the changing pressures of the time. On the other hand, it is argued that if the organization knows where it is going it will, as in the definitions outlined earlier, manage resources and structures in such a way that the aims and objectives can be fulfilled. Weindling (1997) makes use of the ideas of *gap analysis* – where we are compared with where we want to be. He also considers the importance of the stakeholders – all those concerned with a school or college – in contributing to the long-term planning process to enhance their 'ownership' of policy and practice. Recent research into the way in which strategic planning is used in schools (Glover *et al.*, 1996) suggests that the process involves:

- assessing the current position of the school or college related to its environment;
- assessing the current strengths and weaknesses in the use of human and financial resources in the organization;
- reviewing the aims of the organization and whether these should be changed in the light of this strategic audit process;
- considering, and costing, the alternative ways in which the organization could develop to meet its objectives;
- reaching decisions on the priorities for future planning;
- developing the longer-term, medium-term and action plans for the use of resources to meet aims.

The way in which all these are undertaken varies from organization to organization. This variation may be because of the long-term stability of a school or college with inherent tendencies to historic rather than creative development; the leadership style which varies along a continuum from the collegial to the bureaucratic and sometimes has no recognizable pattern at all; the way in which people work together, known as the culture of the unit; and the structure of decision-making which again varies from the autocratic to the consensual. Scheerens (1997) brings these factors together as either *synoptic* planning characterized by high predictability and sequencing of actions, or *retroactive* planning characterized by reaction to events and incremental development. Levačić *et al.* (1999) offers a typology of planning approaches based upon this distinction and suggests that in a detailed study of the management of four secondary and nine primary schools the following were evident:

- embraced rationality – maintaining the fully planned approach;
- accommodated rationality – using plans as guides rather than blueprints;
- managed flexibility – as a pragmatic response to plans but reacting to prevailing conditions;
- value-based resistance – where leaders believe that they can attain objectives without rigid planning.

However, the basic relationship between the ends and the means of financial management is the key to resource use and this is the theoretical basis of all school and college financial planning. Where adherence to the strategic plan is paramount, financial, and hence resource, flexibility is inhibited but stated objectives are more likely to be realized. Where strategic planning is non-existent, or a guide only, short-termism and micropolitical activity may predominate as shown by Siciliano (1997) in an assessment of planning and performance in non-profit-making organizations.

PLANNING, FINANCE AND THE ROLE OF THE MIDDLE MANAGER

The link between strategic planning and financial management appears to vary from school to school. In the research into school management outlined above it was clear that a spectrum of practice existed. This was exemplified in the tight linkage in a secondary school in which all expenditure was sanctioned only if it had been planned for, prioritized and approved, and in the loose linkage in another where expenditure was allowed by senior managers if it was felt to be appropriate and its significance for longer-term planning was then subsequently reviewed.

Management practices within schools can unintentionally inhibit a rational approach. The allocation of funds to subject areas in schools and colleges exemplifies this approach. Traditionally in schools, the percentage of funding devolved to departments is less than 5 per cent of the total, and staffing and accommodation costs are subject to centralized budgeting. In colleges of further education and higher education practice varies but many departments have to manage the costs of staff, accommodation and materials of instruction. The greater the percentage of total resource costs devolved within the institution, the greater the impact of the allocation system. An investigation of practice in 25 large secondary schools undertaken by Glover *et al.* (1998) shows that, despite the pressure for totally rational, objective-driven approaches, a variety of financial allocation systems continue to operate. These include the following types of budgeting.

Historic budgeting

In this approach, each 'cost centre' or budget-holder receives a share of the total according to previous expenditure. The allocation may be 'tinkered with', but remains substantially the same from year to year. It is neither related to actual expenditure needs nor to the possibly changing priorities of the organization.

Modifications to this system may overcome some of the problems of inherent stability. In one modification of the scheme, for example, the central pool may retain a proportion of the total, say 20 per cent, which is then open to bids according to need. In another modification, there may be an agreed formula which is related to the actual costs of teaching certain subjects and the proportion of the timetable taught by particular subjects. Thus, for example, if within a school there is a subject weighting of 1.5 for English on the basis that it is a two-subject GCSE examination, and if the subject is allocated 20 per cent of the teaching periods, it will get an inflated share of the budget. However, it must be remembered that where the weighting is increased for some subjects it will take from the share per unit and other subjects will lose. Thus 'baronial' politics are perpetuated in the power structure of the organization, and, however refined the formula may be, it does not recognize institution-wide (i.e. 'whole-school') planning policies. In the words of one head of faculty interviewed: 'We like to know where we are from year to year, and I am against any attempt to take away our ability to plan for ourselves.'

Zero-base budgeting

Zero-budgeting is one response to the difficulties inherent in the historic budgeting approach. In essence, zero-budgeting means that the cost centre has to calculate its financial needs afresh each year, knowing what its commitments will be: it is then possible to meet demands according to need. One major problem is that over-estimation can occur to ensure that sufficient funds are allocated. One interviewee commented that: 'you get to know the system and put in for more than you think you will realistically get – especially where there is no check later to see that you have spent on what you have asked for.'

The process of negotiation can also continue to be a reflection of power group relationships within the organization. In attempting to introduce the system into American schools, Hartley (1979) provided one approach to this together with an in-built system of criteria, known in advance and by which strategists can plan their bids. He suggests that it is not just the financial requirement of a budget bid which should be taken into account, but also its justification in terms of both curriculum and environmental need.

Programme planning budgeting

To overcome the problems of manipulation which might occur, Caldwell and Spinks (1988) provide an account of their attempt to establish a totally objective method of financial planning in a school context. They argue that the costing of the component parts of the institution's curricular offer can be a precursor to making informed decisions about priorities to be adopted by that organization. They also outline the way in which this might be done. They suggest that if each element of the total programme is costed and subject to collaborative prioritization then the collegiality of the institution will be enhanced and the power politics will be shifted to the capacity which various people have to influence their colleagues. Consequently, whole-institution planning becomes a reality. In one of the sample schools in the investigation, programme planning is used to fund all curriculum changes which are needed to achieve the strategic aims of the school and these are prioritized from year to year but this is not liked by middle managers who feel that they have to work extremely hard to convince senior managers of their case: 'It might mean that we know all spending is on school priorities but it does little for those little schemes which we might want to try in the department.'

The limited plan approach

This approach demonstrates an attempt to bring together the best features of the various schemes. 'Limited planning' argues that there will be a certain basic programme offered by the organization year in year out, and that decisions about change are the most important element of the budgeting process. To achieve this, a formula allocation may be used for, say, 60 per cent of the financing of the organization. Plans are then put forward for the implementation of change, e.g. in the introduction of a health-related fitness programme for a year group; or of a road safety programme in a primary school. Each programme/plan is costed to include staff time, the necessary teaching materials and equipment, and, in some cases, the cost of accommodation and central services are apportioned according to the time the programme operates. Costs may then be set against any saving resulting from the changes – if one subject is developed then it may be that another must be curtailed. Problems may arise out of the complexity of the calculations involved but sample schools using the approach generally cost limited plans in terms of additional staffing, staff training and additional resources to secure specific objectives. In the words of one respondent: 'giving a spur to pilot projects which might be more broadly adopted'.

In reality there is a tendency to use a combination of systems to provide a basic funding but then to encourage 'bidding' for additional resources to foster development and innovation. In practice in the 25 secondary schools in the investigation, 21 used basic formula funding for allocations to departments for educational resources and elements of professional development, and of these, five used a weighting system – one, a system of great complexity which was changed from year to year to meet the needs of the strategic plan. Two of the schools make allocations according to submissions in the school development plan and in a subsequent departmental review. One school uses a combination of zero-budgeting and bidding to fund action plans, whilst the remaining school relies solely on bidding – with consequent emphasis on 'lobbying for funds' as part of the perceived role of subject leaders.

From another source, the OFSTED model of good practice is shown in the contrast between these sections from two reports:

School A
To date, links between curriculum planning and financial planning have not always been precise or explicit. This is the consequence partly of the difficulty of financial prediction, and partly of a wish not to constrain the development of educational vision by subjecting it too early to financial considerations. However, separation of the two

elements can lead to losses of efficiency, whether this is embarking on developments which cannot be sustained in the long run, or moving ahead with new developments at the cost of existing provision. In addition, time can be wasted on the development of plans which ultimately have to be postponed or abandoned because the resources are not available.

School B
The school development plan is very comprehensive and gives a very detailed picture of the school's priorities for development. Financial planning is becoming closely linked to the school's aims and priorities, with funding appropriately targeted. Governors are closely involved with the strategic management of resources and there are detailed policies for charging and pay. The school recognises the importance of value for money and carefully assesses the benefits of expenditure on staffing, premises and learning resources.

In looking at the management of resources in colleges of further education (National Audit Office, 1995) it was reported that, in the early years following incorporation giving them autonomous status, colleges had used an historic approach devolving funds to departments for staff and resources according to formulae based upon student uptake in the period before incorporation. Changed funding arrangements and the need to reassess the staffing situation to keep within tighter financial constraints led initially to bidding systems within colleges. By the time of this report there had been a change to systems which were student related in that an element of funding was fee driven, but which were also requiring departments to determine their contribution to strategic planning through the development of new courses, new teaching approaches and links with the educational and commercial community. In this way strategic aims were funded at departmental level.

Downward devolution of funds, by whatever means, is not without problems. Office for Standards in Education reports frequently indicate the need for the use of a system which requires cost-centre holders to identify the costs of any proposals they are making and the senior managers to allocate the necessary funding according to the priorities established in the development plan. The experience in the schools investigated above (Glover *et al.*, 1998) shows that three problems arise unless the link between planning and allocation is made clear. Where involvement in the micropolitics of the organization is essential in order to maximize the departmental share of resources, it is possible that middle managers become involved in what Fullan (1991) refers to as 'balkanisation'. This in turn, inhibits open discussion and diverts attention away from whole organizational aims towards sectional interests and leads to isolation of groups as a cultural element within the school, department or college. Further, whilst individual departments may develop tactics for 'bending the ear' of those responsible for the allocation of funds, they may be diverted away from the main purpose of their work – that of effective teaching and learning. The response in one of the sample schools is to use an annual review which:

- looks back in terms of assessed and measured progress towards departmental and whole-school aims;
- looks at the immediate plans to ensure that they will be monitored in the light of this review;
- looks forward to order the priorities of plans to ensure that resource allocations are appropriate.

IMPLEMENTING PLANS: USING THE BUDGET AS A FRAMEWORK FOR ACTION

In order for schools and colleges to function efficiently, budget-planning has to be undertaken according to a formalized timetable. Even in schools, where in the past the focus on finance was very much the prerogative of the local authority, the days of a few calculations on the back of an envelope would appear to be long gone! This change and formalization of responsibility at institutional level derives largely from the fact that, overall, the financing of education is now more closely scrutinized and controlled by central government and its agencies. Accountability for the use of public funds now stems from the point of delivery and the Audit Commission is concerned with the way in which local education authorities (LEAs) help schools to maximize the value for money through structured decision-making processes (Audit Commission, 1998; OFSTED, 1998). The Further Education Funding Council pursues a similar course with colleges of further education. This is because:

- the amount of money devolved to local units is now much greater than previously;
- the necessity for consultation with a wider audience of stakeholders is more frequently recognized;
- the systems and mechanisms for the release and control of money are more sophisticated as data management becomes the norm.

Arnold and Hope (1983) developed the budget-making process as the opportunity for schools and colleges to review their current position, identify the eventual aims, develop plans for their achievement and establish criteria by which success can be measured. Through this process the opportunities for collective management in identifying goals, choosing the basis of decision-making, ranking alternatives and monitoring progress may be indicated. The process also implies the need for full information as a basis for decision-making. However, they demonstrate that the budget is more than a statement of intent. Initial school experience, as reported by Levačić

(1995), suggests that the management of decision-making has now become much more regulated than previously in order that the four stages of the budget process can be monitored and evaluated. These four stages are:

- the establishment of goals through the strategic plan;
- the scheduling and refinement of the processes of decision-making;
- the monitoring of the implementation of agreed plans so that resource allocation proceeds as intended;
- the evaluation of the impact of the allocation according to the budget in one year on the achievement of objectives.

The importance of this is seen in the process outlined as part of the job description for a new headteacher in a 'fresh-start' school in an Education Action Zone established to increase the chances of the achievement of educational improvement in a deprived area. The job description included reference to the establishment of a junior college forming a bridge between traditional schooling and lifelong learning as a given strategic aim; the establishment of effective decision-making teams to ensure that both human and educational resource allocations are consistent with the curriculum of the junior college; responsibility for the implementation of the agreed development and budget plans; and evaluation of the effect that these have had on the overarching LEA requirement for educational improvement.

The practicalities of the budget process are not always easy. Glover *et al.* (1998) identify four problems in schools.

1) Whilst there is considerable initial interest on the part of subject leaders and other middle managers in budget preparation, this interest wanes after the allocation has been finalized and subsequent implementation is seen as an administrative chore and evaluation becomes a passing exercise.
2) The system is dependent upon readily accessible data on income, expenditure and educational outcomes but problems of data processing, especially at LEA level, may inhibit this.
3) The situation is worsened where isolationism of the departmental groups exists so that whole-organization aims and objectives are seen as a senior management concern to the detriment of cross-curricular initiatives.
4) Above all, this lack of coherence may mean that whilst expenditure achieves value for money in one department it may fail to do so in another – a point recognized in many OFSTED secondary reports.

Glover *et al.* (1998) also considered the professional development needs of middle managers in the sample of schools they investigated. Provision of training in some general financial management skills was recognized as a need by 94 per cent of the respondents, and accorded the highest priority by 43 per cent. This need, linked with a similarly high need for training and development in monitoring and evaluation, suggests that many middle managers are coping with complex resource allocation without appropriate training. Indeed, in a sentiment expressed in different ways by several respondents: 'I have grown into the job by copying the practices of my past head of department and it has come as a surprise to know that I should be proactive in planning for resources, rather than reactive so that I can manage with what I get.' This comment suggests that whilst professional development is offered at whole-school level there is a lack of specific training for middle managers. There is some value in considering the way in which structures, cultures and practices within a school or college operate. The model proposed by Meyerson and Martin (1997) recognized the relationship between the organization as a whole and the constituent parts. This could be:

- integrated – where there is consistency, consensus and whole-organizational focus;
- differentiated – where there is diversity, lack of consensus and sub-unit focus;
- ambiguous – where there is lack of complexity, lack of clarity and uncertain focus.

Integration is shown in the practice of one school outlined by Gambling (1998). Here the culture that prevails has a clear strategic aim of securing increased pupil numbers in the future through enhanced academic achievement in the present. To this end there are a set of school strategic aims including attendance, numeracy, literacy and information technology achievement targets. All departments have evolved their departmental plans in order to secure these aims through their own work and, in the annual presentation of these development plans to headteacher and governors, a standard format is used. This format includes desired expenditure on staffing, professional development, equipment and materials of instruction. The pro forma highlights the way in which the department will contribute to whole-school aims. The initial budget procedure, involving review of the current readiness to contribute to the whole programme, with costed and timed plans, is revisited as the basis for review in future years. Whilst the system appears to be restrictive, in that expenditure is constrained by whole-school objectives, those who are working with it feel that it has heightened whole-school awareness, led to more effective expenditure and promoted better monitoring and evaluation because of the importance of the review process.

ACHIEVING PROGRESS: LINKING REVIEW TO FUTURE PLANNING

One of the ways in which this linkage can be achieved has been outlined in the previous paragraph. The fundamental requirement is that the process of review should be regular, active, in that it involves all those who must deliver a particular programme, and perceived as an important starting-point for annual budgeting. The importance of recognizing the difference between monitoring and evaluation is paramount in considering progress towards strategic aims. In the school described previously this difference is recognized by a structured review process which asks one group of questions about the way in which previous expenditure has been managed with probity. Monitoring is achieved by seeking evidence that expenditure has taken place on those items for which plans had been approved, that value for money has been obtained through competitive tendering for major items, and that quality assurance processes have been used to ensure that staff have used the resources as agreed. The second group of questions asks for detail of the impact of expenditure on achievement within the department and on achievement within the school. All departmental review reports are then used in the compilation of a 'report on work in progress' which is used by the headteacher and governors in their annual review of strategic aims and long- and medium-term plans.

The structure of the process and the detail of the review in this school are exceptional and the school has thereby avoided one of the problems in developing school-based autonomy – that staff may fail to see the relevance of budgetary control and evaluation. Audit functions are understood in terms of ensuring that each item of expenditure is legal and documented, but it remains the case – even with the development of a 'quality' focus – that it is less well understood in terms of getting 'value for money'. Even within the classroom situation there is a need to ensure that resources are used to maximize educational effectiveness and this may require consideration of the quality of purchases, information about alternative sources of supply and the development of criteria by which the teacher can recognize whether particular patterns of resource use achieve success. The longer-term impact of resource allocation is considered by assessing outcomes against the quality and pattern of resources used. An example may be the annual assessment of the GNVQ results of a college cohort against the additional expenditure made for staffing or for information technology within a department. But evaluation, in current official terms, is seen as being more than this – it is the use of resources to support the aims of the school which determines the outcomes achieved – movement towards strategic objectives. Many staff and governors may feel that the budget is only of value for the current year and that it does not contribute to the strategic plans of the organization – again isolationism prevails.

The importance of evaluation in financial management has been recognized in the OFSTED and National Audit Office reporting systems. Schools and colleges are encouraged to have:

- clear financial procedures to ensure that, when money has been allocated, it is spent according to intention – *monitored*;

- a consistent audit control to ensure that there is no possibility of fraud or misuse of funds – *monitored*;
- an awareness of procedures for ensuring value for money purchasing – *evaluated*;
- a system which ensures that the long-term effects of expenditure are reviewed against the achievement of planned objectives – *evaluated*.

To help with this process much publicity has been given to the use of benchmarking. This involves recording the expenditure in various areas of educational practice and then using this as a mean against which the performance of individual schools and colleges can be measured. In this way it is possible for a school to consider how it stands in relation to other schools of similar size and context, for example in the use of staffing as part of the total budget, and then to ask the questions 'why?' and 'to what effect?' Practices have been outlined by DfEE (1995, p. 5) with results such as: 'Another headteacher used the benchmarking data to review spending in different staffing areas and found that there was some duplication of management tasks. A revised management structure released funds for other priorities.'

A further approach is through the use of auditing procedures, not in the more narrow financial accounting sense but with a broader perspective based upon the questions:

- What progress have we made towards our strategic objectives?
- What factors have inhibited this progress?
- What are the current favouring and inhibiting factors for future development?

The answer to these questions will establish the 'gap' mentioned by Weindling (1997) and will indicate the areas of future planning which need modification or rethinking. In this way the strategic aim is kept at the forefront of debate and consequently drives future financial planning. Cuttance (1994), in an assessment of systems for monitoring educational quality, stresses the importance of a strategic view of teaching and learning as the driving force for all resource use. Without effective review and evaluation no school or college can ascertain the way in which resources affect educational outcomes. Similarly without review and evaluation strategic aims may become no more than an occasionally acknowledged pipe dream.

It is therefore appropriate that the systems by which schools and colleges operate are sufficiently flexible to avoid strategic aims being immutably set in one year and then not revisited for the next three to five years. Contexts and conditions may change over a period of months and, whilst there is little to be gained from a 'talking shop' activity which, because it is oft-repeated, then loses its value, it is important that senior managers at organizational level, and middle managers at departmental or unit level, maintain the longer view. In one of the secondary schools mentioned earlier

(Glover *et al.*, 1998), the annual school review process undertaken by head-teacher and governors briefly revisits the strategic aims each year and revises them fully on a four-year cycle. In this way the departments are aware of their main direction in the coming years and have to adapt their planning to accord with minor changes, but they are assured that no major change will be considered unless it has been the subject of a whole-school review. Perhaps, in this way, direction is maintained, staff ownership is facilitated and resource planning is possible over a longer period. As a result, financial planning, although subject to change as a result of changing funding, can be seen to be working towards known objectives.

REFERENCES

Ansoff, I. (1987) *Corporate Strategy*, Harmondsworth, Penguin.

Arnold, J. and Hope, T. (1983) *Accounting for Management Decisions*, Hemel Hempstead, Prentice Hall.

Audit Commission (1993) *Adding up the Sums: Schools' Management of their Finances*, London, HMSO.

Audit Commission (1998) *Better by Far: Preparing for Best Value*, London, HMSO.

Bailey, A. and Johnson, G. (1997) How strategies develop in organisations, in M. Preedy, R. Glatter and R. Levačić (eds), *Educational Management: Strategy, Quality and Resources*, Buckingham, Open University Press.

Caldwell, B. J. and Spinks, J. (1988) *The Self-Managing School*, London, Falmer Press.

Caldwell, B. J. and Spinks, J (1992) *Leading the Self-Managing School*, London, Falmer Press.

Coopers and Lybrand (1988) *Local Management of Schools*, London, HMSO.

Cuttance, P. (1994) Monitoring educational quality through PIs for school practice, *School Effectiveness and School Improvement*, Vol. 5, no. 2, pp. 101–26.

DfEE (1995) *Benchmarking*, London, DfEE.

Fullan, M. (1991) *The New Meaning of Educational Change*, London, Cassell.

Gambling, M. (1998) Evidence of good practice, in D. Glover, D. Miller, G. Gough and M. Johnson (eds), *Subject Leaders: Work, Organisation and Professional Development*, Keele, Keele University Department of Education.

Glover, D., Levačić, R., Bennett, N. and Earley, P. (1996) Leadership, planning and resource management in four very effective schools. Part I: setting the scene, *School Organisation*, Vol. 16, no. 3, pp. 135–48; Leadership, planning and resource management in four very effective schools. Part II: planning and performance, *School Organisation*, Vol. 16, no. 3, pp. 247–61.

Glover, D., Miller, D., Gough, G. and Johnson, M. (1998) *Subject Leaders: Work, Organisation and Professional Development*, Keele, Keele University Department of Education.

Hartley, H. J. (1979) Zero-based budgeting for secondary schools, *NASSP Bulletin*, Vol. 63, pt 431, pp. 22–8, Virginia, National Association of Secondary School Principals.

Levačić, R. (1995) *Local Management of Schools*, Buckingham, Open University Press.

Levačić, R., Glover, D., Bennett, N. and Crawford, M. (1999) Modern headship for the rationally managed school, in T. Bush, L. Bell, R. Bolam, R. Glatter and P. Ribbins (eds), *Educational Management: Redefining Theory, Policy and Practice*, London, Paul Chapman.

Meyerson, D. and Martin, J. (1997) Cultural change: integration of three different views, in A. Harris, N. Bennett and M. Preedy (eds), *Organisational Effectiveness and Improvement in Education*, Buckingham, Open University Press.

Mintzberg, H. (1994) *The Rise and Fall of Strategic Planning*, London, Prentice Hall.

Mintzberg, H. and Quinn, J. B. (1996) *The Strategy Process: Concepts, Contexts, Cases* (3rd edn), London, Prentice Hall.

National Audit Office (1995) *Managing to be Independent: Management and Financial Control at Colleges in the Further Education Sector*, London, National Audit Office.

OFSTED (1993) *Standards and Quality in Education*, London, HMSO.

OFSTED (1995a) *Guidance on the Inspection of Secondary Schools*, London, HMSO.

OFSTED (1995b) *Guidance on the Inspection of Special Schools*, London: HMSO.

OFSTED (1998) *The Annual Report of Her Majesty's Chief Inspector of Schools 1996/7*, London, The Stationery Office.

Scheerens, J. (1997) Conceptual models and theory-embedded principles on effective schooling, *School Effectiveness and School Improvement*, Vol. 8, no. 3, pp. 269–310.

Siciliano, J. (1997) The relationship between formal planning and performance in non-profit organisations, *Non-Profit Management and Leadership*, Vol. 7, no. 4, pp. 387–403.

Teacher Training Agency (1997) *National Standards for Headteachers*, London, TTA.

Tompkins, P. (1997) Financial and material resources in M. Leask and I. Terrell (eds) *Development Planning and School Improvement for Middle Managers*, London, Kogan Page.

Weindling, D. (1997) Strategic planning in schools: some practical techniques, in M. Preedy, R. Glatter and R. Levačić (eds), *Educational Management: Strategy, Quality and Resources*, Buckingham, Open University Press.

8

BUDGETING IN SCHOOLS

Kevin McAleese

INTRODUCTION

This chapter is written from the perspective of a secondary school head-teacher who leads Harrogate Grammar School, a North Yorkshire 11–18 comprehensive school with 1,620 pupils and 103 teaching staff. The school has been responsible for managing its own budget since 1990. The chapter begins by setting the historical context for the introduction of Local Management of Schools (LMS) in the 1988 Education Reform Act, and goes on to outline from a practitioner's viewpoint the processes which constitute effective management of a delegated school budget, ending with a consideration of the impact of school financial autonomy on the processes of teaching and learning.

Figures used as illustrations (tables) in the chapter are drawn from the 1998/99 members of the National Information Exchange. This is a project involving over 100 secondary schools of every size and type in England, which the author has co-ordinated since 1995. Participating schools voluntarily provide information about their characteristics: the number of pupils on free meals, those with special needs and the annual public exam results. They also provide data about their income and use of resources in a given year. For example, the budget proportions spent on teachers and support staff, the use of promoted posts, their teacher contact ratio and pupil–teacher ratio, even how much the most senior non-teacher is paid. In return they are provided with comparative data about all the other participating schools.

Whilst this chapter is written about UK schools with delegated budgets, the general issues of effectiveness in resource use and management are relevant to any school spending context, irrespective of whether that spending is centrally or locally directed, or located elsewhere on the resource allocation continuum which is developing in the public education systems of many countries.

LMS AND THE SELF-MANAGING SCHOOL: A CULTURE CHANGE

Before LMS, virtually all of a school's spending was centrally directed and managed. A local education authority (LEA) like North Yorkshire administered literally hundreds of primary, secondary and special schools, most usually through a series of regional education offices linked to county hall where elected councillors set the overall strategy for education officers and teams of administrators to implement in detail. Such an arrangement had existed in England and Wales more or less unchanged for nearly a century.

By the mid-1980s it was the Conservative government's view that such a schooling system was inefficient and unresponsive, and a key reason why Britain was lagging behind other developed economies. The system was seen to be inefficient because decision-making was too remote from where resources were actually deployed, and it was unresponsive because LEA cultures were typically bureaucratic and reactive. The solution was seen to be the creation of more or less 'self-managing' schools which would compete for pupils and be directly responsible for the resources they were given, with the role of the LEA shrinking to that of providing key strategic services. The mechanism chosen to make schools self-managing was LMS. Every LEA was required to devise a formula by which the money it spent on all its schools would in future be delegated directly to the schools themselves, apart from some funding kept back for the provision by the LEA of central services such as transport to school and the provision for special educational needs.

It is hard to overstate the impact on culture that the change involved. Having had direct responsibility only for classroom books and equipment, schools took over a hugely increased range of spending headings which they could manage on a more flexible and responsive basis. They could, for example, plan for overall underspends and carry balances from one financial year to the next, or even plan for in-year deficits. Under LMS, heads of department found themselves with annual budgets for books and equipment which could actually be *managed*! For example, if the publication of a set of textbooks was delayed from the planned release date, money could be earmarked and set aside. For middle management post-holders in schools this change has been the major benefit arising from resource delegation.

THE PLANNING PROCESS: FINANCIAL AND ACADEMIC YEARS

Schools in England and Wales operate an academic year which begins each September and ends the following August. Financial years, on the other hand, most commonly operate on a 12-month cycle which begins in April and runs through to the following March. Given that state education is funded from the public purse through taxation, there was never any doubt that LMS would be introduced through the traditional fiscal year beginning in April. As a result, schools have to forward plan their delegated budgets by meshing together a financial year with a curriculum and timetable year beginning five months later. This dichotomy in planning cycles, whilst manageable with experience, has always posed significant problems for schools.

Such problems are particularly acute for schools which, possibly because of falling rolls or an LEA budget cut, or both, have to find significant savings in the following academic year. Curriculum courses are usually organized and planned on an academic year basis, and any reductions – for example, in the number of teaching sets created or part-time teachers employed – are usually only possible from September. This means that any saving is in practice only obtainable in seven-twelfths of the financial year which ends in the April beyond, and therefore measures may have to be more severe to generate the necessary in-financial year reduction.

In practice, most schools with delegated budgets continue to plan from one academic year to the next and accept that resources implications for those 12 months of educational activity will run across two different financial years.

INCOME

The income for schools managing their own budgets comprised mainly the funds delegated by the LEA through its LMS formula, plus the school's self-generated income through activities like premises lettings, community use, contracts for initial teacher training, bank interest on unspent balances, and so on. The figures from schools in the 1998/99 National Information Exchange (Tables 8.1 and 8.2) illustrate the range of such income streams per pupil.

Table 8.1 Overall delegated income, per pupil

	Lowest	Highest	Average
Network 1 (11–16 schools)	£1,865	£2,635	£2,214
Network 2 (11–18 schools)	£1,953	£3,388	£2,269

Table 8.2 Self-generated income, per pupil

	Lowest	Highest	Average
Network 1	£0	£120	£81
Network 2	£3	£149	£98

At least 80 per cent of the school's delegated income from the LEA must be provided on the basis of pupil numbers actually on roll, to ensure that schools have a financial incentive to be mindful of the quality they offer. The pupil number linkage is provided by the 'LMS formula' through which each pupil is allocated a cash value according to their age, known as the 'Age Weighted Pupil Unit' (AWPU). The cash value of an AWPU for a child in any school-year grouping is for the LEA to decide, given its income provided by the government through the Standard Spending Assessment (SSA). Comparisons of AWPU values across England and Wales in the same financial year lead to striking differences in provision for identically aged children, as the extract from the National Information Exchange 'Generosity Table' (Table 8.3) for 1998/99 schools illustrates.

Table 8.3   Comparison of Year 7 AWPU values in a range of LEAs

LEA	£	
Bath and NE Somerset	1,191	
Bradford	1,325	
Norfolk	1,449	
Warwickshire	1,488	
Somerset	1,547	
Cumbria	1,619	
York	1,642	Average:
Devon	1,663	£1,660
Birmingham	1,763	
Camden, London Borough of	1,812	
Coventry	1,824	
North Somerset	1,881	
Hillingdon, London Borough of	1,922	
Newham, London Borough of	2,113	

In addition to delegated and self-generated funds, schools also have access to any of their reserves carried over from previous financial years. In practice, however, many schools have such monies earmarked in one way or another, rather than simply held as contingencies; for example, to fund a building project or to fund a transition in the pupil roll, to finance equipment replacement or indeed to fulfil Development Plan commitments. Evidence from the National Information Exchange shows that growing numbers of secondary schools are running down their reserves as a short-term measure, by setting budgets which utilize unspent balances from previous years to support planned spending.

When the three elements of delegated income, self-generated income and any reserves utilized are put together, the income available to the school in a financial year becomes clear, as the actual example in Table 8.4 from the National Information Exchange illustrates.

Table 8.4 Income side of the planned budget in an 11–18 comprehensive, 1998/99 financial year

	£
Delegated income from the LEA: AWPU funding	3,370,639
Size-related and lump sum funding	339,538
Bank interest	6,000
Standards funding from LEA	13,000
Premises lettings/rents	15,000
Initial teacher training contract	15,400
Other miscellaneous income	7,500
Reserves used	30,000
Total school income in 1998/99	3,797,077

PATTERNS OF SPENDING

Table 8.5 shows the planned spending side of the same school's budget whose income was illustrated in Table 8.4. Even the most cursory observation will reveal the extent to which staffing costs are the largest single element in a school budget. In both primary and secondary schools, expenditure is dominated by the salaries of the staff in general and the teachers in particular. Comparative data from schools of different types throughout England and Wales in the National Information Exchange confirm the extent to which the school in Table 8.5 is typical in its planned use of resources (see Table 8.6).

Consideration of staffing costs

The size of staffing costs as part of the total budget means that it is good practice to break salary costs of teachers down into their constituent parts, which can then be tracked separately over time. These parts include the spread of Common Pay Scale (CPS) costs and promoted post costs, and also incremental movement, the cost of non-contact time and the total management costs of the school. In addition, what is the average age of the teaching staff in the school? How long has the average teacher worked there? How many have worked in any other school than their present one? Such questions can be used to create an internal profile for every department that includes patterns of age, gender, time in the school and total teaching experience.

Comparison of an individual school's profile to that of a national average may be helpful. How many teachers in the school are moving through experience towards the top of the CPS, and what proportion is that of the total staffing complement? It is an economic fact that an unchanged teaching force costs more each September, as individuals move by 'incremental

Table 8.5 Planned expenditure budget in an 11–18 comprehensive, 1998/99 financial year

	£	% of budget
Administrative and clerical salaries	129,000	
Technician salaries	83,500	
Teacher salaries	2,752,000	
Supply teacher costs	26,000	
Midday supervisors	23,700	
Foreign language assistants	10,500	
Site staff costs	40,200	
Other staff costs (advertising, interviews, free meals)	19,500	
Total staffing	3,084,400	81.2
Premises maintenance	73,000	
Grounds maintenance	15,000	
Energy (electricity, gas)	58,000	
Rates, water, sewerage	125,700	
Cleaning	98,800	
Staff travel and minibus	2,900	
Total premises	373,400	9.8
Furniture and supplies	20,000	
Departmental books and classroom materials	114,000	
Central services (administration)	38,000	
Hired/leased equipment and services	45,500	
Standards funding	13,000	
Quality assurance/initial teacher training contract	13,000	
Public examination fees	68,000	
Total supplies and services	311,500	8.2
Postage/telephones/fax	11,500	
Governors' discretionary fund	3,000	
Insurances	5,500	
Provision for contingencies	10,000	
Total communications and miscellaneous	30,000	0.8
Total school expenditure	3,799,300	100

drift' up the CPS on the basis of accumulated experience. In small primary schools it is not uncommon for the cost of incremental drift to exceed that of any annual pay rise, placing disproportionate pressure on the budget as a whole.

A key starting-point for planning salaries in April is the salary bill for *the previous month*, not the one a year before in the last initial budget. The March salary costs are the first building block for the new financial year, and in most schools they will remain unaltered, apart from any pay rise in April, until the end of August when most resignations will take effect. September, the start of the new academic year, will be when incremental

Table 8.6 Staffing spending in a range of 11–18 mixed secondary schools (comprehensive intake unless otherwise shown) as a percentage of total spending

	School A	School B	School C	School D	School E
LEA: type	Shire	Metro-politan	New unitary	Metro-politan	Shire
Other	Selective				Church (RC)
Intake: Free school meals	4%	10%	13%	40%	8%
% special needs	0%	1%	3%	3%	1%
% A*–C GCSE results	99%	54%	47%	33%	58%
Clerical salaries	3.6	4.4	5.5	3.7	4.5
Technician salaries	2.6	2.6	1.9	2.2	1.8
Teacher salaries	71.7	71.1	73.4	72.0	76.4
Supply teachers	1.5	1.9	1.0	2.3	1.2
Midday supervisors	0.6	0.6	0.5	0.4	0.7
Foreign language assistants	0.4	0.2	0.0	0.2	0.7
Site staff	2.0	2.4	0.5	2.3	1.2
Other staffing costs	0.1	1.0	2.2	0.1	0.3
Total staffing	82.5	84.2	85.0	83.2	86.8

drift adds costs for teachers. At current values, a teacher moving incrementally from Point 7 to Point 8 of the CPS receives a September increase equivalent to a pay rise of around 6 per cent. September will also be the first month when any planned curricular and staffing changes will begin, with cost or savings consequences.

The easiest way to put together the teacher salaries element of the new initial budget is by using a payroll spreadsheet or software package, broken down into as much detail as needed, month by month. Such management information tools take staged pay awards as well as September increments in their stride, and can model the pattern of salaries, including on-costs, over the financial year. The school has to meet the employer's contributions to both National Insurance and superannuation for every member of staff, and therefore net salaries need to have been increased by some 16 per cent in the initial budget to ensure that the provision is accurate.

A growing number of schools have reviewed their management teams and taken opportunities to flatten structures, using the resources freed to create more junior responsibility posts or to shift a role across the teacher/non-teacher interface. For example, one teacher responsibility point would add around £1,600 to the annual salary bill, at December 1998 values. Alternatively, it would provide at least six hours a week of Scale 1 clerical assistance for the full school year. Such decisions are likely to be made in light of the potential impact on learning outcomes. Similarly, management costs are worthy of careful and continuing consideration in school because they can increase without any assessment of demonstrable gain for pupils. Above CPS level, practice varies enormously in how much non-contact time is given to holders of promoted posts.

What can be safely assumed is that illnesses will strike a proportion of the staff in the average school in any year. Whilst some will be long term, most illness will be short term and self-certified under statutory sick pay arrangements. Illness strikes individuals differently: every school has its staff who will soldier on and those who will fold at the first sign of being unwell. Staff sickness is a sensitive issue to manage, and the adverse effect upon classes, particularly in examination years, must be addressed by the recruitment of a supply teacher who can cover the work set by the absent member of staff or his or her head of department, at a daily cost of around £130 and with a consequent impact on the budget. Some schools regard the average sickness absence for the staff as a termly or yearly benchmark.

Provision will also be needed for maternity leaves, whether by insurance or not. Every maternity leave costs the school budget up to a net £3,000, depending on the salary point of the absent teacher, because the Statutory Maternity Pay scheme does not fully reimburse the school for the cost of the absent teacher to offset the salary of their temporary replacement. It is good practice, on the basis of annual data, to make provision for such costs in the staffing element of the initial budget by allocating money to cover the statistical likelihood that maternity leaves *will* occur: some schools see 10 per cent of female staff as a prudent figure, depending on the age profile involved.

It is good practice for the school to keep annual records on both issues of sickness and maternity leave, and an allocation in the supply budget can be made for annual long-term sickness absence on the basis of what the trends show. Within the supply budget, an allocation can also be made for spending on planned absence like in-service training and examination board work, most if not all of which will have been matched on the income side with Standards funding and release vouchers.

With support staff, it is important to be sure that both contracted hours and any overtime or additional hours are included in the calculation of total salaries, plus the costs of any benefits like free meals for midday supervisors. In addition, because administrative and technical staff have a pay rise in a different month from teachers, it is likely that AWPU values will not have been increased to cover any projected pay rise falling in the financial year. The necessary funds will often come as a supplementary allocation.

Consideration of costs other than staffing

The initial budget for costs other than staffing normally covers about 20 per cent of total planned expenditure, distributed between premises, and supplies and services to the school. For some headings like energy and water use, examination of consumption figures over previous years will permit an accurate allocation to be made. In this 20 per cent of the school budget which is not consumed by staffing costs there are important questions to be asked. Classroom supplies and services are usually the largest element in supplies and services spending. Yet how are different courses funded, year on year? Does the amount of books and equipment reflect the number of pupils actually opting for the subject at 14 and 16, or its historic level? What proportion of funding is necessary for standstill as distinct from growth? In many schools such questions have led to a review of subject weightings and the allocation of at least some funding on a bidding basis against school Development Plan priorities.

All schools face the problem of upgrading or replacing major items of equipment, and very few have ever made any systematic provision for annual replacement costs. Some schools have concluded that the answer lies in leasing rather than capital purchase. It is possible to buy major equipment (computers, musical instruments, reprographics) on a three-, four- or five-year lease with competitive rates of interest fixed at the outset, plus a maintenance contract over the same period.

Within premises budgets there are well-established methods of conserving energy costs. Most LEAs offer bulk purchase schemes for gas or oil which are highly competitive. Service contracts for boilers and heating systems can still be retained by the LEA. However, other contracts for fire extinguishers, gym equipment and intruder alarm systems may already be delegated and it may be false economy not to fund them.

School furniture often suffers from the same lack of planned replacement funding as equipment. A school is likely to have chairs and tables for 120 per cent of its pupils, and the age and condition of the stock will vary enormously with boisterous use, particularly at breaks and lunch times. Given that school-quality classroom furniture has a planned life of ten years, 10 per cent of total stock per year seems a realistic replacement assumption, that is, around £6,000 per year in a large secondary school. Surroundings have an impact on student behaviour, and like lack of paint, furniture in poor condition has a negative effect on both pupils and staff.

SETTING THE ANNUAL SCHOOL BUDGET

In setting the annual budget, schools will normally have the most accurate predictions for:

- the school's total income for the new financial year;
- the likely budget outturn for the financial year which has just ended;
- the likely school roll next September;
- the curriculum for the remainder of this academic year and for next September, with particular reference in the secondary school to Year 10 GCSE groups and the lower sixth option blocks;
- the teacher and other staffing requirement for the remainder of this academic year and for next September as far as it can be known, with resignations possible until the end of May;

- unexpected changes which were implemented after last September (for example, increased SEN provision) and which are now part of the spending baseline;
- spending implications within the school Development Plan for the new financial year.

Each January, the annual Department for Education and Employment Form 7 exercise allows the school to know exactly what pupil numbers will be used as the basis of the LEA's formula allocation of funds for the new financial year. Because at least 80 per cent of delegated income from the LEA must be driven by pupil numbers, the school will know whether it is facing a cut or increase in real terms because of growth or decline in its pupil roll in comparison to January of the previous year. By March the school will have received its delegated allocation from the LEA.

What matters most are the strategic assumptions behind the cash values. As Davies (1994, p. 329) points out: 'the budget process is a dynamic one with competing forces vying for funds'. For example, have the AWPU values increased by sufficient to fully meet the increased costs associated with the new financial year, of which inflation and the annual pay rise for teachers are the largest elements? If the LEA has been *unable* to increase AWPU levels sufficiently to, for example, fully fund the teachers' pay award, then provision will need to be made for finding the shortfall. Failing to meet the national award in full is not an option, any more than it is with support staff pay awards. In a medium-sized secondary school every 1 per cent of income represents some £30,000 in cash terms. Therefore, if the LEA has had to reduce the value of its delegated funding by 1.5 per cent below the level necessary to fully cover inflation and pay awards, then the school has to find £45,000 from elsewhere in the budget.

The continual problem with cash values in budgets, however, is making common sense of them. To say that a school spends £2.6 million on teachers or £30,000 on electricity, for example, is to use figures which are not easy to relate to. It may make more sense to express the new initial budget to governors and parents in a more accessible way; for example, by relating the budget to each pupil on roll, as in the example from a school in the National Information Exchange (Table 8.7).

Table 8.7 Budget

	£
Income per pupil:	2,050
Spending per pupil:	2,009
Difference per pupil:	41

However, the analysis can be taken further in order to make even more sense of the spending plans in the new initial budget. The budget which is going to spend £2,009 per pupil can also be analysed (Table 8.8).

Table 8.8   In this financial year, the amount the school plans to spend for every pupil

	plus	and
£82 on clerical salaries	£30 on maintenance	£6 on furniture
£56 on technician salaries	£12 on grounds maintenance	£67 on books and equipment
£1,407 on teacher salaries	£19 on electricity	£58 on administration
£28 on supply teachers	£15 on gas	£8 on staff training
£11 on midday supervisors	£60 on rates	£8 on equipment
£2 on foreign language assistants	£8 on water and sewerage	£7 on phones and postage
£39 on caretaking	£47 on cleaning contract	£25 on public examination fees
£14 on other staffing costs		

Such an analysis of the spending plans in the new initial budget will generate new questions as well as answering others about the school's priorities. By placing the average figures for the LEA as a whole, or for 'similar' schools, alongside the school's spending in each category, a wider comparison of priorities is also made possible and lessons can be learnt about where scope for future review might lie.

In setting the initial budget for the new financial year, it is obviously desirable not to commit the entire income to spending, in order to allow for costs which might arise unexpectedly. At the same time, it makes sense to spend as much as possible of the available resources on the pupils on roll, because they are the intended beneficiaries of the delegated funds from the LEA. As a result, schools are under considerable pressure not to accumulate massive reserves which could arguably be put to better use in current spending. In practice, however, a typical school budget profile of annual results is most likely to show that some financial years were in planned surplus and others were in planned deficit.

BUDGET MONITORING AND REVIEW

The school's running view of how the budget is operating can be regularly informed by the monthly monitoring reports of income and expenditure, which will be automatically produced by the school's financial information software and which senior management (for example, the head and the bursar or equivalent) can keep under review on a regular basis. An hour a week is sufficient for the head, deputy head or bursar to keep a management overview of the budget without becoming overburdened by the detail of particular transactions.

It is likely that around October the school management will have asked governors to agree some *mid-year corrections* as resources within the initial budget were vired from one heading to another in response to trends in spending. Many governing bodies have a budget policy which will limit such virements to a certain sum without approval, or which identify certain principles for mid-year corrections; for example, resources can be moved *within* staffing headings (i.e. from teachers to non-teachers), but should never be moved *between* budget headings (i.e. staffing and premises).

It should also be recognized that the process of monitoring and review is inconsistently applied in many schools, particularly in terms of checking the relationship between intention and outcome; for example, what has been the actual effect of increased investment in special needs staffing? As Knight (1997, p. 148) reports: 'these processes are often quite superficial, sometimes invisible.' However, the spread of national comparative statistics from the Department for Education and Employment, the Chartered Institute of Public Finance and Accountancy, and the National Information Exchange, amongst others, is significant. In addition, the provision to each individual school of an annual comparative performance report from the Office for Standards in Education (OFSTED) is important. It is becoming harder for schools to avoid embarking upon the process of review, with the increased accountability which arises from the national programme of OFSTED inspections.

ISSUES OF EFFICIENCY

Attention to the detail of budgeting is important, but there is need to consider some of the wider issues underlying patterns of spending including attention to data which might generally indicate the efficiency with which the school is using available resources in the current financial year. *Efficiency* is defined clearly in Part 6.3 of the OFSTED *Guidance on the Inspection of Secondary Schools*: 'An efficient school makes good use of all its available resources to achieve the best possible educational outcomes for all its pupils – and in doing so provides excellent value for money' (OFSTED, 1995, p. 121). The *Guidance* also explains that judgements by the inspecting team about the efficiency of the school will be based on the extent to which:

> educational developments are supported through careful financial planning; effective use is made of staff, accommodation and learning resources; there is efficient financial control and school administration; the school provides value for money in terms of the educational standards achieved, and the quality of education provided in relation to the school's context and income.
>
> (ibid.)

Reality is likely to be more complex, however, as Levačić and Glover (1994) point out in their study of 66 inspection reports. Largely because of the lack of any agreed model of school performance which would show that a given input of teachers would lead to a given output of examination results, inspectors tend to concentrate on *what can be found* in a school, that is, on the school's decision-making and management systems as a measure of its efficiency, and on unit cost per pupil as an indicator of value for money.

There will be year-on-year arrangements in place for ensuring that the head, senior staff and governors keep abreast of developments within departments, whether by a formal programme of annual review, the attachment of senior management team members to subject teams or simply the analysis of annual development plans. However, financial management is likely to involve the regular monitoring of some key efficiency data, at least on an annual basis. In September each year the deployment of the teaching staff will have been planned and implemented. The allocation of non-contact time and remission from teaching will have led to at least three measures of the use of staff resources: contact ratio, pupil–teacher ratio and the proportion of the school budget spent on teachers.

Contact ratio (CR) expresses the relationship between the total number of periods actually taught in the school's curriculum and the total number of periods theoretically available if every teacher was teaching for every period of the timetable. In the demanding business of teaching, the CR is held to a level which is judged as reasonable to ensure consistently effective teaching over the secondary school year. This means in practice that all secondary teachers have a proportion of their time which is designated as non-contact or 'free' from teaching. So, if in a large secondary school 6,300 periods of teaching were carried out by the staff whilst 8,000 periods were theoretically available per timetable cycle, then the CR would be 78.75 per cent. The situation in primary schools is very different, with only the head and deputy head likely to have non-contact time.

Pupil–teacher ratio (PTR) expresses the relationship between the total roll of the school and the total teacher complement employed. So if there were 1,200 pupils on roll and 73 full-time equivalent teachers in post, the school's overall PTR would be 16.44, that is, there would be 16.44 pupils for every teacher employed. Pupil–teacher ratios can also be calculated for particular ages of pupils, and kept under more detailed review: broadly, as the pupils increase in age the PTR will be expected to fall, reflecting the curriculum pattern and the planned reduction of class sizes. So a typical Year 7 PTR might be 28 pupils to every teacher, with 24 to every teacher at the beginning of Key Stage 4 and 12 students to a teacher in the sixth form.

Budget proportion spent on teachers (BPT) is one of the key pieces of information shared between schools in the National Information Exchange. It is calculated by expressing the full teacher salary bill as a percentage of total expenditure by the school. Therefore, an annual salary cost of £2.6 million on total spending of £3.4 million would create a BPT of 76.5 per cent.

There are no national benchmarks to indicate what the most effective levels of the three measures would be, and local management permits each school to set what it judges to be the most efficient levels. Broadly, an 11–18 secondary school may want to hold its budget proportion spent on teachers to a target close to 70 per cent, its overall PTR to around 16 pupils per teacher, and its CR in the range from 75 per cent to 79 per cent. For a school reviewing its efficiency, the starting-point is likely to be that those responsible collect such data systematically year on year, and keep them under review. In carrying out this process, the school will have evidence to demonstrate the OFSTED requirement that *effective use is made of staff.*

IMPLICATIONS FOR TEACHING AND LEARNING

The beginning of this chapter explained that, through the move to a system of self-managing schools with delegated budgets in the 1980s, the government of the day sought to achieve greater efficiency and effectiveness within the education service. That process of structural reform in England and Wales has been replicated in parts of the USA, Australia, New Zealand and elsewhere, as public education systems have devolved responsibilities and resources to local management level. The assumption behind such structural devolution must have been that the changes would lead to improved efficiency and effectiveness at school level, not just in the use of resources but also in improved teaching and learning outcomes. After all, teaching and learning is the core business of schools, and a significant and positive impact upon standards might be expected to justify the significant upheavals associated with structural reform: 'in the final analysis, the case for self-management must be based on benefits for students in terms of gains in learning outcomes' (Caldwell and Spinks, 1992, p. 57).

It is undoubtedly true that LMS has driven down the *unit cost* of delivering an education to pupils. Locally managed schools are certainly more efficient at using resources than central bureaucracies, not least because of the sense of scrutiny and ownership created by being directly accountable for service quality. An illustration of this is the deputy head who, on taking over responsibility for a taxi contract servicing a shared sixth form site, discovered that overcharging for non-existent journeys had gone on for years. A monthly invoice had been submitted to the local education office, who had paid it without question because they were only responsible for paying the bill, not for the quality of what was provided. Six months later an improved service was operating at half the cost, with a different company.

It is also true that LMS has permitted more varied and adventurous resource mixes than was ever apparent under LEA directed spending. Schools have learned how to benefit from marginal switches of spending in, say, support staff rather than teachers or classroom decoration rather than furniture. As a result, schools have been able to plan investment over more than one financial year in major projects like information technology, without having to wait for LEA support. Schools have also gained experience that significant funding for particular initiatives such as the achievement of Technology College status undoubtedly enhances classroom practice and learning outcomes.

But has LMS had a generally positive impact upon teaching and learning outcomes? Have schools raised the quality of learning outcomes as they have become more self-managing? That is an extraordinarily difficult question to answer with any certainty (see Caldwell, Chapter 2 in this volume).

There is no doubt that LMS has significantly altered the work of the head and senior staff in schools. But it has gone further. There are schools where local management and its associated culture has taken root, with heads of teaching departments holding significant delegated budgets and having the power to vire funds between, say, classroom equipment, furniture and staff training. In such schools, many staff participate actively in the local management of school resources.

However, in many other schools in the UK, LMS has yet to transform the professional culture of the staffroom: teachers continue to be paid monthly in the same way, their heads of department continue to oversee books and equipment, and in their daily classroom lives and interactions with pupils little else has changed. As a result, LMS can seem something which 'management' does, as distinct from those working in the classroom. It therefore becomes difficult to track any significant changes in pedagogy and classroom practice which are attributable to the growth of devolved resourcing. I believe the best that can be said is that there *is* linkage of some kind between LMS and improved student outcomes, but the relationship is not a straightforward or demonstrably causal one. In my experience, it is most likely to be that: *local management encourages schools to make more efficient, effective and innovative arrangements for the physical environment for learning, for the resources available in the classroom and for the quality of the teaching which is then likely to occur.*

NOTE

Comparative data used in this chapter is drawn from material published annually to participants in the National Information Exchange. Further details can be obtained from the author at Harrogate Grammar School, Arthurs Avenue, Harrogate, North Yorkshire HG2 0DZ

REFERENCES

Caldwell, B. J. and Spinks, J. M. (1992) *Leading the Self-Managing School*, London, Falmer Press.

Davies, B. (1994) Managing resources, in T. Bush and J. West-Burnham (eds), *The Principles of Educational Management*, Harlow, Longman.

Knight, B. (1997) Budget analysis and construction, in M. Preedy, R. Glatter and R. Levačić (eds), *Educational Management: Strategy, Quality and Resources*, Buckingham, Open University Press.

Levačić, R. and Glover, D. (1994) *OFSTED Assessment of Schools' Efficiency*, Milton Keynes, Open University.

McAleese, K. (1996) *Managing the Margins*, Leicester, Secondary Heads Association.

OFSTED (1995) *Guidance on the Inspection of Secondary Schools*, London, Office for Standards in Education.

9

THE ROLE OF THE BURSAR

Fergus O'Sullivan, Angela Thody and Elizabeth Wood

INTRODUCTION

This chapter discusses the contribution of the bursar to the management of finance and resources, particularly in schools, but also with reference to colleges of further education. The title 'bursar' is a generic term for the person who administers or manages educational resources and leads the support services in schools. This is primarily a non-teaching role that is well established in independent schools but is relatively new in the state sector. The International Educational Leadership Centre (IELC) began an exploratory study of bursarship in 1996, with assistance from the National Bursars' Association and the Teacher Training Agency. The research design used case studies to explore the background and life history of bursars and develop a holistic picture of the bursar at work. The informants of this indicative research were an opportunity sample of 62 bursars who were attending the MBA programme from schools, mainly secondary but primary and cross-phase schools were also represented. Job descriptions and curriculum vitae (CVs) were analysed, structured interviews were held, bursars were observed in a small sample of schools, and focus groups discussed bursarship in schools of the twenty-first century. The study concentrated on the period in schools and colleges between 1986 and 1998 and on those institutions located in England and Wales.

Since the end of the 1980s, when power began to be devolved to the site level, there has been an increase in the appointment of bursars in state schools. In general the role evolved from that of the school secretary or resulted from the replacement of a deputy headteacher at a lower salary rate. Although their job titles vary, the bursar's main responsibility is to ensure that all non-teaching functions are effectively carried out, freeing teaching staff to concentrate on curricular issues. However, this role has become much wider as schools take up more of the options of self-management that come with site-based management. Currently, they manage a growing number of support staff and come into contact with a wide variety of people during their working day. The bursar's role has also been evolving in many schools to include the management of all the school's resources and some are now full members of the senior management team (SMT). Because of their diverse backgrounds, they have brought different qualifications to their wide-ranging jobs, and need a variety of knowledge, skills and competencies.

In schools with successful experience of site-based management, the appointment of a bursar able to work at the levels of manager and leader is a significant factor. Bursars' responsibilities for administration, finance, human resource management (HRM), facilities, information and communications technology (ICT), marketing and teaching and learning can involve them in all areas of resource management at all levels of operation as listed in Table 9.1. It is, therefore, important that the school investigates the type of bursar it needs to match its management, operational and ethos requirements. A bursar operating as a school business manager, will not fit well into a school that needs an administration manager to function at a purely clerical level.

Working as a school business manager, however, the bursar can plan the future requirements for support staff and train them appropriately. Operation at this strategic level in schools requires an understanding of teaching and learning, full participation in SMT meetings and a substantial liaison role with the governing body. In summary they would:

- provide comprehensive financial and management information;
- expand the marketing, promotion and fund-raising capabilities of the school;
- manage all clerical and contract staff to provide effective and efficient support for the school;
- ensure that the school is a safe and user-friendly environment for all staff and students.

Within these areas they would be managing contracts, generating income and monitoring the budget. Their knowledge of the detail of the school's finances would enable them to manage costs efficiently and equitably and to provide information to the SMT and teachers at all levels, especially those acting as budget-holders.

The development of the bursar as school business manager explores and reaffirms the democratic values of the worth of the individual, the need for freedom and intelligent inquiry and the responsibility of stakeholders to discover communal ways of achieving practical ends (Maxcy, 1995). School business managers have a central role in the transformation of

Table 9.1   Bursars' responsibilities and levels of operation

Responsibility area	Administration	Management	Leadership
Administration	Prepare and produce records and returns Ensure the adequacy and safe operation of school transport Ensure the adequate and efficient provision of food services Ensure the maximum level of security consonant with the ethos of the school Maintain pupil records including examination results, teachers records, exclusions and survey results of prospective pupils	Manage the administrative, clerical and other support functions of the school Manage information and communication systems Manage legal, public and statutory matters Ensure the continuing availability of supplies, services and equipment Review management information systems Manage risk/fire control, safe systems of work and medical aid Manage all support contracts to the school Ensure conformity with health and safety legislation Analyse and report trends in pupil numbers, examination results and exclusions	Participate in strategic planning Initiate and manage change and improvement in pursuit of the school's goals Develop management information sysems
Finance	Keep accurate financial accounts Comply with sound principles of school finance	Maximize income through lettings and additional activities Manage the budget cycle Analyse costs to ensure value for money Report accounting, auditing and financial information Manage cash, investments and credit control	Evaluate and plan the budget Develop sound financial systems and practice Develop financial strategy and planning
HRM	Keep accurate staff records Adminster personnel remuneration Follow clear and fair principles of recruitment, retention and discipline	Supervise and deploy support staff Manage staff contracts Manage supply staff cover Appoint and induct support staff Secure good labour relations through individual and collective negotiations	Appraise and develop support staff Develop good labour relations
Premises	Keep records of equipment, furnishings, school maintenance Follow sound practices in real estate management and grounds maintenance	Ensure the safe maintenance and operation of all buildings Manage support contracts Supervise planning and construction services	Establish and monitor a site security policy

Responsibility area	Administration	Management	Leadership
ICT	Keep records of computer hardware and software	Manage maintenance of the computer system Ensure compliance with legal requirements for ITC	Develop the school's computerized administration system
Marketing	Maintain positive relationships among all members of staff	Manage support staff to promote the school positively to all stakeholders Manage marketing matters	Develop relationships with community and business to secure support for school Create positive relationships among all members of staff Develop supportive relationships with parents
Teaching and learning	Keep accurate records of learning resources and equipment	Maintain learning resources	Articulate the curriculum philosophy of the school Teach pupils when required

schools into organizations working in supportive cross-functional teams, including support staff, thus concentrating on acquiring the optimum level of resources and fully exploring the best use of such resources to facilitate pupil learning.

THE EMERGENCE OF THE BURSAR IN LITERATURE

During the 1990s, as a direct consequence of the increased site-based resource management responsibilities brought about by the Education Acts of 1986 and 1988, there has been a growth in the use of the post of bursar or its equivalent in state schools. Harrold and Hough (1988, p. 14) suggested that 'the financial responsibilities [in schools] will be so time-consuming that it cannot be doubted that the appointment of a bursar with specialist accountancy qualifications and/or experience will be essential'. Headteachers and their deputies, in particular, were concerned that the increased workload of local school management prevented them from concentrating on leading teaching and learning in schools (Emerson and Goddard, 1993) and, as governors were free to appoint teaching or support staff in line with the school's needs, they were able to look outside education for managers with financial and business backgrounds to take responsibility for resources and the larger numbers of support staff in the schools (Bush, Coleman and

Glover, 1993). The person that was appointed to this educational resource management role has usually taken the job title of bursar.

By 1992, Bowe, Ball and Gold quote a secondary school headteacher who stresses the importance of this role:

> They are administering the budget and they are controlling finances. And that includes equipment and the school's and the administration's systems, and all the non-teaching staff, so they would be making recommendations about the efficient use of resources, they will be looking at not just the servicing end of things – what do we do to get this equipment repaired – but what equipment should we have and who will use what. There would be someone in charge of all the cleaning and caretaking who would report to them. They will be in charge of all the staff in the office, and their job will be devising efficient structures, of people and for administration. To make the whole school run efficiently and effectively, in order to leave teaching staff free to actually get on with teaching.
>
> (Bowe, Ball and Gold, 1992, p. 154)

From 1989, schools that opted to become grant maintained (GM) were delegated further control of their own resource management and financial systems and began to operate as small businesses (Davies and Anderson, 1992). Many of these schools made it a priority to appoint a bursar as soon as they had greater control of their budgets (Bush, Coleman and Glover, 1993). Grant maintained schools were, then, able to take advantage of their new managerial freedom to make more imaginative use of support staff both inside and outside the classroom (Bush and Middlewood, 1997). Furthermore, Evetts (in 1996) identified the bursar's role in generating income and their contribution to the new commercial imperative driving schools. As the role evolved, many bursars took on supervisory and leadership responsibilities (Mortimore, Mortimore and Thomas, 1995, p. 53; Nathan, 1996) and were involved to various degrees with the senior management team (Hall, 1997; Thomas and Martin, 1994; 1996; Wallace and Hall, 1994).

The Mortimore, Mortimore and Thomas's (1995) study of associate staff in a number of schools catalogued bursars' management responsibilities, which included administration, finance, premises, HRM, income generation and marketing. Wood, Thody and O'Sullivan (1999) showed that health and safety is also a remit of bursars. Thomas and Martin (1996) discussed the appointment of an administrator, where the school benefited from receiving prompt, specific and detailed information for its management decision-making as well as enabling deputy headteachers to concentrate on teaching and learning responsibilities. Mortimore, Mortimore and Thomas (1995) indicated that bursars could also free middle managers from some management/administration work and O'Sullivan, Thody and Wood

(2000) describe how bursars are contributing to strategic management and decision-making.

Thus, by the end of the twentieth century, bursars can be said to be contributing significantly to the management of schools, reflecting Dean's (1993, p. 108) list of four school management tasks:

1) Oversee the administrative work of the school (including marketing and human resource management).
2) Control the school finances.
3) Be responsible for the building and environment.
4) Ensure conformity with health and safety legislation.

THE BURSAR AND RESOURCE MANAGEMENT

The resource management process can be conceptualized as a cycle covering both strategic and operational levels. Often, at school level, the budget cycle is regarded as the principal resource management process, starting at the point of receipt of the budget share figure and concluding at the reconciliation of outturn budgets. In reality, however, most schools are involved in capturing additional income and must carry out extensive analysis of the balance of their expenditure at some stage. If schools consider all the inputs to the Evaluation, Analysis and Aims stages illustrated in Figure 9.1 they will be in a much better position to understand and adjust their resource management strategy to get the best from the opportunities of increased devolution of resources and decision-making to site level. In schools with a high degree of autonomy, the bursar is usually best placed to gather, analyse and present budget data to inform the resource management decision-making process.

Levels of school autonomy and the role of the bursar

Bursarship is a relatively new, but developing, role in state schools (Wood, Thody and O'Sullivan, 1998). In this sector there is no established career route into bursarship and schools have appointed from commercial, administrative, armed forces and educational backgrounds (Harrold and Hough, 1988). Although most bursars were appointed to fulfil mainly financial posts, some were upgraded from administrative posts and the role of the bursar has expanded to cover many other responsibilities (Emerson and Goddard, 1993). Bursars, therefore, bring experience to their post that ranges from detailed understanding of budget and resource management to almost no knowledge of this area but a contribution to other areas such as administration or marketing and income generation. The level of operation can also vary widely from administration by the ex-school secretary to leadership and management by a company executive. Thus the diversity of

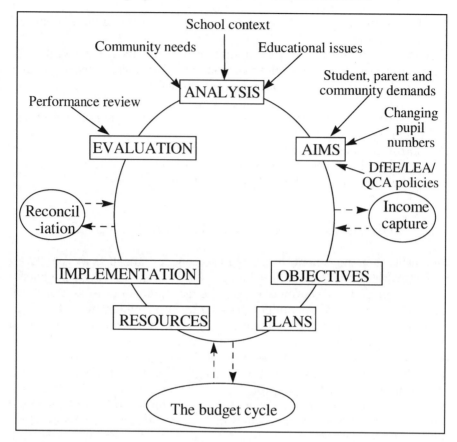

Figure 9.1 The resource management process

backgrounds has varied the emphasis on the areas and levels of bursars' responsibilities in accordance with the individual needs of each school and the type of person appointed.

The link between the needs of the school and the level of operation of the bursar is illustrated in Figure 9.2. Bursars' responsibilities at administrative, management and leadership levels reflect the degree of autonomy enjoyed or aspired to by the school. Administration is defined as consisting of routine work, usually carried out alone, such as organizing and filing, management includes decision-making and supervision of others, whilst leadership is characterized by strategic thinking, policy formulation, evaluation and review (West-Burnham, 1997). The top part of Figure 9.2 shows that schools are operating on a continuum between dependency and autonomy. District managed schools are exemplified by those under special measures in England and by some US School Boards. Locally managed schools are characterized as those managed in England by LEAs and those

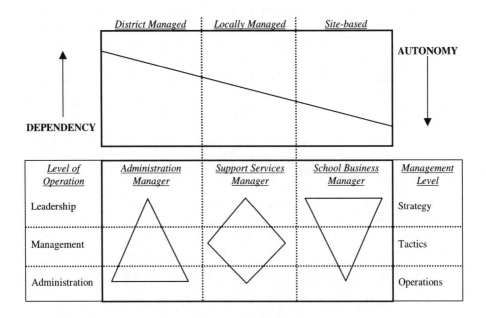

Figure 9.2   Levels of autonomy in school management

in some Australian states such as Victoria. Site-based schools are found in England's city technology colleges, grant maintained schools, 1989–99, and in the independent sector as well as charter schools in the USA.

The lower part of Figure 9.2 illustrates the level of operation and management of the bursar best suited to the level of autonomy/dependency. District managed schools need Administration Managers who spend the majority of their time on operational and functional tasks, but who can assume some supervisory and management responsibilities. Such bursars are focusing largely on providing support systems for the learning core of the school (the 'organizational support' circle in Levačić's model, see Chapter 1 in this volume).

Support Service Managers are found in schools with more autonomy and less district control. These bursars operate mainly at the managerial level but their role also incorporates administration and leadership elements. This level requires the bursar to have a greater understanding of the educational business of teaching and learning, thus including the 'learning core' with the organizational support circle.

Schools with site-based management and a high degree of autonomy are likely to need School Business Managers who can think strategically and operate at a leadership level. These people lead their own teams, manage outsourced contracts, are full members of the senior management team, and analyse and evaluate data for strategic decision-making. As well as providing organizational support and understanding the learning core, the bursar at this level has an increasing role to play in the interface between the school and the external environment. This role requires a strategic and operational relationship across all three circles of Levačić's model. The model enables senior leaders, having determined their actual or desired level of autonomy, to specify the appropriate mix of strategic leadership and operational administration responsibilities of their site-level resource manager.

THE ROLE OF THE BURSAR

The IELC's research into bursars reveals that their roles are as diverse as the schools in which they work. Observations and job descriptions depict working days that cover a variety of activities requiring a wide range of skills in many areas. An analysis of the job descriptions indicates that the bursar's role covers six main areas of responsibility (Figure 9.3).

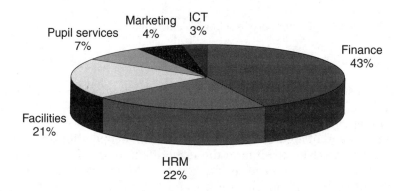

Figure 9.3   Bursars' areas of responsibility from the job descriptions

Almost half of bursars' work is linked to finance, with facilities and HRM together accounting for a further 43 per cent of their responsibilities. Information and communication technology, pupil services, and marketing feature in some job descriptions, but are minor functions of the role. A range of activities is listed within each of these areas encompassing both operational and strategic responsibilities. Additionally over half the bursars act as clerk to the governors and a quarter serve on governing body committees.

In comparison, observations of bursars at work demonstrate that routine clerical work (e.g. filing, drafting letters and reports) are the most frequent activity (Figure 9.4). Of the responsibilities evident in the job descriptions, finance, HRM and facilities work again take up the bulk of the working day. Bursars are also working on aspects of curriculum and learning such as the purchase and organization of cognitive acceleration programmes and integrated learning systems, and the deployment of classroom support staff. They are particularly involved with recording and issuing test/examination results and organizing visits and trips. Marketing and ICT take up the smallest amount of time. The job descriptions and observations, therefore, indicate that bursars are playing an important role in the school's resource management and in state schools some are beginning to play a part in teaching and learning by being, for example, form tutors or teaching NVQ business studies.

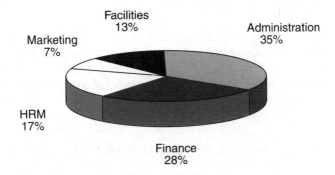

Figure 9.4   Bursars' activities from observations

The job descriptions provide a wealth of detail on the activities of the bursar within their areas of responsibility and these findings will be discussed in the next section.

Financial management

Financial management is an important aspect of resource management that encompasses and impinges on all responsibility areas. It is, therefore, not surprising to find financial responsibilities, along with a wide range of other activities and levels of operation, included in every job description (Figure 9.5).

Every bursar's job description requires them to maintain the school's accounts, although for many it is a supervisory role. They are involved in all aspects of purchasing, administer the payroll system and ensure adequate insurance coverage for the school. They are also crucial in providing advice to governors and the SMT on budget issues and cost management, as well as being the source of information for any financial queries.

A further important role for bursars is income generation. They are in a vital position as the school's facilities managers and, through their

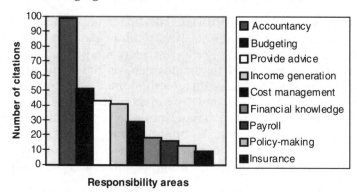

Figure 9.5   Financial responsibilities of bursars

interaction with external organizations and stakeholders, are able to match the needs of others with any spare capacity that the school may have. With the level of knowledge that bursars have on the financial health of schools, it is perhaps surprising that only 12 per cent of job descriptions expect them to become involved more generally in policy-making decisions.

Human resource management

A key resource in schools is its teaching and support staff and 80 per cent of the budget is spent on them. It is, therefore, crucial that this resource is efficiently and effectively employed to provide best value for money. As resource managers, bursars have a strong involvement in HRM at administration, management and leadership levels, and HRM is included in all the job descriptions surveyed and identified as the second largest responsibility area (Figure 9.6).

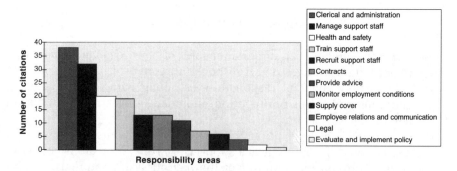

Figure 9.6   HRM responsibilities of bursars

The largest single area of responsibility involves personnel administration for all staff with particular emphasis on maintaining confidential school records. As managers of the school's personnel records, bursars have access to data that indicates employment trends in schools and can provide vital management information to the SMT and governors. Fifty per cent of the job descriptions feature responsibilities for health and safety and 25 per cent include supporting the governing body in devising and implementing the school's HRM policy.

As leaders of the support staff, bursars are expected to play a major role in recruiting, deploying, training and managing their staff. Seventy-five per cent of bursars manage and deploy support staff and 60 per cent are responsible for their training and development. Bursars' roles with teaching staff are generally administrative and concentrate on recruitment procedures and issuing contracts. Some are expected to supply specialist advice, monitor employment conditions and provide supply cover.

Bursars are also leaders of a large group of staff in the school and as such can influence the effectiveness of this staff through induction, training, communication of the school's values and ethos, and their development as flexible and responsive contributors to the school's learning and teaching environment.

Facilities management

> [The bursar is] in charge of everything other than the learning inter-
> face. School can be represented as one class in one classroom with
> one teacher. On first sight the bursar has nothing to do with it but s/he
> is responsible for building, maintenance, heating and lighting, provi-
> sion of desks and chairs, purchasing of books, paying salary, collect-
> ing fees [for] independent schools, flogging uniform, feeding children
> in the classroom. If none of these happen there is no learning. If even
> one doesn't happen learning is damaged.
>
> (From interview with bursar, grant maintained school, 1997)

The above quote highlights how important facilities management is to the smooth delivery of teaching in schools. Facilities management is included in 80 per cent of bursars' job descriptions and involves a range of responsibilities linked to the site in general, buildings and equipment (Figure 9.7).

Facilities management is one area where the job descriptions increase the bursar's contribution to management and leadership and reduces their involvement in administration. Responsibilities range from administration of records to health and safety, maintenance and development of the site and its use.

Bursars are expected to manage the security of the site and supervise contracts for cleaning and building and grounds maintenance. They also ensure that school equipment is maintained. Twelve and a half per cent of the job descriptions charge bursars with maximizing the use of the premises through timetabling rooms and/or promoting the school to outside agencies. Although this is an area normally seen as the responsibility of

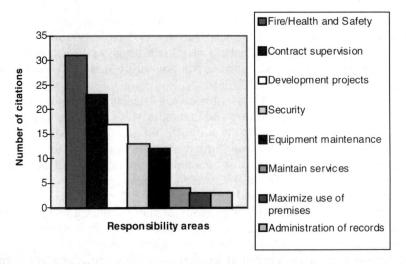

Figure 9.7   Facilities management responsibilities of bursars

teachers, it can be seen as a wise use of a resource manager who has intimate knowledge of the requirements and use of the buildings and grounds. Bursars also liaise with contractors and manage the process of capital and development projects.

'To arrange building development projects, inviting tenders for maintenance and services. To ensure that contractors perform duties according to the contract. To renew contracts and recommend termination or renewal to the headteacher' (Job description, locally managed school, 1997). Contract specification, tendering and supervision feature in both facilities and human resource management. This is an area which is likely to grow under the 'Fair Funding' initiative as more decision-making is devolved to the site level enabling schools to match their resources to their own teaching and learning requirements.

Although LEAs have offered a 'buy back' option to schools, they cannot be as immediately responsive to the needs of a single school as a bursar who, from a position within the senior management of that school, can assess the school's immediate needs.

Other resource management responsibilities

Although finance, human and facilities resource management are major responsibilities for bursars, these are only three aspects of supporting the learning environment. Information and communication technology is gaining in significance as a teaching tool, pupils require direct and indirect services, and without positive marketing the school will not attract the pupils on which its income is calculated.

Information and communication technology

As resource managers, bursars set up and administer networks both for teaching (e.g. 'SuccessMaker') and administrative purposes (e.g. 'SIMS'). 'To take responsibility for the management of comprehensive information systems, participating in developments to ensure that the changing needs of professional staff and the school are met' (Job description, locally managed school, 1997). As leaders of support staff and systems managers, however, their main responsibility in this area is to develop the use of computers for administration and to organize staff training for those who use the systems. They act as the point of contact for technicians from outside, liaise with those inside the school and apply data protection legislation.

Pupils

Most references to the provision of resources for pupils are found in facilities management, particularly the maintenance of premises and equipment. The bursar is, therefore, providing indirect services, which may not motivate pupils but would certainly demotivate them if they are not correctly resourced ('hygiene' factors in Herzberg, 1966). Such pupil services also include managing the provision of teaching aids such as photocopying and supervising travel and catering arrangements. In particular the provision of a catering service which pupils and teachers want to use is an important responsibility for bursars. When such a service is effectively resourced and responsive to its customers, it not only increases income to the school but also promotes the school as a community as more staff and students opt to stay in school during the lunch break and, in some schools, for breakfast.

A further service operated within the school office, and evident in 7 per cent of the job descriptions analysed, is the administration of admissions, pupil records and examinations. Although the keeping of records is a routine clerical operation, with the right software and computer network it is possible for the bursar to maintain a system that provides a wide range of information with minimum effort.

'Monitor and report on admissions and other pupil administrative matters. Supervise staff and pupil administrative duties. Maintain pupil records. Prepare printing and distribution of college termly calendar. Complete DfEE returns related to college pupils . . . Attend to examination entries' (Job description, grant maintained school, 1997). Direct contact with pupils is acknowledged as an aspect of the bursar's role in 17 per cent of the job descriptions and includes mentoring and fostering and maintaining good relations with students. Recent research is indicating that contact with pupils is becoming increasingly important. Some bursars are involved in library and resource management and even teaching.

Marketing

Seventy-five per cent of bursars' job descriptions surveyed include respon-sibility for income generation although there are also other marketing and promotional activities assigned to bursars (Figure 9.8). As schools have not only had to attract pupils in the face of competition from other schools but also supplement their income from alternative sources, marketing has be-come an important aspect of school management that impinges on the level of the school's operational budget. The bursar as resource manager and leader of support staff is on the front line, both in promoting the school through the responses and attitudes of line-managed staff and in dealing with resources linked to pupil numbers and extra income generation. Less than 25 per cent of job descriptions, however, recognize the importance of the bursar to the school's marketing strategy.

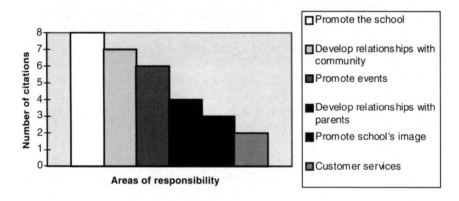

Figure 9.8   Marketing responsibilities of bursars

Bursars' levels of operation

The data from the interviews, job descriptions and bursars' CVs enable an analysis to be carried out of bursars' statuses and levels of operation. Although all act as advisers to the senior management team, only around half the sample are full members. The relationship with governors is closer, however, par-ticularly in giving advice and assistance to committees and the governing body as a whole. Many bursars also act as clerk to the governing body.

The observation field notes were also analysed for evidence of the bursars' level of operation and these show an equal emphasis on administration and management with leadership activities only accounting for an average of 7 per cent of their time (Figure 9.9). However, this figure hides a differential ranging from no time spent on leadership at all to as much as 25 per cent of the day. From this analysis it would appear that most bursars are currently working at the level of 'Support Services Manager' identified in Figure 9.2.

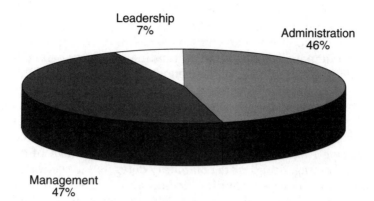

Figure 9.9   Bursars' levels of operation during observations
Source: Wood, Thody and O'Sullivan (1998)

RESOURCE MANAGEMENT IN FURTHER EDUCATION

Although the focus of the research reported here has been on the school sector, many of the issues raised resonate with resource managers in further education (FE) colleges. The findings of our research with schools have shown a high degree of internal consistency between the various aspects of the research and responses from practitioners, thus indicating that the research has considerable face validity. The writers were, therefore, confident that the main outcomes were likely to be relevant in the post-compulsory sector and extended the research to include the role of the bursar in FE colleges. This extension was achieved through a limited number of additional interviews in such organizations. The aim of this aspect of the research was to explore the different context rather than replicate the earlier investigation. Thus, the preliminary findings must be regarded as speculative.

Prior to the visit, a letter was sent to FE resource managers explaining the aim of the research, the question prompts for the interviews, the resource management cycle (Figure 9.1) and a table listing the main areas of responsibility of school resource managers (Table 9.1). The focus of the visits was a semi-structured interview with the resource manager covering such aspects as the organization of resource management in the college, the resource managers' functions and tasks, their involvement in strategic planning, relationships with student outcomes and any general issues for the future. The background and context of the college, including the physical site, were also noted.

This fieldwork suggests that college resource managers come from a similarly wide range of backgrounds as those of school bursars, although there is more likelihood of their having had experience in the teaching side before moving into management. It is much more common, however, for college resource managers to be at vice-principal level and to act as clerk to the corporation board. In this sense they are more in line with bursars of independent schools. The funding of colleges since incorporation, and indeed even before this, is much more complicated than that of schools as it comes from a variety of sources (traditional post-16 courses, vocational qualifications, professional, adult and leisure provision) and across the student experience (enrolment, progression and outcome). The tendency, therefore, is for the resource manager to be deeply concerned with strategic issues of corporate finance and a huge load of day-to-day finance processing. Budgets are commonly delegated to section heads and the connection between funding income and student outcome can be rather tenuous, though colleges are becoming much more aware of such issues.

The functions of marketing, premises management, HRM, ICT and student services are very similar to those in schools and the resource management process illustrated in Figure 9.1 is identical except for the funding and quality assurance bodies. The detail of their management, however, is different in character as FE colleges usually have more access to and experience of resource management issues for a longer period, even though they have been incorporated for a shorter time than many GM schools. The impression from our exploratory visits is that there is more recognition of the role of the resource manager in FE but that, again, very little research has been carried out in this area.

THE IMPLICATIONS OF FAIR FUNDING FOR THE ROLE OF THE BURSAR

The introduction of Fair Funding in 1999, which delegated a further £1 billion to schools for services, has impacted on both LM and GM schools. Former GM schools were brought back in line with LM schools and, in terms of funding, experienced reduced operating budgets, and reporting responsibilities returned to LEAs. Locally managed schools have been given increased budgets and responsibility for: building repairs and maintenance; minor capital works; school meals; central support services; ancillary services; curriculum, advisory and training services and school library services, with the option to buy back into LEA services.

Alongside the introduction of Fair Funding, the government is intent on raising standards in schools. As in the late 1980s, its 1998 Green Paper, *Teachers Meeting the Challenge of Change*, recognizes the crucial role and increased level of responsibilities of the headteacher along with the need to spread the load amongst the senior staff: 'not all of these tasks need be carried out by the headteacher . . . [they] should be prepared to delegate tasks to other members of staff – both teachers and others – in order to free up time for their key duties' (DFEE, 1998, para. 77).

The bursar is seen as one of those who can relieve some of the head-teacher's burden as evidenced in the House of Commons Education and Employment Committee (HoC) report which states that school bursars are a: 'seriously under-utilised resource. Their potential contribution as senior managers has significant implications for the future role of headteacher' (HoC, 1998, para. 45).

As resource manager, the bursar is in a position to manage the transition to Fair Funding in an informed manner, thus enabling the headteacher and senior teaching team to lead the developments in curriculum and learning. On one perspective, bursars from the former GM sector have the appropriate experience to provide the senior management team with detailed budget scenarios and information on the effects of reduced income and organize the new reporting systems to the LEA. From the other side, the LM bursar is used to exploring potential benefits of outsourcing services versus providing them in-house or buying back from the LEA. Liaison between ex-GM and LM bursars during the transition would have been beneficial to both parties as one group (LM) has understanding of how best to work with their LEA, whilst the other (GM) is expert at negotiating the most beneficial services for the school. This development requires the bursar to operate at the mainly management and leadership levels of the support services manager or school business manager, depending on the desired level of autonomy (Figure 9.2).

In order to understand what this higher level of management and leadership operation by bursars in schools entails, three focus groups, totalling 49 school bursars, brainstormed how their role could develop and the range of attributes that are particularly important for this. There was general agreement about the six areas of responsibility in which they should be monitoring and evaluating current practice, linking it with the school's Development Plan, managing contracts and providing specialist knowledge. These were finance, HRM, facilities, marketing and promotion, strategy and administration. Moreover, two of the three groups felt that teaching and learning/curriculum should also be part of their remit.

The picture of the future site-based school business manager that emerged from the focus groups indicates that these bursars envisaged a significant shift to leadership and management activities with minimum operation at an administrative level. Such a school business manager is likely to be a proactive education resource manager and member of the school leadership team. Along with headteachers and deputy heads they would be active in strategic development and in establishing procedures to ensure that these developments were communicated and realized in the school. Their growing understanding of the education process would facilitate the building of flexible, interactive systems and support learning teams. As leaders of support staff, they would ensure that administration, finance and premises management were efficiently and effectively carried out by staff who felt valued and able to interact with, and support, teaching staff. Through an understanding of their own role, the school's values and the needs of educators to facilitate learning, the successful site-based school business manager would ensure that the school would be a living and adaptive learning environment, which anticipated and responded to change.

REFERENCES

Bowe, R., Ball, S. J. and Gold, A. (1992) *Reform of Education and Changing Schools: Case Studies in Policy Sociology*, London, Routledge.

Bush, T., Coleman, M. and Glover, D. (1993) *Managing Autonomous Schools: The Grant-Maintained Experience*, London, Paul Chapman.

Bush, T. and Middlewood, D. (1997) *Managing People in Education*, London, Paul Chapman.

Davies, B. and Anderson, L. (1992) *Opting for Self-Management: The Early Experience of Grant-Maintained Schools*, London, Routledge.

Dean, J. (1993) *Managing the Secondary School* (2nd edn), London, Routledge.

DfEE (Department for Education and Employment) (1998) *Teachers: Meeting the Challenge of Change*, London, The Stationery Office.

Emerson, C. and Goddard, I. (1993) *Managing Staff in Schools*, Oxford, Heinemann.

Evetts, J. (1996) The new headteacher: budgetary devolution and the work of secondary headship, in C. J. Pole and R. Chawla-Dinga (eds), *Reshaping Education in the 1990s: Perspectives on Secondary Schooling*, London, Falmer Press.

Hall, V. (1997) Management roles in education, in T. Bush and D. Middlewood (eds), *Managing People in Education*, London, Paul Chapman.

Harrold, R. and Hough, J. (1988) *Curriculum, Finance and Resource Deployment: Toward School Self-Evaluation*, Sheffield, Sheffield Papers in Education Management.

Herzberg, F. (1966) *Work and the Nature of Man*, London, Staples Press.

HoC (House of Commons Education and Employment Committee) (1998) *Ninth Report: The Role of Headteachers*, Session 1997–98, London, The Stationery Office.

Maxcy, S. J. (1995) *Democracy, Chaos, and the New School Order*, Thousand Oaks, CA, Corwin Press.

Mortimore, P., Mortimore, J. and Thomas, H. (1995) *Managing Associate Staff: Innovation in the Primary and Secondary Schools*, London, Paul Chapman.

Nathan, M. (1996) *The Headteacher's Survival Guide*, London, Kogan Page.

O'Sullivan, F., Thody, A. and Wood, E. (2000) *From Bursar to Educational Resource Manager*, London, Financial Times and Prentice Hall.

Thomas, H. and Martin, J. (1994) *The Effectiveness of Schools and Education Resource Management: A Final Report to the Department for Education*, Birmingham, The University of Birmingham.

Thomas, H. and Martin, J. (1996) *Managing Resources for School Improvement: Creating a Cost-Effective School*, London, Routledge.

Wallace, M. and Hall, V. (1994) *Inside the SMT: Teamwork in Secondary School Management*, London, Paul Chapman.

West-Burnham, J. (1997) Reflections on leadership in self-managing schools, in B. Davies and L. Ellison (eds), *School Leadership for the 21st Century: A Competency and Knowledge Approach*, London, Routledge.

Wood, E., Thody, A. and O'Sullivan, F. (1998) The life and times of the school bursar, *Professional Development Today*, Vol. 2, no. 1, pp. 57–68.

Wood, E., Thody, A. and O'Sullivan, F. (1999) The developing role of the school business manager (bursar), in Grant, J. (ed.) Sharing Experience: Value for Money in School Management, York: Funding Agency for Schools.

10

COST ANALYSIS IN EDUCATION

Tim Simkins

INTRODUCTION

Effective cost analysis should be an important part of resource management for a number of reasons which have been spelt out in more detail elsewhere in this book. First, public resources for education are scarce and it is therefore important that they are well used. This is difficult unless we have fairly sophisticated understanding of what things cost and of the factors which affect costs. Second, the establishment of self-managing institutions, with a high degree of control over the deployment of resources coupled with increasing pressures for accountability, makes cost analysis of great relevance to managers at all levels in the system in a way that, perhaps, was not the case in the past. Third, a number of developments in the public sector, such as compulsory competitive tendering, its successor – 'Best Value' – and the 'Fair Funding' regime for schools, increase the degree to which some public services are placed in competitive market contexts. In such contexts, sharp attention both to costs and to the development of appropriate pricing strategies is necessary.

Despite these arguments, there remains an interesting paradox: why have such seemingly relevant forms of analysis been relatively underutilized in the field of education (Rice, 1997, p. 309)? Most of the works which comprehensively address costing issues in education are quite dated, although still valuable (Coombs and Hallak, 1987; Cumming, 1971; Fielden and Pearson, 1978; Hough, 1981). Detailed costing studies are also rare, although becoming less so. This chapter explores the main dimensions of cost analysis as they have been applied to education. It begins by outlining some key underpinning concepts. It then proceeds to describe and illustrate the main forms of cost analysis used in education and the questions that they attempt to answer. Finally, it returns to the question of why cost analysis remains relatively rare and what the possibilities are for the future. Space precludes the inclusion of any worked costing examples, but the references in the text will enable readers to follow up particular cases if they wish.

OPPORTUNITY COST

Cost analysis needs to be viewed not just as a set of techniques but as a way of thinking – as a set of principles as much as an armoury of tools. We can define 'cost' as the value of resources used in some particular activity or incurred as the result of some decision. What do we mean by value? The relevant concept here is 'opportunity cost', which may be defined as the value of the best feasible alternative which is given up by using resources in one way rather than another. This concept embodies the central economic ideas of scarcity and choice (see Simkins, 1981, ch. 2 for an extended discussion) and has a number of important implications.

While opportunity cost may often be best expressed in budgetary terms – for example, the opportunity cost of employing a teacher is the alternative resources which might be purchased from the funds allocated for the teacher's salary and on-costs – this is not always the case. First, organizational choices with resource implications may not affect budgetary expenditure. For example, a cost of increasing the amount of mathematics in the curriculum (perhaps through the numeracy hour) is the other forms of learning lost as a result of the reallocation of teacher time to numeracy teaching. For the numeracy hour to be judged worthwhile the learning gains arising from it should outweigh the value of other learning which has been forgone.

Second, costs are borne not only by institutional budgets. Thus a school which uses parents as in-class helpers or a college which reduces teaching hours in favour of more self-directed learning by students may pay little attention to the opportunity costs of parents' or students' time. The institution's main concerns will be with the budgetary impact, if any, of the resource choices made. For the parents and students themselves, however, the level and nature of their response is likely to be strongly affected by their perceptions of the opportunity costs and benefits involved. These perceptions will affect their behaviour: parents' motivation to help out in school, or students' willingness to spend their extra self-managed time learning, will depend on their respective judgements about the relative values of these as opposed to other forms of activity.

For managers these examples have four implications. They must be aware that:

- *cost consciousness* (i.e. full awareness of the value of alternatives foregone) is a more fundamental concern in management than *budget consciousness* (i.e. awareness only of the financial implications of an activity or decision);

- costs are often borne by a number of parties, not simply by institutional budgets;
- perceptions of cost – especially personal costs – influence behaviour;
- costs on their own are of limited value in making decisions or evaluating resource use. Without some conception of the benefits which particular resource deployments are expected to realize, the value of cost analysis is limited.

Having made these important general points about the concept of cost, the remainder of this chapter will focus on costs viewed from the institutional perspective. However, I will return briefly to other perspectives in the final sections.

PURPOSES AND TYPES OF ANALYSIS

Cost analysis in its various forms can serve a number of purposes, from the relatively mundane to the ambitious and complex. The major differences between them lie in the degree to which they attempt to relate outcomes to costs and the means they use to do so. The main questions which different forms of analysis attempt to answer can be summarized as follows (see also Levin, 1983, ch. 1; Tsang, 1997).

Can we afford it?

Basic *cost analysis* attempts to value the resources which are, or might be, consumed by particular programmes, activities or projects. It addresses issues of feasibility and sustainability: can we afford to do it, and can we afford to sustain the commitment over the longer term? Analyses of this type consider inputs only: the fact that we can afford to do something does not, of itself, demonstrate that it will be worthwhile to do so.

How can costs be managed?

The principle of opportunity cost suggests that we should always be seeking to reduce costs – provided outcomes can be maintained – because resources saved may be used to achieve additional benefits elsewhere. If we are seeking 'cost efficiency' in this way, then we need cost analyses which enable us to understand the components which make up costs and the factors which affect these components. Such analyses are concerned with the *behaviour of costs*.

Which method is better?

We may wish to consider alternative means of achieving particular educational outcomes. If these outcomes can be quantified and the same measure of outcome can be used for each alternative intervention, then it may be possible to undertake a *cost-effectiveness analysis*. Such an analysis relates measures of outcome to cost with the aim of identifying that alternative which has the most attractive cost-effectiveness ratio. Measures of costs and outcomes in cost-effectiveness analysis use different metrics – typically money for costs and achievement scores or similar quantitative measures for outcomes.

Is it worth it?

The most complex – and controversial – form of cost analysis addresses the question of whether a particular form of educational expenditure is a good investment. Cost-effectiveness analysis cannot do this: it can only compare the relative cost-effectiveness of programmes which have commensurable outcomes. To fully evaluate an educational investment against alternative educational and non-educational uses of resources it is necessary to calculate a financial rate of return on the resources invested. Such a calculation requires that both inputs and outcomes are measured using the same metric, namely money. The tool for doing this is *cost-benefit analysis*.

What should we charge for it?

Finally, in an increasingly marketized educational sector, more educational managers are faced with the need to price the services which they provide. Costing helps to inform *pricing decisions*, although it cannot by itself resolve them.

The following sections consider each of these questions in turn.

COST ANALYSIS: CAN WE AFFORD IT?

The underlying principles of costing are common, although each costing exercise presents its own unique problems. All cost analyses require assumptions, and hence choices, to be made about which costs to include and how to measure them. The appropriateness of the assumptions made will profoundly influence the nature and value of the conclusions which are reached. It is important, therefore, for managers who use cost information to understand the basis on which it is derived: *'caveat emptor'* (Bourn, 1993). As a first step in this understanding, it is helpful to distinguish between absorption and incremental costing.

Absorption costing

The main purpose of absorption costing is to contribute to the *evaluation of activities or programmes*. It attempts to assess the 'full' costs of an activity by identifying and valuing all the resources which are expended on it, either directly or indirectly. For example, what is the total cost of providing primary education nationally or within a particular local area? What is the cost of a school or college, or of teaching a particular subject in a school or college, or of providing education for a particular group of students? Absorption costing should attempt ideally to take account of two kinds of cost:

- *direct costs*: expenditure of resources which contributes directly and unambiguously to the activity being costed, e.g. the time which staff spend teaching and preparing for the programme being costed, teaching materials used by the participants, the space used for the programme;
- *indirect costs (or overheads)*: expenditure of resources which are judged to support the activity in question but cannot be directly attributed to it, e.g. senior management time, library facilities, school/college general administration.

Effective absorption costing of a programme requires that all those costs, and only those costs, associated with that programme are included. This may involve the *apportionment* of direct costs (for example, on the basis of a teacher's timetable) and the *allocation* of indirect costs (for example, in relation to staff or student numbers on the programme) (Carr, 1994, ch. 4; FAS, 1998a). The apportionment and allocation of costs requires information about how resources are actually utilized (for example, staff timetable analysis), but it also involves making decisions (for example, about whether teacher salaries should be allocated on the basis of average salaries or actuals, or whether teacher or student numbers are the better basis for allocating administrative overheads). Such decisions can have significant effects on the results of cost analyses.

How might absorption costing inform the management of resources? One possibility is to undertake some simple analysis of the costs of one institution. For example, Knight suggests that a school might calculate a number of 'process unit costs', such as the cost of educating one pupil or one class for a period, a week, a year or even a minute (Knight, 1993, pp. 179–80). This could be done by curriculum area or by pupil group as a basis for identifying high- and low-cost areas of provision. Difficulties clearly arise, however, in interpreting such figures. What level of cost is 'right' or 'reasonable' in particular circumstances?

One way of addressing such questions is to make comparisons with similar activities elsewhere. Carefully designed cost comparisons can help evaluate the 'reasonableness' of programme or institutional costs, through the process of *benchmarking* against the costs of similar institutions or programmes elsewhere (Fidler, 1999). Such an approach is now being increasingly used in relation to schools (Audit Commission, 1996; DfEE, 1995; FAS, 1999a; McAleese, 1996), colleges (FEFC, 1998), and, more recently, special education (Crowther, Dyson and Millward, 1999). Frequently such comparative studies suggest cost variations which raise questions about both the efficiency and the equity of current patterns of resource allocation.

However, such comparisons are subject to a number of dangers. The major problem is to ensure that like is being compared with like. First, different organizations may not collect and classify expenditure data in the same way. So, for example, cost comparisons among schools within an LEA are likely to be more reliable than comparisons across LEAs. Second, assumptions need to be made about the comparability of the programmes being compared. Ideally, for this purpose the unit of analysis should be some comparable indicator of educational outcome. However, because outcomes are often difficult to assess, and because data are usually readily available on enrolments, 'cost per student' is the comparative measure of unit cost most commonly adopted.

There are dangers associated with this measure. In particular, it is often difficult to be sure what particularly high (or particularly low) unit costs signify. It is often possible to hear relatively high unit costs castigated on the one hand as evidence of waste and inefficiency, and praised on the other as evidence of the high quality of provision. In the absence of independent measures of output, it is difficult to adjudicate between these two points of view. For example, differences in costs per student may reflect:

- differences in the purposes of programmes;
- differences in the educational challenges posed by particular clienteles;
- differences in scale, which may give greater or fewer opportunities to obtain benefits from economies of scale.

All these differences may cause legitimate variations in unit costs. Nevertheless, despite the difficulties, unit cost information is increasingly used both as an evaluative tool and as a basis for resource allocation in education. Thus a number of studies have considered the relative costs of course provision within the further and higher education sectors, typically finding significant differences among institutions (Audit Commission, 1993; FEFC/HEFCE, 1998). Such findings are increasingly informing funding policy as the government seeks to expand post-compulsory provision within tight budgetary constraints. Thus both the Further Education Funding Council (FEFC) and the Higher Education Funding Council for England (HEFCE) have included in their funding regimes measures to force higher cost institutions to reduce their unit costs (Dean and Gray, 1998; Leney, Lucas and Taubman, 1998; Lucas, 1998). However, if institutions are to do this, they need to understand their costs better, an issue to which we will return later.

Incremental costing

The main purpose of incremental costing is to contribute to *decision-making*. Unlike absorption costing which focuses on the costs generated by current activities, incremental costing is concerned with doing things differently or doing new things. For example, a proposed policy may involve expanding a school or college, developing new provision for students with special educational needs, or changing the balance of subjects within the curriculum. In such a situation it is necessary to measure *changes* in resource requirements resulting from the decision and hence to separate out those costs which will be affected by the change from those which will not. This requires a distinction to be made between:

- *fixed costs*: those costs which do not alter when the scale or pattern of an activity changes; and
- *variable costs*: those costs which do alter as a result of such a change.

Whether particular costs are fixed or variable depends on the type of change which is being considered. For example, if a class is being expanded in size the teacher clearly represents a fixed cost whereas the cost of textbooks and writing materials (if students are provided with these individually) is variable. On the other hand, if a school or college is being expanded, then the cost of teaching staff is likely to vary broadly with student numbers whereas the cost of the senior management team or of caretaking staff may well be fixed unless the expansion is a considerable one.

One example of the methodology of incremental costing was work on the likely implementation costs of the National Curriculum (NUT, 1992a; 1992b). These studies attempted 'to identify whether there are extra resources required by the National Curriculum over and above those which would have been committed to the curriculum it replaces' (NUT, 1992a, p. 7). The study recognized that the *total* costs of the new curriculum would comprise three components:

- costs associated with the existing curriculum which would continue to be deployed to the new curriculum;
- resources which could be transferred to the new curriculum because they were no longer needed for the old one;
- additional resources.

Only the third of these represents incremental costs. The secondary study (NUT, 1992b) suggested that such costs could arise as a result of:

- increased teacher time allocations for National Curriculum subjects, *provided that* these could not be covered by existing staff being redeployed from elsewhere in the curriculum;

- additional class groups created to reduce class sizes in key subject areas;
- additional time for assessment and meetings;
- additional time for curriculum and materials development;
- additional incentive allowances to manage the new curriculum;
- supply cover and other costs associated with in-service training;
- additional technical support to meet the increased emphasis on technology, science and information technology;
- books, learning materials and software which could not be funded by reallocating existing budgets.

The studies suggested that the likely additional costs of effectively implementing the National Curriculum would be considerable. In the event expenditure increased very little. In part no doubt this was because some of the increased demands on staff time were met by teachers giving more of their own time (i.e. incurring personal opportunity costs) to school work; and in part it was because schools were forced to manage with resourcing levels which were lower than the analyses suggested were desirable.

Nevertheless, incremental costing remains a powerful tool for evaluating proposed developments at both national and institutional levels. The National Curriculum studies represent a relatively rare published example of the systematic use of such costing in education and their methodology is one which could be usefully applied in a variety of other contexts (see, for example, Bibby and Lunt, 1994).

ANALYSING COST BEHAVIOUR: HOW CAN COSTS BE MANAGED?

It is clearly helpful to understand *what* things cost; even more so if comparisons can be made with the costs of similar programmes elsewhere. However, it is of more value to the manager to understand *why* things cost what they do, why costs appear to differ among similar programmes and hence how costs might be influenced. This requires 'an anatomical examination of resource utilisation' (Tsang, 1989, p. 58), and, in particular, an understanding of 'cost behaviour'. The analysis of cost behaviour typically involves the identification and assessment of 'cost drivers', i.e. those factors which determine cost levels and changes in these. A number of examples will be given here.

First, the idea of cost drivers can be used to analyse factors which determine the costs of different patterns of *staff deployment* to the curriculum. An example of this is the so-called 'Pooling Committee Formula' in further and higher education (DES, 1987). This states that:

$$SSR = \frac{AGS \times ALH}{ASH}$$

where:

SSR is student–staff ratio
AGS is average group size
ALH is average lecturer hours
ASH is average student hours

This formula shows that if an institution wishes to reduce its unit teaching staff costs (in effect, increase its SSR) it can do this only by adjusting one or more of the other variables in the equation. It must increase group sizes on average, ask or require lecturers to teach more hours or reduce the average number of hours students are in class, or it could follow some combination of these strategies. Alternatively, the formula shows that if there is a wish to reduce group sizes without increasing staffing levels, the opportunity costs of doing this *must* be an increase in ALH, a decrease in ASH or some combination of these. These principles have been used to help explain differences in college unit costs (Audit Commission, 1993) and to inform internal resource allocation models (Burton, 1998; Jones, 1986). They can also be used to show how both colleges and universities have significantly reduced their unit costs over a period of years through a process of 'decremental drift': the steady dilution of the teaching resource through reductions in average student hours and increases in class sizes and lecturer teaching hours. Similar approaches are used to analyse staff deployment in schools, focusing on average class size, the teacher contact ratio and the pupil–teacher ratio (Davies, 1969).

Second, cost analysis can be used to explore a wider range of factors affecting costs than staff deployment patterns alone. Thus a study of resource provision for pupils with moderate learning difficulties, which found wide cost variations for pupils with broadly similar levels of need (Crowther, Dyson and Millward, 1999), suggested that a number of factors were at work, including:

- different forms of special school and mainstream provision;
- differential use and deployment of learning support assistants;
- different policies about class size;
- differential deployment of special educational needs co-ordinators (SENCOs) and middle and senior managers in relation to pupil needs;
- costs and deployment of support services such as educational psychologists;
- differences in transport costs.

They concluded that many of the differences identified 'would, on the face of it, appear to be unacceptable' (ibid., p. 82) and recommended that much more work needs to be undertaken in relation to both the costs and effectiveness of different patterns of provision if efficiency and equity in resource use are to be ensured.

Third, cost analysis can be used to explore the likely consequences of quite fundamental changes in the technology of educational provision (Rumble, 1997). For example, the decision to replace a traditional course for a large number of students with one based on open learning must take account of the very different cost profiles of the two models. The major costs of traditional provision arise from the teacher time required for face-to-face teaching – a cost which varies with student numbers. Open learning seeks to substitute many of these costs by specially designed teaching materials. This is likely to reduce variable costs considerably. However, the costs of staff time spent in developing the materials – a fixed cost – may well be substantial. Whether open learning is more economic than traditional methods, therefore, depends on the scale of activity and the relationship between the fixed and variable cost components. Most studies show that the cost advantages from open learning arise from economies of scale, with the breakeven point determined by the relationship between fixed and variable costs in each situation (Rowntree, 1992, pp. 180ff.).

Similarly, the decision to increase the number of students in a programme using traditional methods also needs careful analysis. In this context, staff costs are, in fact, 'semi-variable'. In other words, they increase in steps rather than continuously as student numbers increase. Thus the additional costs of expansion depend on whether further students can be fitted into existing classes. If so, incremental costs will be very low; if not, they will be considerable as new teaching groups will need to be created. For example, if the maximum group size is set at 25, the marginal cost of the twenty-fifth student will be virtually zero. Whereas a twenty-sixth student would bring the full costs of creating and supporting a new class.

Finally, analysis of cost drivers can be used to help inform *resourcing decisions*. For example, the requirement for LEAs to develop 'transparent' formulae to fund their schools under local management schemes has led to a number of analyses which have attempted to move away from traditional, incremental costing assumptions and to explore the organizational drivers which actually determine resource needs of schools. For example, Kelly (1992) explored the concept of 'activity-based staffing' through which staffing needs are determined on the basis of 'professional judgement about the amount of teacher time which is necessary to provide a satisfactory educational experience for pupils in each age group' (ibid., p. 24). Thus assumptions about maximum class size and about the amount of non-teaching time necessary to undertake different kinds of duties necessary to support teaching and to manage the school led to the derivation of staffing requirements which could be translated into financial costs. Such analyses have the potential to make much more explicit the resource requirements for compulsory education. However, they suffer from a limitation which is common to many attempts to model costs on the basis of educational 'needs'. They typically lead to the conclusion that current resourcing levels are inadequate; and, in the absence of any independent evidence on the relationship between additional resources and learning outcomes, it is not easy to use them to justify increased expenditure at the expense of other sectors when public sector budgets are tight (Yarnit, 1994).

In each of these cases, an understanding of cost drivers provides information which can facilitate the effective planning and management of resource provision. It can offer the opportunity to achieve higher levels of 'cost efficiency', for example by changing curriculum staffing patterns or by utilizing economies of scale. What it cannot do on its own, however, is to answer more fundamental questions about the relative value of particular patterns of resource deployment. To achieve this, more comprehensive conceptual frameworks are necessary.

COST-EFFECTIVENESS ANALYSIS: WHICH METHOD IS BETTER?

An activity is commonly defined as effective if it achieves its goals. Cost analysis is of limited value without some attempt to relate costs to results. For many years economists have been using production function analyses to explore whether particular inputs have measurable and generalizable effects on educational outcomes which could inform policy choices. Although these studies have produced some controversial findings – including that class size appears to have no general relationship with outcomes – the potential value of such studies in informing policy and management choices seems limited (Hanushek, 1997a; 1997b).

Cost-effectiveness analysis takes a rather different approach (Levin, 1983). It typically comprises the following steps:

1) Identify the objectives to be achieved.
2) Specify the alternative programmes or projects which may lead to the attainment of these objectives.
3) Determine the cost of each programme or project.
4) Assess the outcomes of each programme or project in relation to the objectives to be achieved.
5) Relate the outcomes of each programme or project to its costs.

However, difficulties often arise with the first step. Attempts to operationalize objectives and develop measures of effectiveness in education often prove extremely difficult. For example, it is often difficult to reach agreement on which objectives to use for the analysis because of the close relation between education and deeply held values of individuals and groups. Furthermore, because of the need to quantify outcomes, there is always a temptation to choose outcomes on the basis of their quantifiability rather than their importance. The danger is that programmes will be evaluated and perhaps found wanting on the basis of indicators which fail to measure either the essential purposes or the complexity of the programme in question.

Other steps, too, may create difficulties. It may be difficult to relate particular outcomes to particular inputs, especially where most costs have to be apportioned; and even where both costs and outcomes can be realistically assessed, conclusions may be difficult to draw because factors outside the educational process, such as peer or family influences, have a significant effect on outcomes.

Partly because of these difficulties, cost-effectiveness analysis has been relatively rarely used in education, although some interesting examples are available. They demonstrate that effectiveness can be assessed at a number of levels. Three may be identified as having the most potential:

- completion rates;
- raw achievement scores;
- value added.

For example, the Audit Commission study quoted in an earlier section contains an element of cost-effectiveness analysis. It supplements its unit cost calculations with information on completion rates for both A-level and BTEC courses and a value-added measure for A-level courses alone. It argues, on the basis of its analysis, that there are significant differences among colleges in costs per student but that these differences do not seem to be significantly correlated with outcomes, leading to the conclusion that there is considerable potential to reduce unit costs without affecting quality (Audit Commission, 1993).

Other studies have also attempted to relate costs to educational achievement. For example, Thomas (1990) examined the cost-effectiveness of three sixth form colleges, six schools, two further education colleges and one tertiary college in educating students for A-level examinations. In another study, Levin (1985) explored the relative cost-effectiveness of a number of educational interventions – reducing class size, using computer-assisted instruction, using peer tutoring, and increasing instructional time – in increasing test performance in maths and reading. Finally, a recent study of special education provision, while not undertaking a full analysis of outcomes in relation to costs, demonstrates clearly the need for doing so (Crowther, Dyson and Millward, 1999).

COST-BENEFIT ANALYSIS: IS IT WORTH IT?

Cost-benefit analysis is an economic tool designed to compare systematically the costs of and returns on various investments in order to assess their economic 'profitability' and, as a result, indicate how resources should be allocated among different investment possibilities in order to maximize the returns from such investments. Cost-benefit analysis applied to education, deriving from 'human capital' theory, requires educational expenditures to be treated similarly to other investments. In particular, it requires that educational outcomes as well as costs be measured in monetary terms. This requirement gives rise to a number of conceptual and technical difficulties which mean that the technique remains controversial after more than 30 years of use. Cost-benefit studies typically measure educational outcomes in terms of increased economic productivity as reflected in earnings, after making allowances for factors other than education which may affect earnings (Cohn and Geske, 1990, ch. 5).

Cost-benefit studies have most frequently been used to inform the policy debate about education in developing countries (Psacharopoulos, 1994; Psacharopoulos and Woodhall, 1985, ch. 3). The results of such studies have been used, for example, to argue the case for increased basic education at the expense of higher education and to challenge the relative economic value of vocational education. More generally, analysis of differences between the public and private rates of return to education have been used to justify increased private contributions especially at higher educational levels. At a microlevel, studies have potential for evaluating vocational training activities whose prime purpose is to raise productivity. Beyond this, however, their potential utility in the management of education would seem limited.

PRICING: WHAT SHOULD WE CHARGE FOR IT?

Cost analysis is only one contributory factor in pricing decisions. Others include:

- the organization's objectives;
- the market situation;
- the demand for the product or service;
- the likely scale of activity (Pyke, 1998, p. 86).

Nevertheless, in determining pricing strategy, cost factors will enter in a number of ways. A decision needs to be taken on which costs should be used to inform pricing: full costs (i.e. costs derived from absorption costing), marginal costs only or some middle position so that income makes a partial contribution to overheads. Second, what should be the relationship between the relevant cost calculations and the price charged? Should 'cost plus' be the rule, and if so how much should the markup be? Or is there a case for charging less than cost and subsidizing the activity from income received from elsewhere? Alternatively, is the market situation such that the product or service can be charged at the market rate, with the surplus contributing to 'profit' or used to subsidize other aspects of the organization's work?

Such considerations help explain why it is often argued that 'costing' is a matter of fact whereas pricing is a matter of policy, although, as has been shown earlier, the 'facts' of costing also depend upon assumption and legitimate argument.

CONCLUSION: THE FUTURE OF COST ANALYSIS

For reasons outlined at the beginning of this chapter, pressures for the increased use of cost analysis in education are likely to grow over the next few years. As a US report put it:

> Although some argue that education is too important to be managed by concerns about costs and efficiency, we argue that education is too important not to be managed by those concerns. The United States must do everything possible to ensure that it reaps the largest possible educational gain from the resources available.
>
> (Hanushek, 1994, p. 52)

However, the problems involved are considerable. First, the systematic use of cost analysis raises important questions about management mindsets in education. For many, it is still the case that hard choices about resource use and concerns about educational values and quality do not sit easily together. Second, the limitations of all cost analyses, especially their dependence upon assumptions and value judgements which are contestable, must constantly be borne in mind. Allowing for these two caveats, a number of tentative predictions can be made about future developments in this area.

First, increased emphasis on accountability and delegated responsibility for resource management will cause increasing attention to be given to how costs are incurred and who is responsible for incurring them. This implies both the wider use of cost centres within educational organizations and the continued development of more sophisticated information systems which enable the incidence and behaviour of costs to be better understood.

Second, we can expect cost analysis to be applied more comprehensively and systematically to explore alternative methods of deploying resources that might produce more cost-effective educational solutions. This might involve processes of 'radical audit' which have 'implications for good information on costs, recognition of foregone alternatives as well as anticipated benefits' (Thomas and Martin, 1996, p. 36). There are a growing number of policy initiatives which attempt to manipulate resource variables in particular ways or which target resources in particular directions to achieve particular desired outcomes. For example:

- policies to manage class sizes for particular student groups (Gibbs, Lucas and Simonite, 1996; Jamison, Johnson and Dickson, 1998; NAHT, 1996);
- policies to supplement or substitute support staff for qualified teachers in the educational process (DfEE, 1998, ch. 5; FAS, 1998b; Mortimore and Mortimore, 1993);

- policies to develop open and distance learning alternatives to traditional teaching methods (Crabb, 1990; Rowntree, 1992, unit 6; Rumble, 1997);
- policies to redesign the school or college day (FAS, 1999b).

Each of these embodies implicit assumptions about the relative cost-effectiveness (or even the cost-benefit) ratios associated with innovative patterns of resource use. There is significant potential over the next few years for bringing these assumptions into the open and testing them through careful analysis and evaluation along the lines suggested in this chapter.

Finally, governments' concerns with the impact of policies on the level and distribution of measurable educational outcomes would suggest that more attention will be given in future to the use of cost-effectiveness (or even cost-benefit) analysis to address equity issues. It is rare for either the costs borne or the benefits received as a result of educational innovations to be distributed equitably among different client groups. A government agenda which is increasingly targeting those who have been 'socially excluded' by some aspects of previous policy regimes, as well as by socio-economic factors, implies that much greater attention will need to be given to the distribution of costs (both public expenditure and private contributions) in relation to the benefits obtained in terms of enhanced educational performance and other measures.

REFERENCES

Audit Commission (1993) *Unfinished Business: Full-Time Educational Courses for 16–19 Year Olds,* London, HMSO.

Audit Commission (1996) *Adding Up the Sums 4: Comparative Information for Schools 1995/96,* London, HMSO.

Bibby, P. and Lunt, I. (1994) Special costs, *Managing Schools Today,* Vol. 4, no. 1, pp 7–8.

Bourn, M. (1993) Caveat emptor: some aspects of cost analysis in universities, *Higher Education Policy,* Vol. 6, no. 3, pp. 10–18.

Burton, N. (1998) Calculating the cost of an undergraduate Initial Teacher Education (ITE) course, *International Journal of Educational Management,* Vol. 12, no. 6, pp. 260–9.

Carr, J. G. (1994) *Effective Financial Management in Further and Higher Education,* London, Chartered Association of Certified Accountants.

Cohn, E. and Geske, T. G. (1990) *The Economics of Education* (3rd edn), Oxford, Pergamon.

Coombs, P. H. and Hallak, J. (1987) *Cost Analysis in Education: A Tool for Policy and Planning,* Baltimore, Johns Hopkins University Press.

Crabb. G. (ed.) (1990) *Costing Open and Flexible Learning: A Practical Guide,* London, National Council for Educational Technology.

Crowther, D., Dyson, A. and Millward, A. (1999) *Costs and Outcomes for Pupils with Moderate Learning Difficulties in Special and Mainstream*

Schools, Research Report RR89, London, Department for Education and Employment.

Cumming, C. (1971) *Studies in Educational Costs*, Edinburgh, Scottish Academic Press.

Davies, T. I. (1969) *School Organisation*, London, Pergamon.

Dean, G. S. and Gray, D. E. (1998) Funding maximisation within a further education college: a case study, *Journal of Further and Higher Education*, Vol. 22, no. 1, pp. 41–8.

DES (Department for Education and Science) (1987) *Managing Colleges Efficiently: Report on a Study of Efficiency in Non-Advanced Further Education*, London, HMSO.

DfEE (Department for Education and Employment) (1995) *Benchmarking School Budgets: Sharing Good Practice*, London, HMSO.

DfEE (Department for Education and Employment) (1998) *Teachers: Meeting the Challenge of Change*, London, The Stationery Office.

FAS (Funding Agency for Schools) (1998a) *Cost Effectiveness in Sixth Forms*, York, FAS.

FAS (Funding Agency for Schools) (1998b) *Making Changes: Effective Use of Support Staff in Schools*, York, FAS.

FAS (Funding Agency for Schools) (1999a) *Cost and Performance Comparisons for Grant-Maintained Schools: Expenditure and Income 1997/98*, York, FAS.

FAS (Funding Agency for Schools) (1999b) *Making a Break: New Approaches to Meeting the Need for School Places*, York, FAS.

FEFC (Further Education Funding Council) (1998) *Performance Indicators 1996/97*, Coventry, FEFC.

FEFC/HEFCE (Further Education Funding Council/Higher Education Funding Council for England) (1998) *Study of the Relative Costs of HE Provision in FE Colleges and HE Institutions*, Coventry, FEFC/HEFCE.

Fidler, B. (1999) Benchmarking, in Funding Agency for Schools, *Sharing Experiences: Value for Money in School Management*, York, FAS.

Fielden, J. and Pearson, P. K. (1978) *Costing Educational Practice*, London, Council for Educational Technology.

Gibbs, G., Lucas, L. and Simonite, V. (1996) Class size and student performance: 1984–1994, *Studies in Higher Education*, Vol. 21, no. 3, pp. 261–73.

Hanushek, E. A. (1994) *Making Schools Work: Improving Performance and Controlling Costs*, Washington, DC, The Brookings Institution.

Hanushek, E. A. (1997a) Assessing the effects of school resources on student performance: an update, *Educational Evaluation and Policy Analysis*, Vol. 19, no. 2, pp. 141–64.

Hanushek, E. A. (1997b) Outcomes, incentives and beliefs: reflections on the economics of schools, *Educational Evaluation and Policy Analysis*, Vol. 19, no. 4, pp. 301–8.

Hough, J. (1981) *A Study of School Costs*, Slough, NFER-Nelson.

Jamison, J., Johnson, F. and Dickson, P. (1998) *Every Pupil Counts: The Impact of Class Size at Key Stage 1*, Slough, National Foundation for Educational Research.

Jones, D. (1986) Accountability and budgets in colleges: a practical unit cost approach, *Coombe Lodge Reports*, Vol. 19, no. 1, pp. 15–66, Blagdon, Bristol.

Kelly, A. (1992) Turning the budget on its head, *Managing Schools Today*, Vol. 1, no. 7, pp. 24–7.

Knight, B. (1993) *Financial Management for Schools: The Thinking Manager's Guide*, London, Heinemann.

Leney, T., Lucas, N. and Taubman, D. (1998) *Learning Funding: The Impact of FEFC Funding, Evidence from Twelve FE Colleges*, London, NATFHE/University of London, Institute of Education.

Levin, H. (1983) *Cost-Effectiveness Analysis: A Primer*, London, Sage.

Levin, H. (1985) Costs and cost-effectiveness of computer-assisted instruction, in J. Augenblick (ed.), *Public Schools: Issues in Budgeting and Financial Management*, New Brunswick, NJ, Transaction Books.

Lucas, N. (1998) FEFC funding: research on 12 colleges, *Journal of Further and Higher Education*, Vol. 22, no. 3, pp. 222–306.

McAleese, K. (1996) *Managing the Margins: A Benchmarking Approach to the School*, Leicester, Secondary Heads Association.

Mortimore, P. and Mortimore, J. (1993) *Managing Associate Staff: Innovation in Primary and Secondary Schools*, London, Paul Chapman.

NAHT (National Association of Head Teachers) (1996) *Class Size Research and the Quality of Education*, London, NAHT.

NUT (National Union of Teachers) (1992a) *Costs of the National Curriculum in Primary Schools*, London, NUT.

NUT (National Union of Teachers) (1992b) *Costs of the National Curriculum in Secondary Schools*, London, NUT.

Psacharopoulos, G. (1994) Returns to investment in education: a global update, *World Development*, Vol. 22, no. 9, pp. 1325–43.

Psacharopoulos, G. and Woodhall, M. (1985) *Education for Development: An Analysis of Investment Choices*, Oxford, Oxford University Press.

Pyke, C. J. (1998) Costing and pricing in the public sector, in J. Wilson (ed.), *Financial Management for the Public Services*, Milton Keynes, Open University Press.

Rice, J. K. (1997) Cost analysis in education: paradox and possibility, *Educational Evaluation and Policy Analysis*, Vol. 19, no. 4, pp. 309–17.

Rowntree, D. (1992) *Exploring Open and Distance Learning*, London, Kogan Page.

Rumble, G. (1997) *The Costs and Economics of Open and Distance Learning*, London, Kogan Page.

Simkins, T. (1981) *Economics and the Management of Resources in Education*, Sheffield Papers in Education Management no. 17, Sheffield City Polytechnic.

Thomas, H. (1990) *Education Costs and Performance: A Cost-Effectiveness Analysis*, London, Cassell.

Thomas, H. and Martin, J. (1996) *Managing Resources for School Improvement: Creating a Cost-Effective School*, London, Routledge.

Tsang, M. C. (1989) Cost analysis and decision making in education, *Educational Researcher*, Vol. 18, no. 4, pp. 57–9.

Tsang, M. C. (1997) Cost analysis for improved educational policymaking and evaluation, *Educational Evaluation and Policy Analysis*, Vol. 19, no. 4, pp. 318–24.

Yarnit, M. (1994) Resourcing Sheffield schools: theory and practice, *Educational Management and Administration*, Vol. 22, no. 2, pp. 113–22.

11

THE MANAGEMENT OF STAFF: SOME ISSUES OF EFFICIENCY AND COST-EFFECTIVENESS

Les Bell

INTRODUCTION

There is no doubt that the staff in any school or college is its most expensive resource; Hall (1997) notes, between 75 per cent and 85 per cent of the budget of any educational institution is spent on staffing costs. The successful management of staff, therefore, is a vital part of the overall management of the institution, particularly in relation to cost-effectiveness. As a result of a greater degree of autonomy being devolved to schools, the responsibility for managing staff has increasingly fallen to the senior management of schools in conjunction with the school governors with whom the legal responsibility rests. It has been argued (Bell, 1999) that school management has passed through a number of phases which have culminated in some form of school-based autonomous management. This trend is also evident in many other countries. As Whitty and his colleagues note:

> The past decade has seen an increasing number of attempts in various parts of the world to restructure . . . state schooling. Central to these initiatives are moves to dismantle centralised educational bureaucracies and to create in their place devolved systems . . . entailing significant degrees of autonomy and a variety of forms of school based administration.
>
> (Whitty, Power and Halpin, 1998, p. 3)

This introduction of institution-based management has involved, in particular, the decentralization of the budget so that more and more of the financial resources are deployed at school or college level. This shift of the locus of financial control has increasingly placed the responsibility for the management of staff on senior managers in schools. This trend was indicated in 1985 in the UK when a major government report on improving schools concluded that to improve standards, action was necessary in four areas, one of which was staff management:

1) To secure greater clarity about the objectives and content of the curriculum.
2) To reform the examinations system and improve assessment. . . .
3) To improve the professional effectiveness of teachers and the management of the teaching force.
4) To reform school government and harness more fully the contribution which can be made . . . by parents, employers and others outside the education service (DES, 1985, p. 8).

It was further argued, in England and Wales, that improved teacher effectiveness and better management of staff in schools could only be achieved if information was available about the skills and competences of the individual teacher and if headteachers kept constantly under review the further development and deployment of their staff (Joseph, 1985). As Bolam (1997) points out, there was a growing emphasis on achieving effective school management. Compulsory teacher appraisal, which included classroom observation, a national mentoring scheme for headteachers and a support scheme for newly appointed heads were introduced. Management training courses funded by local education authorities (LEAs) and the Department of Education and Science (DES) gave priority to the management of staff. Management training became a national priority within the education service and a nationally funded development centre for school management training and a task force on school management were established. Furthermore in 1997 a new qualification was introduced for those who aspire to headship and a training programme for experienced heads is about to be launched. These qualifications are part of a national framework that includes, amongst others, standards for subject leadership. All of these initiatives are designed to improve the management of staff in schools.

Staffing is an expensive resource, and Hall (1997) suggests that strategies should be in place to manage that resource at six key stages: recruitment and selection, induction, deployment, development, promotion and exit. A clearly articulated statement about the priorities of the school should inform these strategies, and this can then inform policy at the organizational level and the operational tasks to implement those policies. Recruitment to a vacancy opens up a range of choices, the least effective of which may be to succumb to the temptation to replace like with like. Consideration has to be given to the overall priorities of the school, future developments and the extent to which existing work can be reorganized. In many schools, budgetary constraints often mean that a senior member of staff may need to be replaced by a less experienced and less expensive person. Frequently, the choice may be whether or not to appoint a teacher at all. A significant proportion of primary school heads now prefer to allocate funding to appointing classroom assistants rather than increasing the number of teachers on their staff (Edwards, 1999; TES, 1999). Many schools now participate in various forms of teacher training. School-based initial teacher training, licensed and graduate teacher schemes all help to provide opportunities to recruit new teachers who meet the requirements of children in particular schools. Nevertheless, the decision to recruit a new member of staff should be preceded by a careful analysis of present and future staffing needs.

If recruitment is about attracting appropriate applicants, selection is the process of appointing the most suitable person for the job. Since staff are the most valuable and expensive resource in a school, care must be taken over selection. It must be based on a job description that identifies the key tasks for the post, a person specification that states the knowledge, skills, competences and values that are required, and a clear description of the way in which selection will be carried out. This approach will go a long way towards preventing the appointment of unsuitable staff by limiting the scope for inappropriate subjective judgements. It will facilitate the appointment of staff who meet the needs of the children in the school, have the appropriate experience and expertise to carry out the duties of the post for which they are being considered and who understand what is expected of them.

Once in post, staff should be provided with support throughout their induction phase. Arrangements are now in place to provide induction for newly qualified teachers:

> every teacher should have structured support during the first year of full-time teaching. This should build upon their initial training . . . and continue to develop their skills in areas identified during initial training. Mentor support will be provided. Schools will be expected to provide a planned induction programme for each newly qualified teacher.
>
> (DfEE, 1997, pp. 47–8)

Similar help should be given to all staff who are new to the school in order to ensure that they are deployed effectively and can function efficiently. Teachers should not be expected to take on responsibilities for which they have not been prepared and which is not within their sphere of competence. Nor should their work be subject to arbitrary change. Effective deployment matches the competences and experience of staff with the demands being placed upon them.

More flexible staff deployment can be achieved through various forms of in-service training. All staff in schools should, therefore, benefit from a well-structured professional development programme. Appraisal can contribute to the identification of individuals' training needs but the wider requirements of the school, as expressed through its development plan and other policy documents, must also be given priority. Striking the right balance between the needs of individual members of staff and those of the school community as a whole is difficult to achieve but efficient and effective staff management is likely to be fostered by an open style of management. Similarly, internal promotion opportunities and the nature of support offered to those seeking advancement elsewhere should meet clear criteria. The procedures for obtaining confidential advice in advance of applying for either internal or external posts and feedback after the process should be available. Often such feedback is as important for successful candidates as it is for those who are still seeking promotion. Where a member of staff obtains a post elsewhere it is good practice to conduct an exit interview. This can begin the recruitment process and inform senior managers of many pertinent issues in their schools (Bell and Rhodes, 1996).

It is now clear that staff management in UK schools is to have an added dimension of performance management (DfEE, 1998a). Appraisal is to be relaunched and will be even more rigorous. It will be linked to progression through the pay scale for some teachers as well as performance related pay and promotion to a new grade of Advanced Skills Teacher. The performance of all teachers will be assessed against agreed performance objectives and will be subject to ongoing monitoring. Heads and senior staff will be subject to a similar performance management regime:

> Appraisals of teachers will be conducted . . . on an annual cycle . . . The process will lead to a statement assessing each teacher's performance against the previous year's objectives . . . The statement will also outline objectives for the coming year. The head will then make a recommendation to the governing body about that teacher's pay, based on the outcomes of appraisal . . . Heads will be appraised by the governing body against agreed objectives. Independent advisors will assist . . . In considering the level of pay award, the governing body will take into account the head's performance as reflected in the appraisal report.
>
> (DfEE, 1998a, p. 3)

This rigorous process may or may not lead to the more efficient and effective management of teachers. It is clear, however, that managing staff in education, in the UK at least, is becoming increasing complex and demanding. These complexities require that all of the relevant procedures are known and understood by the staff involved. Hall concludes, therefore, that it is important for effective staff management that all schools have policies for each area of the staff management process and that these policies: 'liberate rather than constrain staff performance. In this way, managing staff in autonomous schools successfully balances management accountability and management for freedom' (Hall, 1997, p. 160). This has to be achieved, however, within a limited budget. In short, in all matters of resource management, including the management of staff, schools must be cost-effective.

THE COST-EFFECTIVE SCHOOL

Resource management in any school can best be considered as a system within which resources are transformed into educational outcomes through a number of stages (Simkins, 1997). Financial resources are the basis of the budget but, in order to achieve any form of outcomes, money must be converted into other forms of resources which, in turn, are deployed to enable the strategic, organizational and operational priorities of the school to be achieved. The most important, and the most expensive, of these resources is the staff of the school. An effective school, therefore, is one which deploys its resources in such a way as to match its results with its stated objectives. An effective school may not be either efficient or economic since these two concepts imply notions of cost. An efficient school is one which achieves its outcomes within its cost limits: 'The efficient school makes good use of all its available resources to achieve the best possible educational outcomes for its children – and in so doing provides excellent value for money' (OFSTED, 1995a, p. 121).

An economic school is similar to this but is one which is able to purchase a given standard of goods or services at the lowest cost. Schools in Britain are not particularly good at establishing procedures to ensure that they are efficient or economic: 'Few primary schools had, for example, procedures to monitor the effectiveness of their deployment of support staff; and while awareness about cost effectiveness is increasing in secondary schools, few schools evaluate the costs of their procedures and plans' (OFSTED, 1995b, p. 24).

The task of establishing how far any school is efficient, effective, economic or even cost-effective is made especially difficult because many of the concepts involved in such an analysis are used imprecisely. As Levačić and Glover (1994) point out, the term efficiency tends to be used when processes are being considered while effectiveness is used to refer to achieving outcomes. Frequently, however, the terms are used either in parallel or interchangeably. The main criterion for making judgements about value for money, that is detailed information on costs and outcomes, appears to lack precision even if it is available, and this may be especially true in the management of staff

The major policy initiative which was introduced in Britain during the late 1980s and early 1990s to seek to make schools cost-effective had five key components which were largely income rather than expenditure driven. These were:

1) The delegation to schools of control over budgets such that, within cash limits, decisions can be taken at school level about numbers and type of staff and other resourcing matters. Thus, schools can make expenditure decisions based on local priorities. This gives senior staff in schools the flexibility to make decisions about the number and type of staff that might be employed in the school.

2) The introduction of a formula to establish how schools are to be funded and to determine what level of funding schools will receive. This is a pupil-driven system through which funding is determined by numbers of pupils on roll and where funding follows pupils. Thus, a popular school which recruits well will receive an increased budget. As a result, more staff may be employed.
3) The delegation to school governors of powers over most staffing matters. The responsibility for identifying the appropriate staffing complement for the school and for certain decisions about the pay of heads and deputies, as well as the appointment of staff, are vested in the governors.
4) The provision of performance information about schools to enable parents to make informed choices about schools. This will, in future, include information about the performance of individual teachers.
5) Admission arrangements which permit relatively easy transfer of pupils between schools.

Here, then, the emphasis is on ways in which the total school budget might be restructured by either gaining or losing pupils, how school policies which determine performance might be influenced to ensure that pupil numbers in any particular school might be increased rather than allowed to decrease and how the overall budget might best be deployed through expenditure on staff and other resources to achieve the school's objectives. As OFSTED inspections reports show, however, there are a wide variety of school based responses to these aspects of policy (OFSTED, 1995b), so what might a cost-effective school look like and how might staff be managed within it?

Thomas and Martin (1996) suggest that these are questions more easily asked than answered. They note that cost-effectiveness is concerned with the relationship between the learning of children and the human and physical resources which contribute to this learning. The analysis of cost-effectiveness is a way of analysing the relationship between the deployment of resources and educational outcomes. As Mortimore and Mortimore with Thomas (1994) argue, cost-effectiveness is a wider and more challenging concept than effectiveness. They suggest that:

> effective schools are those in which pupils of all abilities achieve to their full potential. Whether that performance is achieved using more rather than fewer resources is not, strictly, part of the assessment of effectiveness. On the other hand, the amount of resources is an essential component of cost effectiveness. Thus, if two schools which are comparable in every respect are equally effective in terms of performance, the one that uses the smaller amount of resources is the more cost effective.
>
> (Mortimore and Mortimore with Thomas, 1994, pp. 21–2)

Thus, cost-effectiveness encompasses efficiency but goes beyond it. To enable their school to be cost-effective, senior staff require information about the entire cost of running their school and they also need to use that information to make decisions about, for example, appropriate staffing levels, types of staff and the deployment of staff. Thomas and Martin (1996) suggest a number of features that are likely to be shared by all cost-effective schools. Such schools will base their work on a periodic *radical audit* focusing on the use of staffing and on the identification of professional development needs related to the school's priorities. Decision-making will be informed by detailed information on costs, including staff costs so that alternatives can be assessed in the light of current expenditure. Team meetings, appraisal and surveys will be used to collect information on the quality of teaching and learning from teachers, parents and pupils. Much of this information will be generated independently of the head and senior staff and may lead to the delegation of decision-making about priorities to staff with relevant expertise. A dialogue of accountability will be created which will ensure that decisions about resource deployment are made in the light of an overall strategic plan for the school.

These features, in themselves, cannot ensure that staff are managed in a cost-effective way. They provide a framework within which schools can begin to make appropriate staff management decisions. In their study of 18 schools Thomas and Martin (1996) explored how each school sought to manage its staff in a cost-effective way. Many of the schools achieved this by employing teachers with specific expertise, such as special needs teachers to help colleagues meet the requirements of children with learning difficulties, or an outreach teacher to develop stronger links between the school and its community. Other schools recruited teachers with specific expertise to manage projects for a limited period of time or on contracts which would enable them to cover for absence rather than employing supply staff, thus ensuring some continuity and giving flexibility to staff management. One school tackled its falling pupil numbers and, therefore, its declining resource base by deploying a deputy head to develop community-based programmes to increase the school's intake and change its nature.

Often schools took the opportunity to change teaching roles or to appoint teachers with new or different areas of expertise. In some cases these approaches to cost-effective staffing resulted in a change in the management of the school, sometimes at the strategic decision-making level where the input from a key member of staff whose expertise was not in education brought a different perspective to the work of the school. In one school, this resulted in the collection and presentation of data in a different way to facilitate better decision-making. In another, it produced a total restructuring of the school's management systems through the introduction of financial and staff development databases that provided a wide range of information to inform decision-making. In other cases the changes were at the organizational level and even informed the operational activities. Heads of department received better and more understandable budget information about, for example, the cost of staffing field trips. This enabled informed decisions to be made about whether or not to undertake such trips and how best to plan those that were to continue. At the operational level, teachers were able to take informed decisions about their choice of teaching styles and the cost of teaching in particular ways.

Although the schools had different needs and adopted different solutions, they had in common the use of some form of audit to provide information on costing and to ensure that staffing matched needs on a fitness for purpose basis. In many cases this took the form of changing or enhancing the role of teachers but in others, there was an increased emphasis on the employment of staff with other forms of expertise to support the work of teachers. Several schools used the flexibility that they now had to transfer some administrative functions from senior teaching staff to bursars (see Chapter 9 in this volume), librarians, technicians, site managers and administrative officers or to employ an increased number of clerical and/or technical staff to ease the burden on teaching staff. Mortimore and Mortimore with Thomas (1994) call this group of people who work in schools 'associate staff'.

MANAGING ASSOCIATE STAFF

Research by Mortimore and Mortimore with Thomas (1994) shows that many schools have chosen to manage their staffing resource by bringing non-educational expertise into the school in order to make it more cost-effective. The largest part of any school's budget is spent on its teaching staff, so how might cost-effectiveness be achieved by providing support in classrooms? There is very little systematic evidence about the deployment of associate staff in schools, especially those who work in classrooms, or about the contribution that they might make to the effective and efficient management of schools. It has been clear since 1967, however, that there is considerable variation in both the provision and the impact on teaching and learning of such staff (Central Advisory Council, 1967). The Bullock Report (1975) argued that both teachers and pupils, especially those in disadvantaged areas, 'should have the assistance of trained persons, the nature of whose participation she will herself decide according to the demands of the situation' (Bullock Report, 1975, para 5.32).

In the 1980s concerns over persistent underachievement by certain groups, the increase in number and range of pupils for whom English was not their first language, changes in the curriculum and its assessment all served to focus attention on the provision of support for teachers. Hargreaves (ILEA, 1984) and Thomas (ILEA, 1985) both noted the growing importance of associate staff. By the end of the decade it could be argued that: 'it is a prime management function to choose non-teaching staff . . . with as much care as teachers . . . Thereafter it is desirable . . . to ensure that non-teaching staff are fully recognised for their work and included in as many of the appropriate functions as possible' (Reid, Bullock and Howarth, 1988, p. 3).

In the years following the Education Reform Act the numbers of associate staff in schools increased significantly. Tight financial controls on educational spending, increased class sizes, curriculum and assessment demands, and the growing number of children who are either statemented or regarded as having special needs have combined to lead headteachers and school governors to increase the number of support staff employed in schools:

> According to the most recent official statistics . . . between 1991 and 1996 the number of educational support staff in primary schools more than doubled whilst in the same period the number of teachers rose by only 3.2%. This means that, on average, there is now one full time equivalent non-teaching assistant to every eight teachers.
>
> (Moyles and Suschitzky, 1997a, p. 21)

So what have these support staff done in the past, has their role changed, and what contribution might they make to the effective and efficient management of the school? Razzell, in his commentary on the Plowden Report, described the duties of classroom assistants as follows:

> They issue the milk to the classes, supervise the library, catalogue, classify and cover books with polythene jackets and keep the shelves in good order . . . In other schools aides supply the classes with consumable stock, keep the pencils sharpened, the cupboards and stockrooms tidy, repair damaged equipment, undertake duplicating, act as escorts to children, set out audio visual equipment, sort out lost property and not infrequently make tea for staff at lunch time.
>
> (Razzell, 1968, p. 5)

Kennedy and Duthie (1975) found that many teachers believed that support staff could relieve them of routine non-teaching tasks and so increase the teacher's contact with the children. They note that classroom auxiliaries were used to provide in-class supervision, cleaning and tidying and general school duties such as mounting work and moving furniture. Little appeared to have changed from those activities observed by Razzell, although Marland (1978), quoted in Mortimore and Mortimore with Thomas (1994), was already describing classroom assistants as a valuable and cost-effective component of the teaching team. Brennan (1982) commented that non-teaching staff were frequently employed to provide support for children with sensory handicaps and that the helper was the child's eyes, ears and mobility aid. During the 1980s parents were increasingly being used as volunteers to provide support in classrooms and some were employed as bilingual assistants. There is some evidence that both parents and classroom assistants were starting to be used as apprentice teachers without being trained for the task (Goode, 1982). Hodgson, Clunies-Ross and Hegarty (1984) noted that assistants in special schools were carrying out educational tasks directed by teachers and Hilleard (1988) established, again in special schools, that assistants spent much of their time on instructional tasks designed by teachers and therapists. By 1989 a study on the deployment of classroom assistants concluded that: 'over 90% stated that they frequently supervised and assisted small groups of children engaged in educational activities set by the teacher . . . least time was spent on cleaning and administrative tasks' (Clayton, 1989, p. 106).

Mortimore and Mortimore with Thomas (1994) demonstrate that, by the early 1990s, many classroom assistants were involved in work which previously would have been the domain of teachers. They describe how one classroom assistant had responsibility for supporting practical activities and was given the task of making aspects of the curriculum more accessible to the children, another assisted in language work for Asian children, while a significant number were involved in planning and delivering the curriculum. This marks a significant shift in the role of associate staff who work in classrooms.

This change in the role of classroom assistants from domestic helper to assistant teacher in schools has been recognized in a number of ways (Clayton, 1993). A training programme, The Specialist Teacher Assistant Scheme, was introduced in 1994. Its aim was to develop courses specifically to prepare adults to give support to teachers in classrooms in teaching the basic skills of reading, writing and mathematics (OFSTED, 1996). Unfortunately, no training was provided for teachers on how best to use their classroom assistants. The deployment of teaching assistants and support staff in schools has now become part of government policy:

> Teaching and learning can be strengthened by using the full potential of teaching assistants and school support staff. All staff should be fully integrated into the schools' activities – enhancing their own role and giving teachers support and information . . . Teaching assistants are playing an increasingly important role in schools on tasks such as literacy support and helping pupils with special educational needs. We want that contribution to be fully acknowledged for the first time.
>
> (DfEE, 1998b, pp. 55–6)

Here we see a significant move away from restricting the work of classroom assistants to menial non-teaching tasks, towards a direct contribution to teaching and learning as part of an overall policy intended to improve standards.

Associate staff and cost-effectiveness

In order to contribute to cost-effectiveness in their schools, associate staff must either undertake duties which release teachers to concentrate more on teaching or make a contribution to supporting teachers in educational activities. It has been argued above that increasingly the second approach is being adopted in many schools. Mortimore and Mortimore with Thomas (1994) remind us, however, that three general principles must be born in mind when seeking to establish cost-effectiveness. First, 'fitness for purpose' – has the school the right balance and mixture of staff to meet the needs of the pupils and to achieve its objectives? A school staffed almost entirely by associate staff may be efficient but it is hardly likely to be effective or cost-effective. The second is the use of staff audit. This is much the same as the Thomas and Martin (1996) concept of radical audit and should be used to establish where, if anywhere, are the gaps between staff responsibilities and existing skills. The third principle involves recognizing the cost of implementing any choices that are made. This not only means knowing the full cost of a particular course of action, but also being aware of the cost of alternatives and of what may not be possible because a particular choice is made. In other words, opportunity costs must be taken into account. Thus if a school chooses to spend, say, £20,000 on employing two classroom assistants rather than a teacher, the opportunity cost of the employment of the classroom assistants is the teacher that is not employed. For such a choice to be cost-effective, therefore, the two assistants must contribute more to the school's overall work than any of the alternative staffing possibilities. Mortimore and Mortimore with Thomas (1994) conclude from their study that this focus on costing alternatives, combined with the increased discretion that heads now have over staffing, has enabled heads to manage the staffing of their schools more cost-effectively. Thomas and Martin (1996) go further and suggest that one of the most important consequences of this approach to managing staff in schools is that it has changed the perceptions of heads as to what is possible.

CONCLUSION

This review of some of the research evidence on staff management in schools suggests that some, probably most, school managers are using their autonomy over staffing to achieve increased economy and efficiency and to move towards being cost-effective at the operation level of school management. What is less clear, however, is how far heads and senior staff in schools are taking strategic decisions which link choices about resourcing to explicit educational outcomes. Reports from school inspectors indicate that: 'There is little evidence yet of LMS having any substantial impact on educational standards' (DFE, 1992, p. 11).

Levačić (1995) concludes that there is evidence that local financial management has had a positive impact on the efficiency and effectiveness of schools but it proved difficult to detect any learning improvement as a result of staff or resource management. Researchers, therefore, have to fall back on the perceptions of heads and their staff.

Managing staff in a cost-effective way is about more than simply being creative over the nature of appointments or changing the roles within the school. Cost-effectiveness has to focus on improving the teaching and learning within schools. Even in the limited context of the employment of a classroom assistant for science in one primary school, McGarvey *et al.* (1996) were unable to provide specific evidence of the link between the extra pair of hands and improved pupil performance, although one teacher in the study commented that classroom assistants transform your teaching life. It is dangerous to assume that more adults in classrooms necessarily means better learning opportunities for children (Moyles and Suschitzky, 1997b). While extra pairs of hands may contribute to the operational activities of the school, the evidence to support a close link between cost-effective staff management and improved learning outcomes is, at best, superficial. Nor is it clear exactly how far the increased use of associate staff has contributed to the strategic and organizational management of schools. Caldwell, in Chapter 2 of this volume, considers the links between inputs and improvements in teaching and learning in Australia but much more evidence is still required to establish exactly how cost-effective staff management can have an impact on pupil performance.

REFERENCES

Bell. L. (1999) Back to the future: the development of educational policy in England, *Journal of Educational Administration*, Vol. 37, no. 3/4, pp. 200–28.

Bell. L. and Rhodes, C. (1996) *The Skills of Primary School Management*, London, Routledge.

Bolam, R. (1997) Changes in educational management training. Paper presented to the First ESRC Seminar: Redefining Educational Management, Leicester.

Brennan, W. K. (1982) *Special Education in Mainstream Schools*, Stratford-upon-Avon, National Council for Special Education.

Bullock Report (1975) *Committee of Inquiry into Reading and the Use of English*, London, HMSO.

Central Advisory Council for Education (1967) *Children and their Primary Schools* (The Plowden Report), London, HMSO.

Clayton, T. (1989) The role and management of welfare assistants, in T. Bowers (ed.), *Managing Special Needs*, Milton Keynes, Open University Press.

Clayton, T. (1993) From domestic helper to 'assistant teacher' – the changing role of the British classroom assistant, *European Journal of Special Educational Needs*, Vol. 8, no. 1, pp. 103–15.

DES (1985) *Better Schools*, London, HMSO.

DFE (1992) *The Implementation of Local Management of Schools: A Report by HM Inspectorate*, London, HMSO.

DfEE (1997) *Excellence in Schools*, London, The Stationery Office.

DfEE (1998a) *Teachers: Meeting the Challenge of Change: Technical Consultation Document on Pay and Performance Management*, London, The Stationery Office.

DfEE (1998b) *Teachers: Meeting the Challenge of Change*, London, The Stationery Office.

Edwards, E. (1999) A Study of the development of the Specialist Teacher Assistant Scheme (STA) in England. Unpublished draft of PhD thesis, Liverpool, John Moores University.

Goode, J. (1982) The development of effective home school programmes: a study of parental perspectives in the process of schooling. Unpublished MPhil thesis, University of Nottingham.

Hall, V. (1997) Managing Staff, in B. Fidler, S. Russell and T. Simkins (eds), *Choices for Self Managing Schools*, London, Paul Chapman.

Hilleard, F. (1988) The role of the non-teaching assistant in the special school. Unpublished MEd thesis, King Alfred's College, Winchester.

Hodgson, A., Clunies-Ross, L. and Hegarty, S. (1984) *Learning Together: Teaching Pupils with Special Needs in the Ordinary School*, Windsor, NFER-Nelson.

ILEA (1984) *Improving Secondary Schools* (The Hargreaves Report), London, ILEA.

ILEA (1985) *Improving Primary Schools* (The Thomas Report), London, ILEA.

Joseph, Sir K. (1985) North of England Education Conference, 4 January, Chester.

Kennedy, K. and Duthie, J. (1975) *Auxiliaries in the Classroom*, Edinburgh, Scottish Education Department, HMSO.

Levačić, R. (1995) *Local Management of Schools*, Buckingham, Open University Press.

Levačić, R. and Glover, D. (1994) *OFSTED Assessments of Schools' Efficiency*, Milton Keynes, Centre for Educational Policy and Management, Open University.

Marland, M. (1978) The teacher, the ancillary and inner city education. Unpublished paper, Westminster School.

McGarvey, B., Marriott, S., Morgan, V. and Abbott, L. (1996) A study of auxiliary support in some primary classrooms: extra hands and extra eyes, *Educational Research*, Vol. 38, no. 3, pp. 293–305.

Mortimore, P. and Mortimore, J. with Thomas, H. (1994) *Managing Associate Staff: Innovation in Primary and Secondary Schools*, London, Paul Chapman.

Moyles, J. and Suschitzky, W. (1997a) The employment and deployment of classroom support staff: head teachers' perspectives, *Research in Education*, Vol. 58, pp 21–34.

Moyles, J. and Suschitzky, W. (1997b) *Jills of all Trades? Classroom Assistants in KS1 Classes*, London, Association of Teachers and Lecturers.

OfSTED (1995a) *The OfSTED Handbook: Guidance on the Inspection of Secondary Schools*, London, HMSO.

OfSTED (1995b) *The Annual Report of Her Majesty's Chief Inspector of Schools*, London, HMSO.

OfSTED (1996) *The Specialist Teacher Assistant Pilot Scheme: Final Evaluation Report on the First Year*, London, HMSO.

Razzell, A. (1968) *Juniors, a Postscript to Plowden*, Buckingham, Penguin.

Reid, K., Bullock, R. and Howarth, S. (1988) *An Introduction to Primary Organisation*, London, Hodder and Stoughton.

Simkins, T. (1997) Managing resources, in B. Fidler, S. Russell and T. Simkins (eds), *Choices for Self Managing Schools*, London, Paul Chapman.

Thomas, H. and Martin, J. (1996) *Managing Resources for School Improvement*, London, Routledge.

TES (1999) Heads vote for support staff, *Times Educational Supplement*, 4 February, p. 22.

Whitty, G., Power, S. and Halpin. D. (eds) (1998) *Devolution and Choice in Education: The School, the State and the Market*, Buckingham, Open University Press.

12

MANAGING INFORMATION AS A RESOURCE

Ed Baines

INTRODUCTION

This chapter will further explore the central themes of this book, the links between resources and learning outcomes and the changing environment in which educational organizations operate. The latter links the increased autonomy schools now enjoy and their capacity for adaptation to the changes taking place in education and beyond. The focus, however, will be on information as a resource, its use, the impact of computers and, in particular, a projection of how decision-making, accountability and school or college effectiveness may be improved by management thinking that takes into full account the use of information and communication technology (ICT).

INFORMATION

Lucas (1976) has defined information as: 'some tangible or intangible entity that reduces uncertainty about a state or event.' Davis and Olsen (1985) suggest that it is: 'data that has been processed into a form that is meaningful to the recipient, and is of real perceived value in current or prospective decisions'. The relationship between decision-making and the availability of information is a crucial one in that both the range and quality of our decisions are dependent in part on what we know or can find out.

The current management imperative in education centres on improvement in performance and outcomes. In this context, information can further be defined as what educational managers need to know and understand in order to assess the progress of their organization relative to past performance, to evaluate performance against specified standards (benchmarks), to focus on areas where change is necessary and to demonstrate that they, and others, in the organization are accountable and meeting their responsibilities.

Thus, there are a number of reasons why information is a key concept in the central themes of this book. It is a management resource in its own right and its proper use should, by definition, enhance decision-making at all levels. It provides the evidence for making judgements about other resources and their effective use. It is also central to the new methods of management whose adoption in schools and colleges in the UK was encouraged by the Education Reform Act of 1988 and which owe much to such ideas as effectiveness, efficiency, accountability and 'value for money'. Moreover, the availability of information has been transformed by new technologies, appropriately designated information and communication technologies, and its systematic use is now a central part of educational managers' professional commitment to the maintenance or improvement of standards.

The process of gathering, processing and communicating to managers the information they need is known as a management information system (MIS). This system will, in modern organizations, include elements of ICT, although information can be exchanged in a variety of ways that can be categorized as either formal or informal. Hence, although the term 'information system' is often used to mean a computer network, it includes other networks and channels of communication such as meetings, memoranda, telephone calls and conversations in various contexts. Wilson (1993, p. 3) describes an information system as: 'the nervous system which allows an organisation to respond to opportunities and avoid threats; to be effective'; he continues, 'it must reach into the furthest extremities of the organisation' (ibid., p. 3).

Thus, it is suggested that there are two dimensions to the strategy managers can use to control a complex and multifaceted organization. First, there is a need to create a culture which supports the attainment of the organization's key objectives and, second, there is a need to put in place appropriate management systems. In terms of the latter, an MIS is a vital tool in ensuring that the various facets of resource management such as setting and monitoring budgets, auditing outcomes and agreeing allocation of resources within the scope of the strategic plan are all carried out efficiently and effectively. To this end, information can be statistical, relate to organizational needs, result from demands from outside the organization or to the context in which it operates, be used historically or currently and may be a significant factor in planning and changing learning programmes.

As the term 'management information system' implies: 'it provides information for the management activities carried out within an organisation' (Curtis, 1995, p. 27) and these activities may be at a strategic level, at a tactical level, for operational control or for the processing of transactions. Pounder identifies 'Information Management – Communication' as one of the four performance dimensions of higher education institutions in Hong Kong, describing a top rating on this dimension as: 'Typically in this organization, one would expect mechanisms to have been introduced for the express purpose of cascading information systematically from top to bottom of the organizational hierarchy.' Whilst a low rating is described as: 'Typically, in this organization, one would expect information provision to be "ad hoc" in the sense of being provided when requested if one happens to know that it is available and the relevant party to contact' (Pounder, 1999, p. 396).

Higher education institutions may have more in common with business organizations than do schools. However, at this point, it may be relevant to contrast the use of an MIS in the commercial world and its application to educational organizations. Business information systems are mainly concerned with information inputs and outputs which are relatively easy to determine. However, in educational organizations, inputs are often difficult to cost and some outputs are impossible to quantify. Despite efforts to devise a method that addresses this difficulty, the complexity of schools and colleges as organizations and the subjectivity of many of their success indicators means that the issue remains unresolved (see Levačić, Chapter 1 in this volume). Therefore, attempts to derive worthwhile judgements of the relationship between inputs (resources of many kinds) and outputs (outcomes of many kinds) need to take into account the partial nature of the evidence. Furthermore, the strength of such judgements depends on a wide range of indicators of effectiveness, the experience and professional expertise of those making them and a willingness to draw a broad picture of the life and purposes of the organization.

Management information is a vital tool in effective and efficient school and college management, and it is possible to draw a parallel between the changes that are being brought about in educational management through the impact of ICT and the changes in the core activities of teaching and learning that are occurring as a result of the increasing use of ICT.

A PARALLEL REVOLUTION

It is generally believed that we are living through (many of us participating in) a revolution in the way people are educated (Baines, 1999; Barber, 1996; Bates, 1995; Beare and Slaughter, 1993; Papert, 1988; Raggatt, Edwards and Small, 1996; Stoll and Fink, 1996; Tiffin and Rajasingham, 1995; Usher and Edwards, 1994). The elements of this revolution are becoming clearer as practice is developed in our schools, colleges and universities. One facet of the impact of Information Technology (IT) is on the use of school and college buildings and this is given further consideration in Chapter 13 of this volume.

In the UK there are initiatives which suggest that learning and teaching is being affected to a large degree by the technology shift that has already revolutionized so many areas of our lives. The New Opportunities Fund is providing resources and a framework for the development of teachers' pedagogical skills in the context of the new technologies. The National Grid for Learning (NGFL) sets out to offer a rich set of resources for all those who play a part in our education system, especially teachers. Similar examples are evident elsewhere. In Hong Kong, according to *The 1997 Policy Address*, it is expected that within a few years 25 per cent of the 'content of each subject will be taught with the help of IT' (Education and Manpower Bureau, 1997). Green (1997, p. 16) highlights the use of IT in polytechnics in Singapore: 'The four polytechnics, for example, are state-of-the-art, with fully integrated, robotic manufacturing facilities, and computerised lecture theatres with students answering tests on their desktop PCs and lecturers receiving computer-analysed class results on their consoles.'

At this point, it is worth recalling Sendov's assertion that 'the basic problem now is not how to introduce computers in education, but how to build education in the presence of the computer' (Sendov, 1986, p. 16). Moreover, in claiming that 'an alternative to training educators to use systems that do not meet their core needs is to help them generate and use a system that does', Fulmer and Frank (1997, p. 124) suggest that changes of a radical order must be made in the management of educational organizations if we are to take full advantage of developing management concepts and the facilities made available by the new technologies. We might paraphrase Sendov's insight to help our understanding of the development of educational management thus: 'the basic problem now is not how to introduce computers into educational *management*, but how to build educational *management* in the presence of the computer'.

Close consideration of the key elements of the educational revolution will also help us to draw parallels between changes in the spheres of teaching and learning and changes we might seek in educational management. Such consideration will assist us in our efforts to chart more clearly the information demands that will arise.

Learning and teaching

New ways of accessing information and the increased range of sources available change the relationship between learner and teacher. That relationship can be less hierarchical, and new ways of learning and teaching are emerging.

But information is not *the* key to the radical changes in learning and teaching. The key idea is that educating 'in the presence of' the new technologies offers a clear resolution of the long-standing conflict between student-centred and curriculum-based education in favour of the first and centering on concepts such as:

- empowerment;
- active and experiential learning;

- independence and interdependence;
- lifelong learning;
- negotiation;
- self-motivation;
- clear, staged objectives (targets);
- monitoring of progress and related guidance (an Individual Education Plan for all learners).

Managing learning and teaching

Information is an important element in the changing nature of educational management. New ways of accessing information bring the possibility of new relationships. Open access to information suggests new models of managing educational organizations and new roles for educational managers and for teachers/educators.

But information is not *the* key to the radical changes in managing learning and teaching. The key idea is that managing 'in the presence of' the new technologies offers a possible resolution of the conflict between devolved management and hierarchical management in favour of the first and centering on concepts such as:

- empowerment;
- devolved professional decision-making;
- independence and interdependence;
- membership of a learning organization;
- negotiation;
- self-motivation towards innovation, quality and service;
- clear objectives (targets);
- monitoring of progress and related professional development (an individual professional profile for all educators).

As a result of such an approach, the teacher's role could change to one in which s/he is the key manager with information needs, strategic decision-making responsibilities, a direct relationship to the requirements of accountability and a fundamental involvement in the strategy of improvement.

Baines (1999) explores the transformation of teaching and learning 'in the presence of' the new technologies. From this analysis, is identified four dimensions to the new order that are worthy of consideration here:

1) *Getting, using and presenting information.* Membership of on-line professional forums and development of personal contacts linked to specific management objectives will ensure that managers will be part of a larger management world than is the case at present. For example, databases will be available locally (in school), nationally (NGFL) and globally (web

sites like the 21st Century Teachers' Network or TeacherNet UK). Individuals will include local colleagues (in school, county, region) as well as virtual ones (using e-mail and newsgroups). In using information, managers will draw on a wide range of management skills and, in presenting it, they will employ the full array of the standard ICT applications (word processor, desktop publishing, spreadsheet) at the appropriate level.

2) *Being part of an 'educational management world'.* This will be achieved through membership of on-line professional forums and exploitation of personal contacts linked to specific management objectives. Contacts may be experts (Department for Education and Employment [DfEE], Qualifications and Curriculum Authority [QCA], Office for Standards in Education [OFSTED] or peers (e-mail colleagues) or other providers (individuals' web sites, NGFL, BBC Education, Teleschool, etc.). Central to the idea of such an approach is the development of collaborative research, exploring and building on educationists' intrinsic preference for co-operation over competition.

3) *Communicating.* Managers will communicate within the institution for a specific purpose, for example, to find out or offer information, to elicit or express opinions, to co-operate with peers in some set of tasks.

4) *Greater independence for teachers in management.* Any attempt to break down a management dependency culture which contributes to the weaknesses in our current model of accountability will require a changed view of the teacher/lecturer's role. The notion that the teacher should become a researcher has been proposed (Barber, 1996; Middlewood, Coleman and Lumby, 1999). However, it is argued here that the teacher needs to become a manager of education in a broader, more strategic sense than previously considered. This will require enhanced management skills, agreed criteria for performance evaluation, provision of appropriate information and access to appropriate technologies.

The application of ICT will enable teachers and lecturers to take control of a greater part of their lives. They will no longer be dependent on managers who may be remote from them. They will be able to access students' records, check stock levels, organize on-line meetings, access in-service development. To enable them to carry out these tasks, to work interdependently with a range of colleagues and to maintain records which will contribute to their own evaluation will require a wider range of management skills than they need at present.

Considering the impact of information systems in a business environment, Alter (1999, p. 235) states: 'Across the entire organizational spectrum, information systems have increased the power of people who operate largely on facts and technical competence, and have reduced the ability of people to give orders based on the power of their position.' Educational organizations face, then, the strategic challenge of seeking alternative structures in order to adapt to the new management context. Beare and Slaughter are unequivocal:

Put bluntly, a business which operates on bureaucratic lines cannot compete in a post-industrial economy which guarantees survival only to those firms that are flexible, which can make quick, strategic decisions, which encourage innovation and entrepreneurship, which value creativity rather than conformity, *which give their members the power to take local decisions and to exercise initiative*, and which regard people in the organisation more as partners than property.

(Beare and Slaughter, 1993, p. 78, my italics)

It is likely that there will be some structural centrality as well as some priorities and prescriptions that are accepted and adhered to by all. Hamel and Prahalad (1989) call this aspect 'strategic intent'. However, the notion that an individual or small group can control centrally the daily activities and procedures of an organization, and can make all the strategic decisions the organization needs, conflicts with the management environment as it exists at the start of the twenty-first century.

DECISION-MAKERS AND INFORMATION

There is no doubt that decision-makers rely on information as a resource to underpin the strategic coherence of their judgements. Moreover, this information must be fit for the purpose, relevant to the moment, adequate and accessible. Its value, then, depends upon how it is used, in particular, for evaluating the organization's performance and in deciding the courses of action that follow. Information that meets these criteria, that is accessible to decision-makers who have strong analytic skills and rich experiential background, allows the organization to ask the key questions, 'How are we doing?' and 'What should we do differently?'

Nevertheless, systematic information-gathering is not an end in itself. The expertise and experience that people have can be more useful than facts on a piece of paper or a computer screen. There is some evidence (McKinnon and Bruns, 1992) that most managers do not rely solely on computer-based information to make decisions. A great deal of their information comes from direct interpersonal contact and much of it is derived from documents which are not on the computer system.

Mintzberg (1994, p. 258) points out that studies of organizations reveal that managers actually: 'rely primarily on oral forms of communication, on the order of about 80 per cent of the time.' He goes on to summarize the limitations of information provided by formal MIS:

1) Hard information is often limited in scope and lacks richness.
2) Hard information is often too aggregated for effective use in strategic management.
3) Trends may be spotted before they become identified through hard data.

4) Hard information may be unreliable or may be subject to misinterpretation (adapted from Mintzberg, 1994, pp. 259–68).

Statistical information relating to the progress of schools in England and Wales has been notoriously difficult to interpret. Comparisons of 'raw' results between schools is misleading, and the publication of the Performance and Assessment Reports (PANDAs) now allows the socio-economic status of the area in which the school is located to be taken into account. Nevertheless: 'there are many things that aren't measured, and many things that aren't measurable' (Gann, 1999, p. 30).

THE TECHNOLOGICAL DIMENSION IN EDUCATION

White (1990) claims that, compared with other environments, education has not altered one single basic process that is central to its operation as a result of technology. Clearly, as Riffel and Levin (1997) acknowledge, there is a time-lag between the introduction of technology and its accommodation into current practice, and an even greater delay in changes in current practice that are informed by the potential of the new technology. This is no less true in educational organizations than in others. The thrust in the development of an ICT-based MIS is to enhance the information offered to managers and the processes by which it is gathered and used. In this way the strategic decision-making process may be qualitatively improved because of the changed environment in which managers receive, and use, information. For example, managers may, through a combination of their professional skill and the nature of the information before them, be prompted to ask different questions, seek different information and, ultimately, make better decisions.

An MIS in schools and colleges is now almost entirely interpreted as computer-based systems. Although this has predominately been created with the educational environment in mind, a management information system is likely to share many features with systems from outside education. These features include not only some of their content (assets management, financial control and so on) but also their presentation (increasingly using state-of-the-art interfaces) and their intention (the facilitation of key management functions). They represent, then, a clear manifestation of the organizational response to successive governments' requirement that educational institutions adopt management techniques that work in the commercial and industrial world.

The range of uses to which information systems are put in schools and colleges is already extensive. Fulmer and Frank (1997) have identified some 20 or so such uses, including student records, staff records, financial management, inventory, attendance reporting, assessment reporting and the provision of databases.

LIMITATIONS OF ICT

A major limitation may be the difficulties in recognizing the needs and interests of the range of staff who are affected by the use of ICT as a management tool. An Organization for Economic Co-operation and Development (OECD, 1996) review of information technology in post-secondary education identified some of the differences. In view of the resistance of academic staff: 'What is beyond doubt is that the academic role must change and encouraging staff to adapt will be a major task for any institution' (OECD, 1996, p. 120). Similarly, executives of higher education are said to 'not welcome personal contact with information technology', whilst administrative and secretarial staff 'can make or break effective use of IT . . . Yet because their role is supportive their needs are often neglected' (ibid.).

The successful introduction of ICT to managers must take into account that the system should be 'user-friendly', that is that 'most users can use it easily with minimal start-up time and training' as opposed to 'user hostile when it is difficult to use or makes users feel inept' (Alter, 1999, p. 229). The implications are that issues of training and ownership may be paramount in the successful integration of a computerized information system.

Those who promote the further development of ICT-based management (and, indeed, education) tend to present the modern technologies as the agents of change. The view is that shared access to databases will let people interact with each other, across teams or organizations, and that this new working environment will have its own dynamic and create further opportunities for change. It is chastening to note, however, that outside education some commentators are asking why this promise is still largely unfulfilled. Davenport (1999) suggests that it is because the emphasis is placed too much on the equipment and not enough on the people who will use it. It is essential, he argues, to develop a clear understanding of how, and why, people acquire, use and share information rather than relying on an automatic development of proper information use once the technology is in place. An understanding of the relationship between people and information, combined with an intention to derive improvement from altered management styles, may allow us to determine the information environment we need.

Changing the technological base (hardware or software) of the MIS will not by itself change an organization's information culture. Basic behaviours, attitudes, values, management expectations and incentives relating to information need to be addressed if change is to occur. Simply installing, for example, shared databases will not necessarily encourage the appropriate information-using behaviours. Often the rate of technological change in an organization outstrips the rate of cultural change, rendering the technology advances all but useless. In commenting on the use of ICT in managing colleges of further information, Harper comments:

Too often, discussions relating to information technology policies focus first and foremost on hardware and software. Any policy should, in fact, be based upon the information requirements of the college, commencing with the main issue of insuring people have access to the information they need to do their jobs effectively.

(Harper, 1997, p. 80)

There is a great diversity of information users in educational organizations, and it is increasingly clear that effective information management depends upon our understanding of how they use IT rather than about how they use machines.

The Further Education Unit (FEU, 1993, p. 1) acknowledge that there is, at times, a gap between the information made available by many MISs and its perceived usefulness to college staff: 'All teaching and learning involves information, but the kinds of information required and used by college management can seem alien to lecturers.' One lecturer commenting on the amount of data that was demanded felt that:

The audit requirements are over the top. I have no objection in principle to being monitored. I don't like fraud any more than anyone else and as it's public money I believe it should be accounted for. But the amount of time taken servicing the ISR, the amount of resources going into it, taken away from teaching and students is huge (Curriculum Manager).

(Leney, Lucas and Taubman, 1998, p. 24)

Thinking about the schools of the future, how learning and teaching will take place in them, how they will be organized and managed, has been bedevilled by what Papert (1988) described as 'technocentrism'. The presence of ICT in educational organizations will undoubtedly continue to have a huge impact. In this respect, experience in schools and colleges reflects experience elsewhere. However, those (Papert calls them the 'Utopians') who believe that computers will solve the problems that schools and colleges face and those (the 'Critics') who warn that a surfeit of computers will dehumanize our world are wrong for the same reason. They ask the wrong question. Papert suggests that we should ask not 'What will the computer do to us?' but rather 'What will we make of the computer?' 'The point is not to predict the future. The point is to make it' (Papert, 1988, p. 4). In other words, the computer future will not be determined by the nature of technology, although this will play a part. It will be determined by the decisions made by human beings. Technocentrism is, then, a kind of fallacy that reduces key questions to issues relating to technology. Whenever we ask questions like 'Will using computers to teach mathematics increase our students' arithmetic skills?' or 'Will the use of computers in education create alienated and isolated people?', we are reflecting the technocentric bias in our thinking.

Earlier reference was made to what Davenport (1999) called the 'multi-plicity of meanings' of information. Technology-oriented systems have a tendency to seek to simplify, to restrict these meanings, thus impoverishing the information we receive and use, if they are introduced uncritically.

Reference has also been made to problems in information management arising from internal politics and conflict. These also constitute a principal reason why new technologies do not, of themselves, lead to empowerment and the fruitful sharing of information. In a sense technology can be regarded as neutral. However, the new systems and facilities it affords can support the kind of information use that results in real change in educational practice and management.

ACCOUNTABILITY

Rizvi tells us that the 'purpose[s] of a system of accountability in education is to ensure that public funds are used in accordance with the guidelines set down, to improve the quality of educational provision and, where possible, to provide information to show that this is being done' (Rizvi, 1990, p. 300). It is reasonable to suggest, therefore, that any model of accountability be judged on its ability to fulfil these purposes.

A common model of accountability is that of public accountability (Bush, 1994), based upon the principle that the most senior managers in schools and colleges, particularly the head/principal, must answer for the performance of their establishments to local educational administrators, inspection agencies, governors and, to an extent, parents. In this model of accountability, the head or principal is held accountable for issues within their organization. The 'chain of accountability' is hierarchical and managerial.

However, there are alternative models of accountability. A Department of Education and Science (DES)-funded project (DES, 1988) had earlier made the point that it was not only the senior managers who needed access to information, and Her Majesty's Inspectorate (HMI) reported (HMI/DES, 1990) that some colleges had already begun to develop techniques of data capture to allow computerized creation of management reports on a regular basis, allowing better direction of student learning and more effective course evaluation. The FEU itself (FEU, 1991) heralded greater independence for educational institutions, balanced by greater accountability and the growing interest in monitoring their efficiency and effectiveness which included new ways of quantifying these two measures so that individual student success could be emphasized. Subsequent developments included a focus on MIS used to record the progress of individual learners and on the frequent updating of information, perhaps at course team level. The implication is that there was a determination to decentralize the use of MI and implicitly accountability.

Peters (1987) and Belasco (1990), in identifying a business environment of faster change and greater competition, advocate a flatter, less hierarchical

organizational structure with far less centralised control and the empowerment of people throughout the organization to implement change as a
method of improvement. The teachers and lecturers who may have most
access to key information relevant to future improvement in educational
institutions may be excluded from full access to it. The introduction of a
management structure into schools and colleges that matches Peters's and
Belasco's new decision-making environment can, therefore, shift accountability to the level of the teacher or lecturer. Such a change in management
style and structure would require a change in the nature and management of
information that reflects the key organizational characteristics of openness
and inclusiveness. Murgatroyd puts it succinctly:

> What this means for schools and colleges is a simplification of struc-
> ture: focusing on the person closest to the student . . . as the principal
> manager of the student's experience with the support of a small . . .
> team whose task is to ensure that the resources of the school are used
> to the full to meet the needs of students.
>
> (Murgatroyd, 1991, p. 13)

THE NEW MIS ENVIRONMENT IN EDUCATION

Both in education and elsewhere, information systems deal effectively with
basic management functions such as cost control, inventory maintenance
and development. However, there are key information issues that derive
from the activities and judgements involved in the core activities of teaching and learning.

The model of management which depends on there being a direct relationship between inputs and outputs, in other words if the former is
changed there are predictable effects on the latter, fits educational institutions only approximately. A more appropriate model would be one
where a set of objectives, agreed against a background of previous performance and its evaluation against specified criteria (e.g. benchmarks), is met
in a management context of continuing communication, feedback, review
and tactical flexibility.

Any MIS that is to have a direct effect on the outcomes of an educational
organization will relate directly to, and affect in an immediate way, the
core activities that take place within it – namely, the teaching and learning.
Its related databases will provide information that impacts directly on the
key relationship in the school (teacher–learner) and the teacher's role as
manager.

If information systems are to be devised to meet the needs of decision-
makers, particularly those with the power to direct resources with the
intention of improving effectiveness and efficiency, then the focus will
need to shift from the hierarchically empowered (traditionally, senior
managers) to those who carry on the core business of schools and colleges.

The new MIS will be such that it will develop as its users develop and learn, thereby providing information when it is needed, and be accessible, both actively and passively, at all management levels, particularly that of the classroom teacher and lecturer.

CONCLUSION: THE CHALLENGE FOR EDUCATIONAL MIS

Flinders (1989) asserts that education policy should be founded on an understanding of the realities of teachers' lives in the classroom. While he accepts the professional imperative to improve the quality of instruction, he identifies a mismatch between the demands of curriculum management (lesson planning, marking, teaching and so on) and the limited resources available to teachers in meeting them. He emphasizes the point: 'successful reform is won or lost at the classroom level' (ibid., p. 74). Flinders favours a 'resource management approach' to educational reform, believing that improvement in instructional practice (and therefore outcomes) depends to a great extent on providing the right resources, at the right time, to the right people. His preferred criterion for deciding which changes we make is that they are the ones that *maximize the chances* of the highest quality of educational experiences.

He also proposes a 'user-oriented approach' to educational reform that has particular relevance in the context of such developments as the UK's National Grid for Learning. Focusing on two characteristics of this approach suggests that it is important to create opportunities for policy-makers and teachers to communicate fruitfully and to provide the means for teachers to be directly involved in decision-making. In this way, well-defined and understood management information could be a resource that will enable the reconceptualization of the role of teacher and manager in education and underpin the drive to improve teaching and learning.

Information is a key resource in the management of education. However, the way in which information is managed, and the use that is made of it, is largely dependent on the culture of the institution and the extent to which individuals within the institution have ownership of, and access to, that information.

REFERENCES

Alter, S. (1999) *Information Systems: A Management Perspective*, Reading MA, Addison-Wesley.

Baines, E. (1999) Managing change: twenty-first century classroom, in M. Leask and N. Pachler (eds), *Learning to Teach Using ICT in the Secondary School*, London, Routledge.

Barber, M. (1996) *The Learning Game: Arguments for an Educational Revolution*, London, Victor Gollancz.

Bates, A. W. (1995) *Technology, Open Learning and Distance Education*, London, Routledge.

Beare, H. and Slaughter, R. (1993) *Education for the Twenty-first Century*, London, Routledge.

Belasco, J. A. (1990) *Teaching the Elephant to Dance: Empowering Change in Your Organisation*, London, Hutchinson Business Books.

Bush, T. (1994) Accountability in education, in T. Bush and J. West-Burnham (eds), *The Principles of Educational Management*, Harlow, Longman.

Curtis, G. (1995) *Business Information Systems: Analysis, Design and Practice*, Wokingham, Addison-Wesley.

Davenport, T. H. (1999) Saving IT's soul: human centred information management, in *Harvard Business Review on the Business Value of IT*, Cambridge, MA, Harvard Business School Press.

Davis, G. B. and Olsen, M. (1985) *Management Information Systems: Conceptual Foundations, Structure and Development* (2nd edn), London, McGraw-Hill.

DES (1988) *User Requirements for CMISs in FE*, London, HMSO.

Education and Manpower Bureau (1997) *The 1997 Policy Address*, Hong Kong, Hong Kong Special Administrative Region Government Printer.

FEU (1991) *Grants for Educational Support and Training 1992–3*, London, Further Education Unit.

FEU (1993) *Management Information Systems and the Curriculum*, London, Further Education Unit.

Flinders, D. J. (1989) *Voices From the Classroom*, ERIC (database) Clearing House on Educational Management.

Fulmer, C. L. and Frank, F. P. (1997) Developing information systems for schools of the future. in A. C. W. Fung, A. J. Visscher, B. Barta and D. C. B. Teather, *Information Technology in Educational Management for the Schools of the Future*, London, Chapman and Hall.

Gann, N. (1999) *Targets for Tomorrow's Schools*, London, Falmer Press.

Green, A. (1997) World looks to top of the class nation, *Times Educational Supplement*, 27 June.

Hamel, G. and Prahalad, C. K. (1989) Strategy as stretch and leverage, *Harvard Business Review*, March/April.

Harper, H. (1997) *Management in Further Education: Theory and Practice*, London, David Fulton.

HMI/DES (1990) *CMIS in FE*, London, HMSO.

Leney, T., Lucas, N. and Taubman, D. (1998) *Learning Funding: The Impact of FEFC Funding: Evidence from Twelve Colleges*, London, NATFHE and University of London, Institute of Education.

Lucas, H. (1976) *The Analysis, Design and Implementation of Information Systems*, London, McGraw-Hill.

McKinnon, S. M. and Bruns, W. J. (1992) *The Information Mosaic*, Cambridge, MA, Harvard Business School Press.

Middlewood, D., Coleman, M. and Lumby, J. (1999) *Practitioner Research in Education: Making a Difference*, London, Paul Chapman.

Mintzberg, H. (1994) *The Rise and Fall of Strategic Planning*, Hemel Hempstead, Prentice-Hall.

Murgatroyd, S. (1991) Strategy, structure and quality service: developing school-wide improvement, *School Organisation*, Vol. 11, no. 1, pp. 7–19.

OECD (1996) *Information Technology and the Future of Post-Secondary Education*, Paris, Organisation for Economic Co-operation and Development.

Papert, S. (1988) A critique of technocentrism in thinking about the school of the future, in B. Sendov and I. Stanchev (eds), *Children in the Information Age: Opportunities for Creativity, Innovation and New Activities*, London, Pergamon Press.

Peters, T. (1987) *Thriving on Chaos: Handbook for a Management Revolution*, London, Macmillan.

Pounder, J. (1999) Organizational effectiveness in higher education: managerial implications of a Hong Kong study, *Educational Management and Administration*, Vol. 27, no. 4, pp. 389–400.

Raggatt, P., Edwards, R. and Small, N. (1996) *The Learning Society: Challenges and Trends*, London, Routledge.

Riffel, J. A. and Levin, B. (1997) Schools, coping with the impact of information technology, *Educational Management and Administration*, Vol. 25, no. 1, pp. 51–64.

Rizvi, F. (1990) Horizontal accountability, in J. Chapman (ed.), *School Based Decision Making and Management*, London, Falmer Press.

Sendov, B. (1986) *Information Technology and Education*, Chichester, Ellis Hall.

Stoll, L. and Fink, D. (1996) *Changing Our Schools*, Buckingham, Open University Press.

Tiffin, J. and Rajasingham, L. (1995) *In Search of the Virtual Class*, London, Routledge.

Usher, R. and Edwards, R. (1994) *Postmodernism and Education*, London, Routledge.

White, M. A. (1990,) A curriculum for the information age, in C. Warger (ed.), *Technology in Today's Schools*, ASCD.

Wilson, D. A. (1993) *Managing Information*, London, Butterworth-Heinemann.

MANAGEMENT OF BUILDINGS AND SPACE

Marianne Coleman and Ann R. J. Briggs

INTRODUCTION

Schools, colleges and universities, like most organizations, are committed to spending the largest part of their budgets on staff. Such costs are relatively inflexible in the short term although the creative use of support staff (Mortimore and Mortimore with Thomas, 1994) and the need to cut budgets through the difficult process of redundancy may marginally influence the total spent in this way. In commenting on the benefits of the increased financial freedom enjoyed by schools in the UK, it is recognized that: 'While virement is clearly one of the benefits of LMS [Local Management of Schools], it should be noted that staff salaries constitute a very substantial proportion of total costs, and they cannot be reduced significantly in the short term' (Coleman, Bush and Glover, 1994, p. 26).

Typically, in the region of 80 per cent of the budget of an educational institution may be reserved for staff costs. However, it is likely that the second largest budget heading will relate to the costs involved in the management of educational premises. For this reason alone, managers must be concerned with buildings and their maintenance, although property management is seen as relatively unimportant by some managers. In a survey of management priorities of 80 principals of higher education institutions, only one principal identified property management as a high priority (Warner and Kelly, 1994, p. 1): 'Most senior managers feel happy with money, people and academic issues, but regard property as a technical area to be left to the built environment professionals'.

Nevertheless, the visual impact of a building influences the way its users relate to what goes on within it, and in a budgetary situation where there may be little room for manoeuvre, the creative use of buildings and space may provide opportunities to enhance learning with or without large-scale expenditure. Storage and cloakroom space may be excessive to needs and capable of use as a teaching or office area with minimal structural alteration. A creative approach to the allocation of space can release the potential of educational premises as a major asset. For example, in an overhaul of the South East Essex College of Arts and Technology, the approach was dynamic: 'We tackled our agenda by practical problem-solving, "disjointed incrementalism", making step changes and going with things that worked' (Pitcher, 1995, p. 11). In this instance, the desire to introduce information technology (IT) systems and to integrate the scattered administration of the college led to the removal of internal walls to create open-plan offices, releasing space for teaching rooms where previously offices had been. A standard of interior design standard was adopted, including the use of bright colours, carpets and good quality office furniture, and it was felt that this had a direct and positive impact on the effectiveness and self-esteem of all those working in the college.

Schools and colleges seeking opportunities to maximize efficiency and managers, through creative and entrepreneurial strategies, may be able to achieve higher levels of *cost*-effectiveness. However, possibly the most important aspect of the management of educational properties is the contribution that can be made to the promotion of *educational* effectiveness. Thomas and Martin (1996) link a range of resources including the physical fabric of the building to learning outcomes. The four areas of resources listed are:

- teachers and associate staff;
- physical resources: premises and learning materials;
- administrative support systems;
- external relations and support (ibid., p. 32).

These resources are seen as being linked through management and planning to classroom outcomes in terms of the standard and quality of learning. They are instrumental in creating an appropriate learning environment. Bowring-Carr and West-Burnham identify the relationship between resources and learning:

> The notion that the state of the building, the quantity and state of the books, and the numbers in the classroom are all merely peripheral to learning shows a fine disregard for what learning really is. If one follows the idea that learning is a direct result of a unilinear input from the teacher, then resources, apart from a minimum of heat and light, are probably irrelevant. If, on the other hand, one believes that a child's mind can expand indefinitely if given the right food, then the circumstances, the ambience, into which we put that child are all-important.
>
> (Bowring-Carr and West-Burnham, 1997, p. 27)

The importance of a change of culture in supporting improvement is well documented (Hargreaves, 1997; Stoll and Fink, 1995). It would appear that an impact on the culture of educational institutions can be achieved through the upgrading of physical amenities. A principal graphically recalls his first observations of his new college; the implications for change are clear:

> I recollect some of the scenes which left a marked impression on me and which were crying out for urgent attention: the large unsupervised entrance foyer dominated by drinks machine, litter and smoking students . . . the administrative offices hidden away . . . teaching staff hidden around the College in numerous small cubby-holes.
>
> (Pitcher, 1995, p. 10)

Whilst educational managers may always have been aware of the need to maintain and improve property, it is the increased autonomy of educational institutions that has actually enabled managers to explore the innovative use of buildings. Reviewing the pre-incorporation situation of colleges of further education in England and Wales, Gray (1992) refers to: 'the tortuous means whereby (very occasionally) additional space might be acquired encouraged cynicism rather than positive approaches to the management of premises and assets' (in Kelly and Kedney, 1992, p. 99). In some cases, the additional freedom and favourable circumstances have allowed the development of an entrepreneurial approach to the finance of building projects, evidence of which can be seen both in two of the later case examples in this chapter and also in Chapter 4 of this volume.

In the remainder of this chapter we take a fresh look at the use of buildings in education and then go on to consider how the management of educational premises relates to both efficiency and effectiveness in schools and colleges. Illustrative qualitative data were derived from four interviews undertaken specifically for this chapter. Most schools and colleges face challenges in the management of premises, but the schools and college chosen are not intended to be representative in any way. However, they all indicate aspects of good practice in terms of the management of buildings and space, and illustrate how the management of premises can contribute to changes in culture and improved academic outcomes. The approach of the two secondary schools could be regarded as entrepreneurial; both have been fortunate in securing large grants from a range of sources. The examples of the primary school and the college indicate how space within existing buildings can be managed creatively with the use of relatively little additional income. The interviewees are listed below with brief details of their schools and college.

A deputy head of Northampton School for Boys, a comprehensive school for ages 13–19, which was identified amongst those schools most improved in England and Wales in 1997 and 1998. The school has Technology College status, and since 1992 has acquired a sports hall, has refurbished the provision for science and is about to open a new expressive arts centre.

The headteacher of Dartford Boys Grammar School, a selective school for ages 11–19, with examination results that are excellent within the context of selective schools and continue to improve. The school has Language College status, and during the 1990s has acquired a sports centre shared with the community, a humanities block and a performing arts centre. In addition they have upgraded the provision for both science and technology.

The headteacher of Harpole V.C. primary school, a village school with 190 pupils. Since the arrival of the headteacher in 1997, the school has a new library area, a room for information technology and plans to develop an area specifically for design and technology.

The Learning Resources Manager of Rugby College, a medium-sized college of further education. During the late 1990s, a range of building reorganization and refurbishment projects was carried out, using both external funding and the college's capital budget. The initiative focused on here is the development of the college's learning resource centre.

A REASSESSMENT OF THE IMPORTANCE OF BUILDINGS IN EDUCATION

Educational buildings are primarily intended to provide a location for learning. However, this statement has a number of implications which might be questioned and which may affect decisions about the planning and management of buildings. The idea that learning takes place *only* in schools and colleges is challenged from many quarters. Meighan sums up what may be the main themes:

1) That learning takes place in many locations, e.g. home and work as well as schools and colleges.
2) That parents have a role as partners in educating children with schools.
3) That teachers do not actually have to be present in order for learning to take place, distance learning being given as an example (based on Meighan, 1988, p. 2).

Aspects of these themes have been developed to speculate about the nature of education in the future (Bowring-Carr and West-Burnham, 1997). Kerry (1999) points to the need to 're-vision' the school in the light of the changes to education that are taking place.

It is perhaps the implications of the advent of information technology as a tool of learning, teaching and communication that is likely to have most impact on the reassessment of the importance and the use of buildings in education. At its most extreme, the increase in the use of information and communication technology (ICT) brings into question the traditional nature of schools and colleges. 'Globalization', implying the irrelevance of national frontiers for students of higher education through the use of the Internet, is envisaged (Kingston, 1999). Further education students are increasingly able to receive tuition on a range of academic and vocational subjects through ICT without setting foot in the college to which they are enrolled.

At the very least, the implications of the increased usage of ICT implies a revision of the uses of the school, college and community library and an increased stress on its centrality as a resource. The city technology colleges (CTCs) were purpose built as 'flagships' to promote science and technology and involve partnership and funding from commercial and industrial sponsors. In a review of six of the colleges it was stated that: 'it is important for the library to occupy a central space in the college, so that it can be easily reached from all parts . . . Ideally, it should be visually linked to the main circulation or reception area' (DES, 1991, p. 66).

The challenge of planning premises management for the future is recognized in the further education sector following incorporation: 'Ownership and common-sense, let alone the calls from the funding councils, point to the need to plan ahead and develop an accommodation strategy' (Kedney, 1993, p. 15). In further education colleges, the development of learning resource centres as communal resource bases and access points to ICT has been a dominant feature of the decade. These were often initially based on small specialist subject workshops or college libraries; their emergence as large, complex learning environments has tested the ingenuity of college managers in creating space to satisfy both existing and predicted future need.

It has already been noted that learning takes place outside the confines of designated educational buildings. Schools may recognize this formally or informally. Sergiovanni gives the example of an elementary school in Texas where students might spend two days a week in the community: 'using the community as a classroom. They believe that schooling without walls is both motivating to students and pedagogically sound' (Sergiovanni, 1998, p. 19).

In addition to the idea that learning can take place outside school and college buildings, the linkage of such buildings only with teaching and learning is an oversimplification, since buildings intended for education actually serve other functions as well. Such functions could include acting as a social centre both informally for the students in break times and more formally as a centre for the community. This is true in the case of intentions for the new arts centres of both of the example secondary schools and for the sports centre attached to the Dartford school. Strengthened links between schools or colleges and their communities can in their turn foster positive attitudes towards education, and lead to enhanced learning achievements.

This situation highlights the major contribution of buildings to the marketing of the organization (Warner and Kelly, 1994). Schools and colleges are increasingly aware of their image in the more open environment where they compete for students; and 'place' meaning location and facilities, along with 'product', 'price', 'promotion' and 'people', constitute the marketing mix which provides the basis for planning a marketing strategy in education (Coleman, 1994; Gray, 1991). The deputy head of Northampton School for Boys stated that:

> the buildings can be seen as a marketing tool; this will keep us over-subscribed for the next three or four years at least. The feedback from new parents is that they are impressed, first by the changes in the standard of buildings and the environment and, secondly, by the enthusiasm of the teachers and pupils.
>
> First of all, they like the traditional building of the school. Then they are impressed by the new sports hall, by ICT equipment, by the refurbished science building and finally by the new expressive arts building. The first impression is generally of buildings and equipment being up to date.

The Learning Resources Manager of Rugby College noted: 'When prospective students visit the college – often with their parents or teachers – they measure the learning resource centre against the facilities they have in school, or have seen on other college visits. I am convinced that it is a major factor in their assessment of the college as a whole'.

The reassessment of the use and improvement of educational buildings may be achieved by the adoption of a re-engineering approach which challenges received thinking. Thomas and Martin (1996, p. 36) refer to the principle of a 'radical audit' which would involve 'creativity and diversity in the use of premises', that would impact on the approaches to teaching and the management of learning and the use and deployment of resources. Examples of such 'radical auditing' may be seen in the case studies identified in this chapter where at Dartford Grammar School, an architectural plan was commissioned in 1991 and at Northampton School for Boys, an estimate for the refurbishment of the whole school was costed at £21 million in 1995. Both plans served as a marker for what might be achieved.

However, even when presented with the radical prospect of the building of a new school, it is not always possible to incorporate thinking that will best deliver the curriculum. In describing the building of a new CTC, the principal commented that 'the decisions taken by the [building] consultants would have profound effects on the way that the curriculum was to be delivered' (Lewis, 1997, p. 48). The fact that the effects were considered negative by the principal relates to his view that in planning the building 'there was neither a clear overall vision nor an effective co-ordination'.

Thinking about the future of education and the impact of ICT on schools and colleges raises questions about the continuation of traditional educational buildings. However, in current practice, the existence of an educational institution implies the presence of at least some buildings that must be managed in as efficient a way as possible.

EFFICIENCY IN THE MANAGEMENT OF BUILDINGS AND SPACE

A fresh look at the way in which space is used may reveal untapped potential. In the case of the primary school, considered in greater detail below, the knocking out of a wall allowed some space previously used for storage to be converted to a purpose-built ICT room for the children.

One of the key aspects of the efficient use of buildings is the extent to which that building is occupied. The claim that schools make poor use of the space available to them in terms of occupancy over the year is well rehearsed (OECD, 1996). The argument has been made strongly for the adoption of the five-term year partly on the grounds of improving the occupancy rate (Kerry, 1999). Indeed the adoption of the five-term year in some of the CTCs has meant the extension of the school year to 40 weeks as opposed to the normal 38 (Lewis, 1997). However, this is still a fairly minimal improvement in total occupancy.

In some cases, educational priorities, as in the provision of accommodation for pupils with special needs, may need to take priority over issues of pure efficiency: 'In adapting mainstream buildings there is likely to be a "loose fit" necessitating a greater overall area than for new construction, with associated higher running costs' (DFE, 1992, p. 2).

The partial use of school buildings for community purposes goes some way to improve the overall occupancy rate and, depending on the nature of the arrangement, may raise revenue for the school. The use of school buildings for adult evening classes extends both the occupancy of the building and the educational opportunities for the community. The most logical way of extracting the maximum usage from school buildings is through the multiple-shift system. Bray (1990), in an overview of research on the use of this system in countries as diverse as the USA, Malaysia and Zambia, identifies that clear financial benefit is likely to accrue in terms of the costs of schooling, but that levels of achievement do not appear to suffer. He is able to conclude that: 'The overall balance of this international research therefore seems positive' (Bray, 1990, p. 76).

However, Bray does point out that schools operating double shifts do tend to run a shorter than average school day and there is evidence that teaching focuses on narrow areas of language, mathematics and science, neglecting wider aspects of the curriculum. There may be compensations where funding allows. For example, where there is a double school population there is more justification for investment in sports facilities and equipment. Exactly the reverse may be true for educational institutions, particularly schools, operating on split sites. Whilst colleges may be large enough to warrant the duplication of equipment made necessary by split sites, schools are less likely to be so. In a study of split-site schools, Whitehouse and Busher (1990) identified the need to duplicate resources as one amongst a range of problems that impede the efficient and effective working of such schools.

Low occupancy rates are not the prerogative of schools. In colleges of further education: 'In the past, systematic studies have indicated surprisingly low levels of occupancy when compared with college expectations and national targets' (Kedney, 1993, p. 2). Even where users complain of overcrowding it has been common to find that actual occupancy rates are of the order of 0.20 to 0.25 (quoted in Kedney and Kelly, 1992), and given the constraints on individual room usage, 37 per cent occupancy can be regarded as good. The range of costs incurred in respect of premises in further education lead Kedney and Kelly (1992, p. 108) to argue that: 'Colleges that can reduce their estate related costs will enjoy a significant advantage over competitors.' They also point to the fact that space management can further enhance efficiency through facilitating the effective deployment of staff and technology.

The task of managers is made more difficult by the inadequacy of information about the use of rooms and of the changing needs which are apparent in both further and higher education. In respect of such information, Murphy (1994, p. 53) comments: 'Getting to grips with an institution's rooms, their use and ways of improving their utilization is a daunting, messy and long-term task.' Micropolitical factors may also be relevant. Murphy (1994) also refers to the issue of supposed 'ownership' of rooms where departments or faculties may feel that through historical precedent they have the right to specified accommodation: 'It is not uncommon for departments to regard a certain group of rooms for "their use" . . . Old plans are produced "proving" the claim; and there are anecdotal tales of locks being changed to keep out "undesirable" members of the institution' (ibid., p. 52). In undertaking the refurbishment of South East Essex College of Arts and Technology, the principal was initially met by: 'a prevailing culture of private spaces and rights-of-way' (Pitcher, 1995, p. 12).

LINKS WITH EFFECTIVENESS AND IMPROVEMENT

The link between use of rooms and micropolitics illustrates the relevance of buildings to the culture of the institution. There is considerable complexity in the range of factors that bring about school and college effectiveness and improvement. However, a clear link has been made between the culture of the institution and its capacity for improvement:

No school or teacher culture can be shown to have a *direct* impact on student learning and achievement, and claims to that end are vacuous. But the effects of culture can be conceptualized as trickling down, so to speak, through the architecture – political and micro-political, maintenance and development and service – until they eventually make some impact on what goes on in classrooms.

(Hargreaves, 1997, p. 249)

The interviews undertaken for this chapter give clear indications of the ways in which changes in buildings and their use have impacted on insti-tutional culture: 'Buildings enable the changes to happen. Just the decora-tive state has had a big impact on culture' (headteacher, Dartford Boys Grammar School). Other changes occurred in this school as a result of the building work: the learning resource centre created within the school has encouraged more independent learning and the sports centre, which is shared with the community, has a community feel to it enhancing the perception of the school as part of the community.

In the primary school, the impact of the development of the ICT room, funded by a successful bid to the National Grid for Learning, has been a change in the confidence and competence of all staff. Those that were inexperienced are now confident in teaching whole-class ICT, and also use the computer room in the lunch time, and before and after school. They are finding their own way round the system. The headteacher stated: 'The phobias have gone. Those that were competent are now even more so, their skills are improved and their ability to teach enhanced. Staff are using the facilities personally as well as professionally, e.g. accessing the Internet'.

There has also been a direct effect on children's learning: 'The impact on the children has been phenomenal. Before, about 5 per cent of the top age group were competent in handling text, graphics and layout. Now 95–100 per cent can do that and we have only been running the timetable in the computer room since January [one term]'. Similarly the change in library facilities funded through the PTA, a local charity and the school's own budget has had perceived effects both on the culture of the school and on learning outcomes. The head stated that the new facility:

- has raised the status of library and library skills;
- has raised community involvement in the school – a sponsored spell raised money for the computer;
- has enhanced the official and physical environment – it is now a welcom-ing place for people to go and do research;
- is more accessible to the pupils;
- has enhanced access to information.

Following the changes, an audit of the children's library skills has been carried out in order to enhance teaching. Further audits in the future will allow the progress of the children to be monitored.

In the further education college, rooms which were 'invisible' to students, i.e. the finance, examinations and management information system offices, were stripped out and brought into the student domain as a much needed expansion of the college library to create a learning resource centre. In turn, the administrative teams located in those offices were moved into converted classrooms which had been designated as surplus to teaching requirements. The developments took place at the same time as the college was being cabled for improved computer access: this enabled both the computer-dependent administration systems and the ICT needs of the students to be catered for effectively.

As in the primary school, the physical changes to the building enabled increased confidence and competence in the use of ICT to take place. Initiatives which seemed experimental at the beginning of the development of the learning resource centre – the focused use of the Internet as an information source and communication tool, the production of Powerpoint presentations by students as assessed work, the use of 'on-line' learning packages and assignments – became commonplace within a year of inception.

> There are still some staff who are wary about their own competence in ICT. But even they have found that they can't live without the college's new e-mail system, and they expect ICT competence in their students. Having the learning resource centre at the heart of the building has increased everyone's expectations, and it acts as a focus of support for staff and students alike.
>
> (Learning Resources Manager)

In the case study schools and college, building works were just one of the changes that were occurring. Research undertaken by Gray (1998) has shown that schools seeking improvement often initiate change through a range of approaches:

> Teachers reported to us that their schools had been changing the ways they were run and organized, changing their attitudes and approaches to planning, changing the ways the curriculum was organized and changing the schools' ethos or culture. Sometimes schools were moving on all four fronts at the same time, launching, in the process, a dozen or more initiatives.
>
> (Ibid., p. 22)

This approach is particularly evident in the two secondary schools, where the period of change under review was roughly that of the decade of the 1990s. The deputy head of Northampton School for Boys found it impossible to differentiate out the effects of the range of initiatives that had been introduced during this period. The school has been particularly successful in increasing the number of students gaining five A–C grades at GCSE:

1994: 33 per cent;
1995: 46 per cent;
1996: 56 per cent;
1997: 59 per cent;
1998: 63 per cent.

These changes occurred despite the fact that in the years 1994 to 1996 there was no significant improvement in the ability profile of the intake. The deputy head stated:

> changes in the building and the environment of the school have obviously had an effect. However, the changes in the A–C grades only came when we concentrated our strategy on teaching and learning in the classroom – we then got impressive, improved results . . . It is hard to estimate the importance of target-setting, and the strategic plan targeting teaching and learning and the involvement of parents. We don't know, we can't stop doing anything . . . I know that the SDP [School Development Plan] process had a big impact. It started in 1993/1994 focusing on teaching and learning and also target setting particularly for borderline groups.

The changes at Dartford Boys Grammar School had also been as a result of a range of initiatives. The headteacher, summing up the change in culture, stated that:

> there has been a vast change in culture over the last 10–12 years. When I came the school was very conservative and lacking in self-confidence. For example, a governor who was concerned at the rate of change said: 'This is a mediocre place for mediocre people. If you try to change this you will make everybody unhappy.' The brightest science student was going to Cambridge for an interview and I asked him why he wanted to do science. He replied, 'in science people know all the answers, everything is cut and dried.'

The headteacher went on to identify the change in culture and its range of possible causes:

> People now feel successful, confident, not threatened by change. They are more ready to innovate. They know they will be supported if they have a good idea. People aren't afraid to try something that may not work. The school is more team based than previously. If there was one single thing that was important it was the culture of middle management. This was a result of staff development projects. A high proportion are internal appointments. All the [present] curriculum managers were taken on as main-scale teachers.

At Rugby College, the changes were driven by the needs of students – principally, but not exclusively, those on vocational courses – for access to a greater range of resource materials and for proactive support in using the materials effectively, both in 'class time' and in their own study time. The majority of students and staff needed better access to computer technology, both as a source of information and as a presentation tool, and access to approachable people who would help them to use it:

> Having a learning resource centre which is open for 57 hours a week, with specialist tutors and librarians offering study support, is invaluable when the time spent in the classroom is at a premium. The demands of most subjects are such that the classroom lecturer cannot present a wide enough range of resources and learning experiences solely within the confines of the classroom.
>
> (Learning Resources Manager)

Innovative use of existing space, allocation of internal capital funding and an approach to IT which encouraged the most effective use of existing college computers within a planned programme of upgrading and replacement of technology enabled a significant shift in the learning culture of the college to be achieved.

CONCLUSION

In a review of British and American literature on effectiveness in schools, the learning environment is identified as one of a number of key factors (Sammons, Hillman and Mortimore, 1995). Similarly Davies (1997, p. 29) lists 'care of the school environment, buildings and working conditions' as a key factor related to educational effectiveness in the developing world and one which can be tackled by educational managers without the necessity of large-scale inputs of finance. In addition, the efficient use of space can be seen to reduce running costs and facilitate innovation.

In this chapter we have sought to indicate that the impact that buildings may have on both the culture and learning outcomes of schools and colleges should not be underestimated by managers. Renovations and new construction can be achieved through obtaining funds externally, as in the case of the two secondary school case examples, or by the energetic and innovative use of internally generated funds, as was largely the case in the college and the primary school examples. However it is funded, a programme of creative premises management can be one of a range of interlocking initiatives that support a school or college in a strategy for improvement.

At a time when the potential impact of ICT calls into question the nature of the education process itself, managers of educational buildings face a considerable challenge. Both the links with institutional improvement and the impact of information technology call for a strategic reassessment of the ways in which educational buildings are used and planned for the future.

REFERENCES

Bowring-Carr, C. and West-Burnham, J. (1997) *Effective Learning in Schools: How to Integrate Learning and Leadership for a Successful School*, London, Pitman.

Bray, M. (1990) The quality of education in multiple-shift schools: how far does a financial saving imply an educational cost? *Comparative Education*, Vol. 26, no. 1, pp. 73–81.

Coleman, M. (1994) Marketing and external relations, in T. Bush and J. West-Burnham (eds) *The Principles of Educational Management*, Harlow, Longman.

Coleman, M., Bush, T. and Glover, D. (1994) *Managing Finance and External Relations*, Harlow, Longman.

Davies, L. (1997) The rise of the school effectiveness movement, in J. White and M. Barber (eds), *Perspectives on School Effectiveness and School Improvement*, University of London, Institute of Education.

DES (1991) *Educational Design Initiatives in City Technology Colleges*, London, HMSO.

DFE (1992) *Designing for Pupils with Special Educational Needs: Special Schools*, Architects and Building Branch, Building Bulletin 77, London, HMSO.

Gray, J. (1998) *The Contribution of Educational Research to the Cause of School Improvement: A Professorial Lecture*, London University, Institute of Education.

Gray, L. (1991) *Marketing Education*, Buckingham, Open University Press.

Gray, L. (1992) Foreword to R. Kedney and J. Kelly, FE: the built environment and incorporation, *Coombe Lodge Report*, Vol. 23, no. 2, Bristol, The Staff College.

Hargreaves, D. (1997) School culture, school effectiveness and school improvement, in A. Harris, N. Bennett and M. Preedy (eds), *Organizational Effectiveness and Improvement in Education*, Buckingham, Open University Press.

Kedney, B. (1993) *Designing a College Accommodation Strategy*, Mendip Paper, MP 053, Bristol, The Staff College.

Kelly, R. and Kedney, J. (1992) FE: the built environment and incorporation, *Coombe Lodge Report*, Vol. 23, no. 2, Bristol, The Staff College.

Kerry, T. (1999) The future for schools and schools for the future, Inaugural lecture for the College of Teachers, *Education Today*, Vol. 49, no. 1, pp. 3–16.

Kingston, P. (1999) Britain has to push the pace, *Guardian*, Higher Education section, 30 March, pp. ii–iii.

Lewis, J. (1997) From a blank sheet of paper, in B. Davies and J. West-Burnham (eds), *Re-engineering and Total Quality in Schools*, London, Pitman.

Meighan, R. (1988) *Flexi-Schooling: Education for Tomorrow, Starting Yesterday*, Ticknall, Education Now.

Mortimore, P. and Mortimore, J. with Thomas, H. (1994) *Managing Associate Staff*, London, Paul Chapman.

Murphy, M. (1994) Managing the use of space, in D. Warner and G. Kelly (eds), *Managing Educational Property: A Handbook for Schools, Colleges and Universities*, Buckingham, Society for Research into Higher Education and Open University Press.

OECD (1996) *Making Better Use of School Buildings*, PEB Paper, Paris, OECD.

Pitcher, T. (1995) Building blocks to transform learning, *Innovations in FE*, no. 2, Spring, pp. 10–19.

Sammons P., Hillman, J. and Mortimore, P. (1995) *Key Characteristics of Effective Schools: A Review of School Effectiveness Research*, a report by the Institute of Education for the Office for Standards in Education.

Sergiovanni, T. J. (1998) Moral authority, community and diversity: leadership challenges for the 21st century. Address given on the occasion of the inauguration of the Center for Educational Leadership, University of Hong Kong, 4–5 December.

Stoll, L. and Fink, D. (1996) *Changing our Schools: Linking School Effectiveness and School Improvement*, Buckingham, Open University Press.

Thomas, H. and Martin, J. (1996) *Managing Resources for School Improvement: Creating a Cost-Effective School*, London, Routledge.

Warner, D. and Kelly, G. (eds) (1994) *Managing Educational Property: A Handbook for Schools, Colleges and Universities*, Buckingham, Society for Research into Higher Education and Open University Press.

Whitehouse, I. and Busher, H. (1990) Teachers' views on teaching in a large split-site junior school, *Educational Management and Administration*, Vol. 18, no. 1, pp. 54–60.

INDEX

Additional Educational Needs
  (AEN) 62, 70, 73, 74
Area Cost Adjustment 63, 74
Audit Commission 62, 73, 82
autonomy – *see* school-based
  management
Age Weighted Pupil Unit
  (AWPU) 135, 141

budgeting – (*see also* strategic planning
  in schools) 132–46
  and a culture of change 133
  and efficiency 143–45
  and implications for teaching and
    learning 145–46
  and income 134–36
  and monitoring and review 142–43
  and patterns of spending 136–40
    other than staffing costs in
      139–40
    staffing costs in 136–39
  and the planning process 133–34
  setting the budget 140–42
bursar xii, 148–66
  and level of operation 162–63
  and resource management 153
  emergence of 151–53
  and Fair Funding 164–66
  in FE 163–64
  responsibilities and levels of
    operation 150–51
    levels of autonomy and role
      of 153–56

roles of 156–62
  facilities management 159–60
  financial management 157–58
  human resource
    management 158–59
  other responsibilities 160–62
  ICT 161
  marketing 162
  pupils 161

Contact Ratio (CR) 144, 145
cost analysis xii, 168–82
  absorption costing 172–73
  and behaviour 175–78
  and effectiveness analysis
    178–80
  and pricing strategy 180–81
  future of 181–82
  incremental costing 174–75
    and the National
      Curriculum 174–75
  opportunity cost 169–70
  types of 170–71

decentralisation (*see also* Local
  Management of Schools) x, 4
Department for Education 69
Department for Education and
  Employment (DfEE) 12, 53, 54, 60,
  61, 78
  and Standards Funding 12
Department of the Environment 61,
  62, 63

229

Department of the Environment,
Transport and the Regions
(DETR)   61, 63, 76, 77

economy   xi, 105
Education Reform Order (ERO)   45, 67
Education Standard Spending
Assessment (SSA)   59, 61, 62, 63,
64, 66, 73, 74, 135
effectiveness   xi, 13, 105, 178–80, ⚡
191
efficiency   xi, 13–14, 105, 143–45, ⚡
221–22
and value for money   14 ⚡
English as an additional language
(EAL)   71, 72
entrepreneurialism   xi, 41–56
and culture   45–8
and management and
leadership   44–5
approaches to   48–55
benefactors   52
bidding   54
fund-raising   48
enterprise   49
support from companies   49–50
partnership   52–3
Private Funding Initiative
(PFI)   53–4
Private Public Partnerships
(PPP)   53–4
professional fund-raisers   55
sponsorship   50–1
definition of   42–4
equity   14–15, 65–6

Fair Funding   68–9, 164–66
finance manager – *see also* bursar
85–94
financial management and strategic
planning   117–30
see also strategic planning
funding   ix
and equity   xi
of colleges   ix, xi, 81–94, 100
budgeting   88–92
changing culture   92–4
future of   94
management of   85–94
and decision-making   87–8
principles of   84–5
of schools   ix
national system of   x, 59–79
distribution from central to local
government   60–3

and alternative methods of
76–9
activity-led staffing   77
needs-based approach   78–9
and problems with   73–5
and local perceptions of   75–6
and distribution of resources from
LEA to schools   67–9
and determination of education
budget   63–7
and Education SSA   66–7
and special educational
needs   69–71
and how schools use money for
SEN and AEN   71–3
and equity   65–6
decisions about education
budget   64–5
setting the budget   64
Funding Agency for Schools (FAS)   55
Further Education and Funding
Council (FEFC)   53, 54, 81, 82, 83,
84, 85, 173
Further Education Unit (FEU)   209

Higher Education Funding Council
(HEFCE)   173

Individual Schools Budget (ISB)   68
information – *see* management of
information

Learning and Skills Council   83
learning outcomes   4–5
and local management   xi, 24–37
and early research   25–7
and mapping the links   34–6
and third generation research
27–34
in Chicago   29–30
in England and Wales   28–9
in Victoria   30–4
and implications for policy-
makers   36–7
Local Education Authority (LEA)   54,
59, 61, 81
see also funding
Local Management of Schools
(LMS)   67, 69, 99, 133, 146
Local Schools Budget (LSB)   68

management
and ICT   xii–xiii, 161
of buildings and space   215–27
efficiency in   221–22

importance of buildings in
education 218–21
and effectiveness and
improvement 222–26
and ICT 219, 223, 224, 226
of information 200–12
and accountability 210–11
and decision-makers 206–7
and ICT 202–6
and limitations of 208–10
definition of 200–1
system for (MIS) 201–2, 211–12
of resources – *see* resources
of staff 186–97
and appraisal 189
and the cost-effective school
190–93, 195, 197
and of associate staff 193–95
and deployment 188–89
and induction 188
and recruitment 187–88
and selection 188
management, models of xi,
99–114
ambiguity models 104
and resource allocation 113
collegial models 102–3
and resource allocation 108–10
political models 103
and resource allocation 110–12
bidding systems in 111–12
rational models 101–2
and resource allocation 104–8
and formula funding 108
and incremental
budgeting 106–7
and zero-based budgeting
107–8
principles of 105–6
impact on finance and
resources 99–114

National Audit Office 124
National Grid for Learning 203,
223
New Opportunities Fund 202–3

Organisation for Economic Co-
operation and Development
(OECD) ix
organisations
and operational core 6
and perspectives 7–9
and task environment 10–11
OFSTED 15–16

Performance and Assessment Report
Data (PANDA) 18, 207
Private Funding Initiative (PFI) 53
Public Private Partnerships (PPP) 53

quasi-market xi, 20

resources ix
allocation of 12
bureaucratic 19
market 20, 41
quasi-market 20
evaluation of 13–15
finance xii
knowledge xii
links with learning x, 3, 4–5
learning outputs x, 4
learning outcomes x, xi, 15–16
management of x
and benchmarking 17–18, 172–73
and effectiveness in secondary
schools 16–17
and improvements 19
and organisational analysis 9–10
and support staff 6
(*see also* management of staff)
and the external environment 6–7
and the internal environment 6
and organisational
perspectives 5–7
material xii
organisational framework for
10–11
obtaining of 11–12
hypothecated grants 12
unhypothecated grants 12
people xii
power xii
use of 13
and evaluation of 13
Revenue Support Grant (RSG) 61

school-based management x
and learning outcomes – *see* local
management and learning
outcomes
and middle management xi
Schools of the Future (SOF) 30–4, 36
self-managing school 99–100
and the external environment 41
definition of 24
Special Educational Needs (SEN) 66,
69–73, 77, 78
Special Educational Needs Co-
ordinator (SENCO) 71, 72

strategic planning
  and achieving progress   127–30
  and use of budget as
    framework   125–27
  links with financial planning   117,
  119
    and role of middle manager
      121–25, 163–64
      and historic budgeting   121–22
      and limited plan

    approach   123–25
    and programme planning
      budgeting   122–23
    and zero-base budgeting   122
  nature of   118–19
  practicalities of   119–20

Total Standard Spending   61
Training and Enterprise Councils
  (TECs)   83